# The Holy Spirit and Moral Action in Thomas Aquinas

# The Holy Spirit and Moral Action in Thomas Aquinas

Jack Mahoney, SJ

LEXINGTON BOOKS/FORTRESS ACADEMIC
*Lanham • Boulder • New York • London*

Published by Lexington Books/Fortress Academic
Lexington Books is an imprint of The Rowman & Littlefield Publishing Group, Inc.
4501 Forbes Boulevard, Suite 200, Lanham, Maryland 20706
www.rowman.com

6 Tinworth Street, London SE11 5AL, United Kingdom

Copyright © 2021 The Rowman & Littlefield Publishing Group, Inc.

*All rights reserved.* No part of this book may be reproduced in any form or by any electronic or mechanical means, including information storage and retrieval systems, without written permission from the publisher, except by a reviewer who may quote passages in a review.

British Library Cataloguing in Publication Information Available

**Library of Congress Cataloging-in-Publication Data**

Names: Mahoney, John, 1931- author.
Title: The Holy Spirit and moral action in Thomas Aquinas / Jack Mahoney.
Description: Lanham : Lexington Books/Fortress Academic, [2021] | Includes bibliographical references and index. | Summary: "This book is a detailed study of how, according to Thomas Aquinas and his works, God's Holy Spirit is continuously at work in and through human moral activity"—Provided by publisher.
Identifiers: LCCN 2020050638 (print) | LCCN 2020050639 (ebook) | ISBN 9781978710443 (cloth) | ISBN 9781978710467 (pbk) ISBN 9781978710450 (epub)
Subjects: LCSH: Thomas, Aquinas, Saint, 1225?-1274. | Holy Spirit. | Christian ethics—Catholic Church.
Classification: LCC B765.T54 M2524 2021 (print) | LCC B765.T54 (ebook) | DDC 231/.3—dc23
LC record available at https://lccn.loc.gov/2020050638
LC ebook record available at https://lccn.loc.gov/2020050639

# Contents

| | | |
|---|---|---|
| Abbreviations | | vii |
| Introduction | | 1 |
| 1 | Understanding the Holy Spirit | 19 |
| 2 | The 'Prompting' of the Holy Spirit | 49 |
| 3 | 'The Law of the Spirit of Life' (Rom. 8.2) | 81 |
| 4 | Moral Decision-Making in the Spirit | 103 |
| 5 | Constants of the Holy Spirit | 121 |
| 6 | All-Embracing Wisdom | 145 |
| Bibliography | | 167 |
| Index | | 181 |
| About the Author | | 185 |

# Abbreviations

| | |
|---|---|
| DS | *Enchiridion Symbolorum* definitionum et declarationum de rebus fidei et morum, edd. H. Denzinger, A. Schönmetzer, Herder, 1963 (ed. 22) |
| DSp | *Dictionnaire de Spiritualité*, Paris, 1932– |
| DTC | *Dictionnaire de théologie catholique*, Paris, 1899–1950 |
| DV | The Holy Bible. Douai-Rheims Version |
| Greg | *Gregorianum*, Rome, 1920– |
| Lyra | *Glosa ordinaria* cum expositione Lyre litterali et morali, necnon additionibus ac Replicis, tt. 6, Basileae, 1506–1508 |
| MScRel | *Mélanges de science religieuse*, Lille, 1944– |
| NB | *New Blackfriars*, Oxford, 1920– |
| NRT | *La nouvelle revue théologique*, Tournai, 1869– |
| PG | J.-P. Migne (ed.), *Patrologiae cursus completus, series graeca* (166 vols.; Paris: Petit-Montrouge, 1857–1883) |
| PL | J.-P. Migne (ed.), *Patrologiae cursus completus, series Latina* (221 vols.; Paris, J.-P.-Migne 1844–1864 |
| RevThom | *Revue thomiste*, Toulouse, 1918– |
| RSPT | *Revue des Sciences philosophiques et théologiques,* Paris, 1907– |
| RTAM | *Recherches de théologie ancienne et médiévale*, Louvain, 1929– |
| RUO | *Revue de l'Université d'Ottawa*, Ottawa, 1930– |
| ST | Aquinas, *Summa of Theology,* Part, question, article, objection |
| TS | *Theological Studies*, Baltimore, 1940– |

# Introduction

This study was born of a wish to know what so great a theologian as Thomas Aquinas thought of the role of the Holy Spirit of God in the process of human moral action. The result strikingly more than satisfied the author's expectation, in making it abundantly clear that Thomas's entire moral theology, or his theological ethics, is pervaded by the presence and the dynamic activity of the Holy Spirit, as this work is now intended to show.

All studies of the thought of Aquinas must depend significantly on his major systematic works, notably his *Summa* of theology. In addition to this, however, we have in our study also taken care to consult regularly his several commentaries on Sacred Scripture, as the most evident source for his teaching on what is a profoundly biblical theme: the power and influence of the Holy Spirit of God in human moral decision-making.

## LIFE AND ACADEMIC CAREER

It is useful, in trying to understand any of Thomas's writings, to aim to locate them at some point in the stages of his comparatively short teaching career, in Dominican study centres and universities around Europe.[1] Born in 1225 in Roccasecca, south of Rome, he received his early education at the neighbouring Benedictine monastery of Monte Cassino, and the monks later recommended he continue as a teenager at the University of Naples. There he was attracted to the new 'Order of Preachers', which had been founded only ten years previously by the Spanish Dominic de Guzmán, and, despite his family's strenuous opposition, he insisted on becoming a friar.[2]

He was sent by his Dominican superiors to their Paris community to complete his studies (1245–1248) and then appointed to join his master, Albert the Great, in Cologne (1248–1252) as a postgraduate student and secretary to Albert, producing transcripts of some of his mentor's lectures.[3] From there, he was appointed to his first teaching period in Paris, as bachelor of the Bible and of the *Sentences* of Peter Lombard (1252–1256), and then graduated and lectured there as master of the Sacred Page from 1256 to 1259. He seems then to have returned to Naples from 1259 to 1261, after which he spent from 1261 to 1265 in Orvieto, north of Rome, teaching and writing at the Dominican priory connected with the papal court,[4] before being sent to Rome itself (1265–1268) to found a study house there on the Aventine for Dominican students.[5] On this development, Simon Tugwell comments that 'for a few years, the convent of Santa Sabina must have housed one of the most remarkable study houses the Order ever possessed'.[6] Subsequently, Thomas returned to Paris for his second teaching period there (1268–1272).[7] Jean-Pierre Torrell passes on a fascinating glimpse into the background of the controversies in which Thomas was professionally and regularly engaged, especially in Paris University, when he quotes Verbeke's analysis of the reason for Thomas's return there: he would have to 'struggle on three fronts simultaneously: he would have to battle the conservative minds in the theology faculty who saw in Aristotle only a danger for the Christian faith; in the other direction, he would have to oppose the Averroist monopsychism; and finally, he would have to provide a defense of the mendicant orders against the secular clergy, led by the ironically-named William of Holy Love, who campaigned to exclude them from university teaching'.[8] Tugwell, too, provides a lively account of the professional jealousy of the secular clergy aroused by the Dominican and Franciscan presence and successes in the University of Paris.[9]

After some four years in Paris, Thomas proceeded to Naples (1272–1273), under instruction to found a Dominican house of studies there, for what turned out to be the last phase of his professional teaching.[10] In January 1274, despite feeling unwell, he undertook the long journey from Naples to Lyons to attend the Church Council that Pope Gregory X had convoked there. On the journey, he fell ill and spent a short time at a niece's house. Moving on to the neighbouring Cistercian abbey in Fossanova, south of Rome, he was looked after there for some weeks by the monks, and he died there, aged some forty-nine years, in 1274, most likely, according to Torrell, of extreme physical and nervous exhaustion.[11] It is intriguing to speculate what contribution the distinguished Dominican theologian might have made to the Second Council of Lyons in its deliberations on union with the Greeks (Thomas had written, on papal commission, a treatise on their 'errors'); on the procession of the Holy Spirit, as held by the sacred Roman Church which is 'mother and teacher of all the faithful'; and on the full profession of the Catholic faith, including the subjects of the final judgement, the number and nature of the seven sacraments, and the Petrine and papal primacy over the entire eastern and western church.[12]

## THOMAS'S SCRIPTURE COMMENTARIES

Thomas's main daily teaching activity throughout his academic career was to lecture on the several books of the Bible; and this resulted in the production of written commentaries in the Old Testament on the books of Isaiah, Job, Jeremiah, Lamentations and the Psalms; and in the New Testament on the Gospels of Matthew and John and the letters of Paul (including the Pastorals and Hebrews).[13] The editors of a welcome modern study of Thomas's biblical commentaries write of them that they 'are in many respects the forgotten corpus of the Angelic Doctor';[14] yet a modern Thomist, Aidan Nichols, has noted that 'St Thomas's reputation as an exegete has probably never stood higher than it does today'.[15] The apparent discrepancy between these two statements may be resolved by recognizing that Thomas's fame as a commentator has certainly grown, but only within the comparatively small body of modern biblical exegetes. Nicholas Healy warmly commends Thomas's scripture commentaries, noting how

> this area of Thomas's work has been too often ignored, perhaps in part because of the commentaries' dry, scholastic style, with its sometimes laborious concern for noting distinctions and categories that seem to have little significance. Yet these works are of vital importance in properly interpreting Thomas's thought, for hidden within them are a multitude of insights that enable a better reading of his more obviously 'theological' works. They give us some idea of which texts he drew upon in treating particular doctrinal issues. They make it clear how much his theology depends upon his reading of Scripture, and how his reading is oriented throughout to Jesus Christ.[16]

Healy provides elsewhere a practical instance of what Thomas's Scripture commentaries often have to offer, when he observes that the classic 'five ways', or arguments, for God's existence are very condensed as they are provided in Thomas's *Summa*,[17] but 'some further insight into Thomas's purpose here can be gleaned from his commentaries', illustrating how the commentaries on Rom. 1.20 and the Prologue of John's Gospel provide more explanation on how God's existence can come to be known.[18] Likewise, a welcoming appreciation by Mary Margaret Pazdan of Thomas's 'interpretative insights' as exemplified in his commentary on Jn 15.15 ('I call you friends') shows that his biblical commentaries are well worthy of rescue from the neglect they have suffered.[19] Summing up her regard for Thomas's biblical works,

Eleanore Stump observes that 'on the whole, the commentaries are clearly the product of the same outstanding mind that composed the *Summa Theologiae*. With the possible exception of the cursory commentaries on the prophets [but surely not Isaiah?] and the Psalms [but see below], all Aquinas's biblical commentaries repay careful study.'[20]

Consulting Thomas's commentaries on Sacred Scripture is not, however, without its difficulties, nor is this due only to the fact that we do not yet possess a critical edition of them, with the exception of the commentaries on Job and on Isaiah produced by the Dominican Fathers of the Canadian centre of the Leonine Commission.[21] Several of Aquinas's Scripture commentaries are, in fact, no more than *reportationes*, or classroom notes, taken during Thomas's lectures, and consequently they must be consulted with an awareness of their indirect character. These notes might not capture all that Thomas said in the lecture hall, they could summarize what he did say, and not always necessarily using the words or phrases which Thomas himself used; they may be hasty and frequently telegrammatic and even, on occasion, inaccurate or just plainly mistaken.[22] It is obvious that those commentaries of Thomas's which are *reportationes* must be treated with a certain reserve, particularly if one is striving to find a development in Thomas's thought underlying a particular passage, or to reconstruct what Thomas said more fully orally in his lecture (*lectura*), as distinct from his own written exposition (*expositio*).

Reassurance is available, however, in Beryl Smalley's authoritative *The Study of the Bible in the Middle Ages*, where she refers to official *reportationes* as 'corrected and approved by the master' and others 'which may be characterized by the university authorities as defective or bad'.[23] Further safeguards to ensure the reliability of Thomas's *reportationes* are forthcoming from accumulating and comparing similar passages elsewhere in his writings; and from a consistent care to use Thomas's dictated or written works – and particularly the *Summa* – as a check and control.

Lack of clear information about the chronology of Thomas's scripture commentaries raises the a priori possibility of a considerable gap in time between repeated courses of lectures on Scripture which might allow for a change or development in Thomas's thought. Not that Thomas's thought did change substantially on any major question from beginning to end of his teaching career. The verdict of Walz and Novarina is that 'to the end of his life he will remain faithful to his first options. With him there is nothing like the considerable evolution that some people knew, like Augustine'.[24] As Mark Jordan also observes, 'there is no prima facie evidence of some grand revolution in his thought. The "late" Aquinas is distinguished from the "early" not by a chronology of reversed opinions but by a maturity in speculative virtue.'[25] Yet there is no doubt that on some individual points, he did modify and refine his teaching,[26] and unless one could place his Scripture commentaries in some satisfactory chronological order, one might perhaps run the risk of misinterpreting a passage or simply missing any nuance or modification which they might contain – granted, of course, that a *reportator* had caught and recorded the nuance.

We should also bear in mind that modern-day academics are not the first to recycle material or to update courses in re-delivering them, so Tugwell makes a pertinent point when he observes on the subject of dating Thomas's works that

> the possibility has to be kept in mind that several of his works, and particularly the commentaries that originated as lecture-courses, were revised, maybe several times, so that Thomas could incorporate material he had not previously known. If this is correct, then of course we need to ask exactly what we are dating when we attempt to fix the chronology of Thomas's works. One and the same work, as we have it now, may contain passages from widely separated periods.[27]

So far as dating Thomas's individual Scripture commentaries is concerned, it is generally agreed that his commentary on Isaiah is the earliest.[28] It is not, moreover, a *reportatio*, but comes partly from Thomas's own pen and partly from that of his secretary to whom he dictated it,[29] as was his custom in most of his major works.[30]

The commentary on Matthew's Gospel has been dated variously by scholars,[31] and most recently Wilhelmus Valkenberg comments that 'the most authoritative scholars nowadays propose ca. 1270 as a probable dating,' with Tugwell identifying the timing as the second Parisian period, 1270–1271.[32] It should be noted that two independent versions were taken down of Thomas's course on Matthew, one by a secular cleric, and the other by a Dominican regular 'reporter' of Thomas, Peter of Andria, which is now identified as the manuscript B.V.12 extant in Basel University Library. The modern English translation of Thomas's *Commentary on Matthew* by Paul M. Kimball incorporates passages transcribed from the Basel Matthew, and it also includes in an appendix an excerpt from the Basel Latin manuscript.[33] In the following study, passages of exegesis from Thomas's traditional *Commentary on Matthew* published by Marietti are checked for accuracy against corresponding passages in the Basel commentary which is contained in Kimball's new translation, with page reference provided in each case. In the event, Kimball considers that 'among St Thomas' works, his lectures on the Gospel of St. Matthew may be classified as a minor work', yet, as will be seen, they do provide matter relevant to our study.[34]

So far as concerns the literal commentary on Job, there was a general tendency to date it from Thomas's second Paris period (1269–1272), but

Eschmann, Tugwell and Torrell prefer 1261–1264 in Viterbo;[35] and it appears likely that the commentaries on Jeremiah and Lamentations were delivered there also.[36] There is general agreement that the commentary on Psalms 1–54 is among Thomas's last works.[37] (Kerr observes the absence of an English translation, 'probably because no one hitherto regarded it as important enough'.)[38] The commentary on John also appears to be late (1269–1272), and, although it is a *reportatio*, it was apparently at least partly revised by Thomas; and Thomas himself may have written the first five chapters.[39] Matthew and John are the only two of the Gospels of which we possess commentaries from Thomas, probably because he considered the commentary on Matthew as theologically adequate to cover all three synoptic gospels. (As Torrell observes, Thomas viewed the three synoptics as covering Jesus's humanity, whereas John concentrated on his divinity.[40])

Finally, of all Thomas's Scripture commentaries, that on the Epistles of St Paul as a whole contains understandably most complications. There is general agreement that external sources indicate that the commentaries on Romans and on First Corinthians chapter 1–10 (written by Thomas) are distinct from the *reportatio* on the remainder of First Corinthians and the rest of the Epistles,[41] but a variety of internal factors show that the commentary on Romans and on First Corinthians 1–10 is later than the rest,[42] and Glorieux argued that Thomas partially revised a *reportatio* of the entire Pauline corpus.[43] There is general agreement on dating the *reportatio* on First Corinthians 11ff during Thomas's Italian period, and although scholars differ on the dating of the commentaries on Romans and First Corinthians 1–10, all agree in placing it after 1265, and Henri Bouillard argued for the second Paris period.[44] Tugwell suggests that Thomas may have lectured on Paul during the second Paris period, but this may have been a reworking by Thomas of the *reportatio* which had been produced in the first Paris period. He also dates the commentary on Romans and the beginning of 1 Corinthians to Thomas's last years in Naples.[45]

It seems, then, that so far as chronology and a possible development of Thomas's thought affect a study of his Scripture commentaries, the problems are not so grave as might have at first appeared. Only one work, the commentary on Isaiah, dates from Thomas's early years in Paris, and all the others that we possess date from after his return to Italy; and since, as we shall have occasion to see, it was during his early years in Italy that Thomas's thought did develop on the power of the Holy Spirit in Christian behaviour, we may reasonably regard all his commentaries, apart from that on Isaiah, as presenting a uniformly mature teaching on the influence of the Spirit.

Although, then, there are no serious difficulties regarding dating to be considered in the case of Thomas's scripture commentaries, it has been suggested there are other troublesome features concerning them. There is, for example, the disconcerting propensity of the mediaeval exegete to regard Sacred Scripture (and particularly the Old Testament) as an encyclopaedia of universal knowledge.[46] This could well include a disquisition on meteorology or zoology, or on the use of music in church and its effects on the listener;[47] and these occasional mini-treatises would, as often as not, be followed by a highly allegorical or mystical interpretation of the verse under consideration.

There were also, at least in Paris University, what Pope Gregory IX judged the dangers attendant on mingling 'the fictions of philosophers with the word of God',[48] or what might be considered today the cultural inconsistencies involved in interpreting Jewish scripture by means of Hellenistic categories, whether Platonic or (later) Aristotelian. Perhaps, indeed, it is the thoroughgoing Aristotelian approach of Thomas to Scripture which most surprises the modern reader of his commentaries. For him, the fourteen Epistles of St Paul, for example, (i.e. including the Pastorals and Hebrews), are not occasional writings, but so many chapters of a single treatise; and each 'chapter' is considered a coherent planned unit, structured logically and even by syllogistically.[49] It proceeds by a process of enquiry from question (*dubium*) to question, in which each word must be minutely analyzed and each argument followed and expounded. As Thomas observed in his commentary on Gal 2.19, 'We should note that the Apostle [Paul] proceeds by asking questions, and he leaves no query without discussing it. His words may seem complicated, but if they are considered carefully he says nothing without good reason, as can be seen in the present instance.'[50] Grammar and logic are the tools of the exegete, and St Paul and St John – and King David, for that matter – are regarded as grammarians, logicians, masters in the skill of distinguishing, and even Aristotelians.[51] In mitigation, however, Vauthier remarks that in the commentaries, 'the thought of St Thomas is relatively easy to grasp, even though it is more spontaneous and flexible than in his systematic works'.[52]

In the circumstances, it is less than encouraging to read Boyle's remark about 'venturing into the thicket of [Thomas's] commentaries on Scripture'.[53] The apparent difficulties in resorting to Thomas's Scripture commentaries are, in fact, very far from insuperable, and they are much outweighed by the advantages to be gained from consulting them. The scholastic and Aristotelian categories which pervade them are in themselves no more unintelligible there than they are in Thomas's systematic works, and they at least contribute the values of clarity and precision of thought to what he understood the sacred writers wished to communicate. Tugwell considers a characteristic of Thomas to be his 'fearless lucidity',[54] while Brian Davies wrote approvingly that

> concern with logical details can be seen in all of Aquinas's writings, even his commentaries on the Bible. People who expound Scripture are not always noted

for going about their task with the skill displayed in the best philosophical essays. But even Aquinas's biblical commentaries are paradigms of philosophical analysis and philosophical reasoning.[55]

Moreover, if Thomas followed the common scholastic practices of loading his commentaries with scientific lore and of drawing allegorical interpretations from the text, he was by no means uncritical, either of the text, or of the views on it of his predecessors or his contemporaries. In reading Thomas, we should remember Ceslaus Spicq's remark that adaptation is not exegesis, and the mediaeval commentator regarded himself as also justified in adapting different senses to the same text, provided that they were true in themselves.[56]

## 'MASTER OF THE SACRED PAGE'

Thomas, in fact, had a keen appreciation of context, as well as a profound respect for the literal sense of Scripture, both of which led him on occasion to reject what he considered mistaken exegesis.[57] In his insistence on the true meaning of the text, and on the primacy of the literal sense over the spiritual sense and over the pastoral applications in which a Pope Gregory or a Bernard delighted, Thomas, along with Albert and Bonaventure, was consolidating the major advance made by Hugh of Saint-Cher,[58] but he also furthered that advance by developing the spiritual sense of scripture less than most of his predecessors,[59] and above all by clarifying precisely what the literal sense is. As Smalley observed, 'The literal sense includes everything which the sacred writer meant it to say',[60] and this included symbol, metaphor, hyperbole and the like; and, as she remarked of Thomas's own commentaries, 'reading these against a background of modern exegesis, one naturally finds the mediaeval element in them startling; [but] approaching them from the twelfth and thirteenth centuries, one is more startled by their modernity. Sometimes he will put fresh life into old conventions and sometimes ignore them.'[61] And it is important to recall that Thomas was firmly of the view that only the literal sense of Scripture could act as the basis for theological arguments.[62] A striking and pertinent example of this is to be found in Thomas's treatment, in the *Summa*, of the patristic and early scholastic development of the doctrine of the seven Gifts of the Holy Spirit. After surveying the possible understandings of the 'Gifts' which have been proposed by Fathers and scholastics, he cuts back to the original text of Isaiah, and contradicts the whole of tradition by pointing out that, actually, the text says nothing about '*gifts*'; it writes of differing '*spirits*'. And that, he concludes, should be the basis for our theologizing on the subject, which Thomas then proceeds to do in a systematic and original manner.[63]

One interesting conclusion which emerges from aiming to use the *Summa Theologiae* as a control, and occasionally as an interpreter, of Thomas's Scripture commentaries, as mentioned above, is that in point of fact, it is often the Scripture commentaries that throw light on the *Summa*. In a comprehensive study of Thomas's attitude to, and use of, Scripture in his teaching career, Terence McGuckin remarks that 'the commentaries, in fact, contain much that contributes to a clearer reading of the *Summa Theologiae*'.[64] Nor, when one considers it, should this be a matter for surprise. Whatever the Aristotelian and scholastic presuppositions which Thomas brought to the study and the teaching of Scripture, he considered his role in the church to be that of a master of the Sacred Page, *Magister in sacra pagina*. In examining Thomas's teaching on the Trinity, Giles Emery makes striking use of Thomas's commentaries on John and Romans alongside the systematic *Summa*, and he makes the interesting point that

> ultimately, the main difference between the biblical Commentary and the *Summa Theologiae* concerns the order of exposition, the organization of the material: whilst the *Summa Theologiae* follows the teaching order (*ordo disciplinae*) which guides us through Trinitarian doctrine as laid out according to the coherence and internal organization of its elements, the biblical Commentary puts its development of doctrinal points into the hands of the text, although the speculative perspective becomes apparent in some specific explanations.[65]

It was, in fact, in daily contact with the word of God that Thomas addressed his students, and the significance of this was well brought out by Henry Denifle in his important discussion on what basic textbooks were used by the mediaeval professors in theology. As he concluded, the basic text was Scripture, and 'the theologian of that day knew no book so well as the Bible'.[66] On Thomas's general approach to his research and teaching, Tugwell provides a striking summary in commenting on his first Paris period that

> from the outset it is clear that Thomas is going to go his own way, politely but firmly, bringing his great gift of lucidity to bear on theological problems and, even in his earliest years as a teacher, exploring ways of making things clearer by reformulating questions, asking new questions, involving a wide range of arguments, and in particular trying to make full use of the resources of philosophy in dealing with theological problems.[67]

For Thomas's systematic works, even the majestic *Summa* of theology, do not constitute his truly magisterial, or teaching, activity. If we wish to see him in action, we must turn to his Scripture commentaries, and if we want to find out the full thought of Aquinas, it should be not just to the *Summa* or the

*Quaestiones disputatae* that we turn, but to his courses on the various books of the Bible, where we have the fortune to possess them.[68] Emery explains that the purpose of Thomas's biblical teaching 'is to disengage the deep meaning of the scriptural text, using reason within faith'.[69] The *Summa* we may regard as the distillation of his thought, but to be fully discerned and explained and appreciated, the *Summa* must be seen as a technical commentary on Sacred Scripture.[70] In his exhaustive study on Thomas, Torrell comments,

> Though long overlooked in favor of the *Sentences* or the *Summa*, this kind of biblical teaching was nevertheless Thomas's ordinary labor. . . . If we wish, therefore, to get a slightly less one-sided idea of the whole theologian and his method, it is imperative to read and use in much deeper fashion these biblical commentaries *in parallel with* the great systematic works.[71]

There existed in the thirteenth century, Grelot remarked, a vital connection between the systematic constructions of the *Summae* and the exegetical work which had prepared the material for them, and if we sever that dynamic link between Thomas's systematic works and his Scripture commentaries, we cut off both Thomas's thought and our appreciation of it, from the source of life, isolating in 'stagnant pools what should be the living water of the Spirit'. [72]

In practice this means, at least, that when Thomas cites a verse of Scripture in the *Summa*, frequently as one of several, and without further comment, one cannot claim to have grasped his full thought on the subject under consideration, unless one consults his exegesis of those verses in his Scripture commentaries. When one then begins to follow up the allusions and associations which Thomas invariably makes to other verses of Scripture, including his favourites, one finds oneself fully launched upon what has been well called Thomas's scriptural ocean, on which one appears to hear only the surge and thunder of the word of God.

Christopher Baglow brings out the significance of what he calls 'the repetition of scriptural *auctoritates*' in Thomas's scripture commentaries; that is, the associated texts which he regularly cites to confirm or to elucidate the theological or biblical point that he is currently making.[73] As we shall see in the context of this study of his moral teaching, Thomas loses no opportunity to invoke, almost as recurring refrains, both Rom. 8.14 on God's children being regularly 'driven' in their wills by God's Spirit, and Ps. 143.10, 'Let your good Spirit "lead" me' in my thinking. These often appear simply as additional and supportive citations, but there can be little doubt that in the lecture hall Brother Thomas would have expanded on them, and would have brought out their nuances and how they enrich the particular verse or passage that he was dealing with at the time. Fergus Kerr, a knowledgeable Dominican describer of the modern scene, acknowledged the present academic emphasis on Thomas as 'an exponent of natural theology and a philosopher', but he found it necessary to add that, in order to develop an alternative and more lifelike portrait, 'one would need to be supported by argumentation and quotations from his biblical commentaries'.[74]

From all this immersion of Thomas in Sacred Scripture, one realizes how pale is the description of him as an Aristotelian or a mediaeval schoolman, far less as just a philosopher. In most English-language university environments until recently, Thomas has been invariably portrayed as just the outstanding figure in mediaeval and scholastic philosophy; and departments of even theology or religion have regularly concentrated in general on his epistemology, in regrettable preference to his metaphysics. One thinks of the favoured syllabus topics, or the essay and examination questions, on Aquinas's 'five ways' of proving that God exists, on his doctrine of the natural law, on his understanding of beatitude, and now, fashionably, of his use of virtue ethics. Kerr has also observed pointedly, 'We are beginning to realise that Thomas's main teaching activity was expounding Scripture, not dictating *Summae* – let alone writing commentaries on Aristotle.'[75]

In the circumstances, it is enlightening to note the difference between the theological project being undertaken in this study, on *The Holy Spirit and Moral Action in Aquinas*, and the philosophical study by the distinguished Thomist scholar, Ralph McInerny, entitled *Aquinas on Human Action: A Theory of Practice*.[76] The latter admirable work is one of pure philosophy. There is regular mention of God, but it is invariably in purely rational terms as First Cause and Supreme Good. By contrast, there is no reference to revelation, nor to the Trinity, far less any mention of the Holy Spirit and his theological role in human action. Nor is any of this to be expected. The difference between a purely philosophical study and our theological one could be usefully compared, we dare to suggest, to that between black-and-white television and colour television, or between a two-dimensional portrait and a three-dimensional one. There is obviously in the pure philosophical study a completeness and integrity, and an inherent value, as it accurately and profitably expounds a highly prized dimension of Thomas's teaching. Yet, a theologian might be forgiven for considering it perfectly valid in its own right, of course, yet also as only an abstraction from Thomas's holistic view of reality; a partial presentation, resulting in a rather 'thin' product, which lacks the ontological depth and the 'thick' theological texture of Thomas's thought taken in its entirety. There is a richness, one might say, about Thomas's theological account of human moral action which finds place for so much more than God as first cause and ultimate end, and which brings out the love – and enhances the mystery – of the divine creative enterprise which we know as human morality. It recognizes the Spirit's grace-laden activity as leading to much more than human natural fulfilment, as he wisely and lovingly 'drives'

(Rom. 8.14) God's sons and daughters progressively through their moral choices to achieving their destined fulfilment as 'participants in the divine nature' (2 Pet. 1.4).

As the recurring ground bass of his theological development, Thomas had a comprehension and a penetration of Scripture which are impressive. He did not speak Scripture almost as a second language, like a St Bernard, but, if we may use the phrase, he walked around inside Scripture. It was his world; and of that world he was a theologian: fully at home in it, appropriating it and savouring it calmly and imperturbably, and fulfilling his mission of showing to others its divine 'sweet reasonableness'. As Otto-Herman Pesch pointed out in a notable article on the relevance of Thomas for theology today,

> For a long time now there has been no doubt among experts that there is no basis for feelings of superiority on the part of Bible scholars towards St Thomas's exegetic writings. Not only did he strive with rare intensity for accurate, even historically accurate information, as far as that was available in his time, but without the benefit of the methods and means available to us today. But he hit on the right solution in interpreting individual biblical texts and arrived at judgements which have not been superseded to this day.[77]

In developing what he claims to be a thorough 'new approach' to Thomas as a biblical exegete, Christopher Baglow draws attention to what he considers the anomaly that much of the increasing recent writing on Thomas and the Bible has concentrated on methodological issues rather than on theological content; that is, on scrutinizing Thomas's principles as exegete and theologian in his attitude to Scripture, and on exploring his historical and systematic presuppositions and his method in approaching the biblical text. By contrast, Baglow observed, little of substance has been produced in practice to exemplify and apply all this theory, and to show Thomas actually at work 'as an exegete in action, dealing with specific texts'.

Baglow himself proceeded to illustrate, and substantiate, his 'new' approach by studying with impressive results one of Thomas's scriptural works, his commentary on Ephesians, as a whole and as a unity,[78] thus building on his earlier achievement of expounding 'The Doctrine of the Eucharist in Thomas's *Commentary on the Gospel of St John*'.[79] Similarly, J.F. Boyle devoted part of his University of Dallas Aquinas Lecture to a brief analysis of the theme of 'life' in Thomas's commentary on John's Gospel, especially as this emerges from Thomas's introductory division and systematic analysis of the Johannine text.[80] And more recently, John Meinert, in his study of the relationship between grace and the Gifts of the Holy Spirit, strikingly draws on Thomas's commentaries, especially on Romans, and shows what theological riches they contain.[81] By contrast, our aim in this study is to be more ambitious and more holistic, to explore a specific moral theme, namely, the role of the Holy Spirit in human moral action, as this is found treated in the whole of Thomas's writings, but not least in the corpus of his exegetical work.

## ADVANCING THE ARGUMENT

In pursuing this theme, it is appropriate to begin by considering the Holy Spirit himself, in terms of Anselm's famous definition of theology as 'faith seeking understanding'. Accordingly, our opening chapter, 'Understanding the Spirit of God', concentrates on the Holy Spirit in the life of the Trinity as understood by Aquinas, before providing a biblical portrait of the Spirit as commented on by Thomas, and then introducing a consideration of his compendious idea of 'the grace of the Holy Spirit'.

After this preparation, we proceed in chapter 2 to consider Thomas's accounts of the outstanding manifestation of the Spirit's activity in human moral action, in terms of *The Prompting (instinctus) of the Holy Spirit* in those 'spiritual' men and women who are 'driven' (*aguntur,* Rom. 8.14, properly understood) by the Spirit, in being subordinated totally, yet freely, to his dynamism. This is followed in chapter 3 by considering the equally significant, and often surprising, ways in which, according to Thomas, the Holy Spirit enlightens and leads God's children, to discern, and to apply in their lives, the true wisdom of the *'Law of the Spirit of life'* (Rom. 8.2).

In the light of these considerations of the Holy Spirit's intimate influence on the decisions as well as the minds of God's children, we turn to consider in chapter 4 how Thomas understands and explains the process of their *Moral Decision-Making in the Holy Spirit*, drawing on examples and problematic incidents in the Bible, and the subsequent history of the Christian community. Following on this, we identify in chapter 5 what we consider three *Constants of the Holy Spirit*, which characterize, for Thomas, the work of the Spirit in influencing human moral behaviour: first, his being one and 'the same Spirit', acting consistently throughout salvation history; then, his being invariably 'the Spirit of Christ', both acting on him and being subsequently imparted by him; and finally, the Spirit's being regularly active within the church, which is for Thomas, significantly characterized as 'the Church of the Holy Spirit'. Finally, in chapter 6, we examine the *All-embracing' Wisdom of God*, considering how the Holy Spirit's activity within God's human creatures is recognized above all for Thomas as an active and creative sharing with them, and by them, of the wise ordering of God's creation. Through the grace of the Holy Spirit, God's children are enabled to judge everything in their lives by godly principles, and to discern the wise and provident ordering of the whole of creation and history as it involves them individually. In this way, God's sons and daughters are destined, and driven under the influence of God's own Spirit, to contribute in their moral acts to bringing about the ordered design of God's loving and all-embracing wisdom for the totality of his creation, as this involves themselves, their fellow humans and the world they share as their common home.

## A NOTE ON TRANSLATIONS, GENDER AND TEXTS

All English biblical quotations in the following work are taken from the New Revised Standard Version (1989, 1995) unless otherwise noted. This version of the Bible is usefully aimed, as it explains, at eliminating 'masculine-oriented language' and at avoiding 'the danger of linguistic sexism arising from the inherent bias of the English language towards the masculine gender' (xvii). Normally this desirable purpose can be achieved without fuss by verbal dexterity, but following it here could raise a theological question, among others, concerning the translation of Rom. 8.14, which, this study argues, is central for Thomas to the activity of the Holy Spirit in human moral behaviour. In the original Greek, the sentence runs, *hosoi gar pneumati theou agontai, houtoi huioi eisin theou*, which in the Latin Vulgate became *quicumque enim spiritu Dei aguntur, ii sunt filii Dei*, and was translated by the earlier Revised Standard Version as 'For all who are led by the Spirit of God are sons of God.'

It might seem that this could now be sensitively and obviously translated 'sons and daughters of God', or just 'children of God', as in the NRSV. However, in Paul, the idea of a 'son' of God partly includes the Roman ideology of a male son-and-heir, with legal implications of inheritance, as Paul himself concludes in the Latin: 'if sons [Latin *filii*, but Greek *tekna*], then heirs, heirs of God and joint heirs with Christ' (Rom. 8.17). This juridical strand of Paul's theological argumentation could appear to be weakened in verse 14 if one refers to 'children' rather than 'sons'; but we prefer to sacrifice the theological nuance, if such it is, rather than appear to continue subscribing to sexual discrimination. (We deal in chapter 2 with the theological inadequacy of using in this famous verse the English verb 'led' to translate the more powerful Greek verb *agontai* and Latin *aguntur*.)

A further gender quandary applies to which English pronoun should be used to refer to God and to the Holy Spirit. The apparent ascribing of gender to God (Is God he or she?) is a familiar challenge today, on which the modern classic has become Elizabeth A. Johnson's *She Who Is: The Mystery of God in Feminist Theological Discourse*.[82] And now, in this study, is the Spirit to be he or she – or it, in pursuit of gender neutrality? This apparently simple issue is a recurring instance of the sheer difficulty of applying inherently limited human terminology in attempts to express divine reality, as we shall have much occasion to consider in the course of this study. There is, of course, no grammatical basis for referring to the New Testament Spirit as 'she', because although the Greek term *pneuma* ends in what may appear to be a feminine 'a', it is neutral in gender (*to pneuma*). Moreover, to refer to the Spirit as 'she', as appears attractive, in some respects,[83] incurs objections parallel to those involved in referring to God simply as 'he'. Nicola Slee points out, following Sarah Coakley, that 'the female naming of the Spirit relies on essentialising stereotypes of the feminine', on which Johnson too has cogent criticisms.[84] Yet, awareness of this risk also in feminist pneumatology, and, as a result, resorting to referring to the Spirit as 'it', appears to imply that the Spirit is somehow a non-personal reality. The NRSV avoids this dilemma in translating the famous chapter 8 of Romans by ingeniously not using any personal pronoun of the Spirit. Our theologically lame conclusion is that every instance has to be considered in context, but our decision is to write mostly of the Spirit as 'he', thus giving theological priority to personhood, while aiming always to bear in mind the cautions to be attached to analogical predication, on which much more anon.

Translations of passages from Thomas's writings and from foreign secondary sources are by the author unless otherwise noted.

For convenience's sake, references to the Fathers and early theologians are regularly made to the easily accessible Migne, *Patres Latini* and *Patres Graeci*. Later critical editions can be accessed, if wished, through the textual references provided for each passage quoted.

Early versions of some parts of the following appeared in the author's *Seeking the Spirit. Essays in Moral and Pastoral Theology* (Sheed & Ward, 1981).

## NOTES

1. Cf Jean-Pierre Torrell, *Saint Thomas Aquinas*, vol. 1, The Person and his Work (Washington, D.C.: Catholic University of America, 1996). For a knowledgeable account of Thomas's life and times provided by a fellow Dominican, see Aidan Nichols, *Discovering Aquinas: An Introduction to his Life, Works and Influence* (London: Darton, Longman and Todd, 2002), 3–18. For a warming account of his family connections, see Fergus Kerr, 'Thomas Aquinas and his Family', *NB* 91, 1031, January 2010, 1–3.

2. Tugwell, Simon, *Albert & Thomas. Selected Writings* (New York: Paulist Press, 1988), 201–3.

3. Tugwell, 208–10.

4. Torrell, 99; Tugwell, 118.

5. Torrell, 142–5.

6. Tugwell, 224.

7. Torrell, 179–82.
8. Torrell, 182, quoting G. Verbeke, *Jean Philopon. Commentaire sur le De anima d'Aristote* (Louvain-Paris, 1966), lxxiv–lxxv.
9. Tugwell, 213–16.
10. Torrell, 247–9.
11. Torrell, 289–95.
12. Second Council of Lyons, Decrees, *DS* 850.
13. Eleonore Stump, Biblical commentary and philosophy, in Norman Kretzmann and Eleonore Stump, edd., *The Cambridge Companion to Aquinas* (Cambridge: Cambridge University Press, 1993), 252.
14. Thomas G Weinandy, Daniel A. Keating and John P. Yocum, edd., *Aquinas on Scripture. An Introduction to the Biblical Commentaries* (London/New York: T & T Clark International), 2005, ix.
15. Aidan Nichols, Book Reviews, *New Blackfriars* 87, 1012 (Nov 2006) 660.
16. Healy, Nicholas H., Introduction, Weinandy, Keating and Yocum, 3.
17. *ST* I, 2, 3.
18. Healy, Nicholas H., *Thomas Aquinas Theologian of the Christian Life* (Aldershot: Ashgate, 2003), 57–8. Cf *Sup Rom.* 1.20 (M 116-22); *Sup. Ioan.* Prol, nn. 6–7.
19. Mary Margaret Pazdan, OP, 'Thomas Aquinas and Contemporary Biblical Interpreters: "I Call You Friends" (John 15.15)', *New Blackfriars* 86, 1005 (September 2005), 465–77.
20. Stump, Biblical commentary, 260.
21. *S Thomae de Aquino Expositio super Job ad litteram*, ed. Leonina, Rome, Opera Omnia, t. 26, 1965; *Expositio super Isaiam ad litteram*, ed. Leonina, t. 28, 1974.
22. Cf Antoine Dondaine, *Secrétaires de saint Thomas* (Rome, 1956), t. 1, p. 15; P. Glorieux, 'Essai sur les commentaires scripturaires de saint Thomas et leur chronologie', *RTAM* 117 (1950), 242; J. Holmes, Aquinas' *Lectura in Matthaeum*, in *Aquinas on Scripture: An Introduction to his Biblical Commentaries*, edd. Thomas G. Weinandy, Daniel A. Keating, Jon P. Yocum (New York: T & T. International, 2005), 74–6.
23. Smalley, B., *The Study of the Bible in the Middle Ages*, ed. 2 (Oxford, 1952), 204.
24. A. Walz – P. Novarina, *Saint Thomas d'Aquin* (Louvain, 1962), 87–8.
25. Mark D. Jordan, *Ordering Wisdom. The Hierarchy of Philosophical Discourses in Aquinas* (Notre Dame: University of Notre Dame Press, 1986), xv.
26. The classic statement on this subject is the study of J. De Guibert, *Les Doublets de Saint Thomas d'Aquin. Leur étude méthodique, quelques réflexions, quelques exemples* (Paris, 1926).
27. Tugwell, 245.
28. Dondaine, t. 1, 200; Torrell, 28–30; Tugwell, 211.
29. Dondaine, t. 1, 201, n. 50.
30. Walz-Novarina, 101, n.43.
31. I. T. Eschmann, 'The Quotation of Aristotle's *Politics* in St Thomas's *lectura super Matthaeum*', *Mediaeval Studies* 18 (1956) 232–40; C. Dozois, 'Sources

patristiques chez saint Thomas d'Aquin', *RUO* 33 (1963), 165*; Torrell, 55–7, 197; Jeremy Holmes, 'Aquinas' *Lectura in Matthaeum*', in Weinandy, Keating and Yocum, 73.

32. Wilhelmus G.B.M. Valkenberg, *Words of the Living God. Place and Function of Holy Scripture in the Theology of St Thomas Aquinas* (Leuven: Peeters, 2000), 167. Valkenberg, pp. 165–85, provides some detailed useful information on the chronology of Thomas's Scripture Commentaries. See also Tugwell, 231.

33. Tugwell, 246–7, and 331, n. 461. P. M. Kimball, *Commentary on the Gospel of Saint Matthew* (Bristol: Dolorosa Press, 2012), pp. *vii–xix*. For the *Appendix: Transcription of Basel Manuscript B.V. 12* [Reportatio Petri de Andria], ed. H. Kraml, see ibid., 971–97. On the whole, see Holmes, 74–6.

34. Kimball, *vii*.

35. Glorieux, *Essai*, p. 260. Eschmann and Torrell consider 1261–64 more likely. Cf Eschmann's Catalogue of St Thomas's Works, in E Gilson, *The Christian Philosophy of St Thomas Aquinas* (New York, 1957), 394; Tugwell, 246; Torrell, 120–1.

36. Glorieux, *Essai*, 258–9.

37. Glorieux, *Essai*, 250–1; Torrell, 257–61; Tugwell, 332–3, n. 475.

38. Fergus Kerr, 'Recent Thomistica: I', *NB* 83, 975 (May 2002), 246.

39. Glorieux, *Essai*, 245. Tugwell, 246. Cf Torrell, 198–201; Tugwell, 331, n. 457.

40. Torrell, 199–200.

41. Tugwell, 247.

42. Cf. H Bouillard, *Conversion et grâce chez saint Thomas d'Aquin*. Apppendice: Date du Commentaire de saint Thomas sur l'épitre aux Romains (Paris: Aubier, 1944), 225–41. Glorieux, *Essai* 254–5.

43. *Essai*, 256.

44. *Essai* 257–8. Cf Torrell, 250–7.

45. Tugwell, 247–8.

46. Ceslaus Spicq, *Esquisse d'une histoire de l'exégèse latine au moyen âge* (Paris, 1944), 282.

47. Cf Thomas, *In Ps.* 32, lect 2–3, on the verse 'Praise the Lord with the lyre, make melody to him with the harp', Ps. 33.2.

48. Smalley, *Study*, 309.

49. Spicq, Esquisse, p. 66, quotes the explanation of the ancient Roman, Honorius (Migne *PL* 172, 279), that syllogisms lie hid in holy Scripture like fish in deep water waiting to be hauled out for our benefit.

50. *In Gal.*, cap 2, lect. 6 (M102).

51. See Walz-Novarina, 97–8.

52. E. Vauthier, 'Le Saint Esprit principe d'unité de l'Eglise d'après Saint Thomas d'Aquin', *Melanges de science religieuse,* 5 (1948) 187.

53. Boyle, J. F., *Master Thomas Aquinas and the Fullness of Life* (South Bend, Indiana: St Augustine's Press, 2014), 55.

54. Tugwell, Simon, *Albert & Thomas. Selected Writings* (New York: Paulist Press, 1988), xi.

55. Davies, Brian, 'Aquinas and the Academic life', *NB*, 83, 977 (July 2002), 337.

56. Spicq, *Esquisse*, 282–3.
57. Spicq, *Esquisse*, 206, 250–1. See Healy, Preface, in Weinandy, Keating and Yocum, 7–9.
58. Walz-Novarina, 97.
59. Spicq, *Esquisse*, 285.
60. Smalley, 101.
61. Smalley, 301.
62. ST I.1.10 ad 1. Smalley, 300.
63. *ST* 1–2.9.4 and 6. See below, pp. 68–70.
64. Terence McGuckin, 'Saint Thomas Aquinas and Theological Exegesis of Sacred Scripture', *NB* 74, 870 (April 1993), 200.
65. Gilles Emery, *The Trinitarian Theology of Saint Thomas Aquinas* (Oxford: Oxford University Press, 2007), 21.
66. H. Denifle, 'Quel livre servait de base à l'enseignment des maîtres en théologie dans l'université de Paris?' *RevThom* 2 (1948) 161.
67. Tugwell, 212.
68. Cf Glorieux, Essai, p. 237.
69. Emery, p. 22.
70. Cf M.-J. Le Guillou, *Le Christ et l'Eglise théologie du mystère* (Paris, 1963), 150.
71. J.-P. Torrell, *Saint Thomas Aquinas, Vol 1. The Person and His Work* (Washington, D.C.: The Catholic University of America, 1996), 55. Emphasis added.
72. P. Grelot, 'Exégèse, théologie et pastorale', *NRT* 88 (1966) 11.
73. Baglow, 272.
74. Fergus Kerr, 'The Varieties of Interpreting Aquinas', in idem, ed., *Contemplating Aquinas. On the Varieties of Interpretations* (London: SCM, 2003), 3.
75. Fergus Kerr, 'Recent Thomistica: I', *NB* 83, 975 (May 2002), 251.
76. Ralph McInerny, *Aquinas on Human Action. A Theory of Practice* (Washington, D.C.: Catholic University of America, 1992).
77. Pesch, Otto-Herman, 'Thomas Aquinas and Contemporary Theology', in Kerr, *Contemplating*, 207.
78. Christopher T. Baglow, *"Modus et Forma": A New Approach to the Exegesis of Saint Thomas Aquinas with an Application to the* Lectura super Epistolam ad Ephesios, *Analecta Biblica* 149, Pontifical Biblical Institute (Rome, 2002), p. 15.
79. C. T. Baglow, 'The Doctrine of the Eucharist in St Thomas Aquinas' *Commentary on the Gospel of St John'* (Dallas: University of Dallas, 1996).
80. Boyle, 61–74; 77–80.
81. John M. Meinert, *The Love of God Poured Out. Grace and the Gifts of the Holy Spirit in St. Thomas Aquinas* (Steubenville, OH: Emmaus Academic, 2018).
82. New York, Crossroad, 1992.
83. Cf Yves M.-J Congar, *I Believe in the Holy Spirit*, vol. 3 (New York: Seabury Press, 1983), pp. 155–64.
84. Nicola Slee, 'The Holy Spirit and Spirituality', in Susan Frank Parsons, ed., *The Cambridge Companion to Feminist Theology* (Cambridge: Cambridge University Press, 2002), 171–89 at 183. On 'the problem of stereotyping', see Johnson, pp. 52–6.

*Chapter 1*

# Understanding the Holy Spirit

## THE HOLY SPIRIT IN THE TRINITY

In composing his *Summa* of theology for his students, Thomas Aquinas stressed their need for a brief systematic approach to the study of theology, with its parts identified, pursued and integrated in a manner which would not only make it easier for 'beginners' to grasp and retain the content, but it would also present an intellectually and faith-satisfying schema for their Christian belief.[1] Within the logical progression of his subject matter, Thomas began with a First Part introducing how 'sacred teaching' provides a privileged knowledge of God, and he then concentrated on the subject of God, first within the divine nature as triune, and then as the origin and goal of all created things, especially those creatures endowed with the power of reason. Thomas's Second Part, divided into two sections, moved on to focus in detail on 'the moving of the rational creature towards God'; and finally in his Third Part, which was interrupted by his death and completed by a disciple drawing on Thomas's earlier commentary on the *Sentences* of Peter Lombard, Thomas concluded with treating of 'Christ, who as a human being is our "way" [Jn 14.6] of tending towards God'.[2]

The Holy Spirit, of course, figures prominently throughout the whole of the *Summa*, but the fullest systematic treatment by Thomas is to be found in the First Part, where he explores God's existence, nature and attributes (questions 2–4, 6–14, 18–26), acknowledges God as a Trinity of divine Persons (questions 27–32, 39–42), and then directs his attention to each of the three Persons in turn (questions 33–38), dealing specifically with 'the Person of the Holy Spirit' in questions 36–38. A useful analysis of the section on 'The Person of the Holy Spirit' in Thomas is provided by Matthew Levering, building on Jean-Pierre Torrell's survey of a wide range of relevant literature. These, with

Gilles Emery's rich treatment of the Holy Spirit, including his position within the Trinity and his appropriation and mission, together form an authoritative trio of authoritative commentators on Thomas's text.[3]

It is entirely appropriate, Thomas maintains, to give to a Person of the Trinity the name of 'Holy Spirit'. Scripture itself does this, he points out, in stating that 'there are three that testify in heaven, the Father, the Word, and the Holy Spirit'.[4] Moreover, as Augustine had explained, the Father is spirit and holy, and the Son is also spirit and holy; so, the third Person, being common to both Father and Son, is appropriately called the Holy Spirit.[5] Additionally, in created things, the word 'spirit' is like breath and wind, involving impulsion and movement; and it is typical of love to move and impel the will of the lover to the object of its love, while holiness is ascribed to those things which are ordered towards God. Hence, since a divine Person proceeds by way of love in God, it is appropriately named the Holy Spirit.[6]

Moreover, Thomas proceeds, if we follow the teaching of the early Pope, St Gregory the Great, we shall hold that an outstanding immanent characteristic of the Holy Spirit within the life of the Trinity is that of love.[7] As Thomas argues, 'The Holy Spirit is said to be the bond between the Father and the Son insofar as he is Love . . . . From the very fact that the Father and the Son love one another, their mutual love, that is, the Holy Spirit, must proceed from them both.'[8] For similar reasons, a second outstanding characteristic of the Holy Spirit within the Trinity of divine Persons is that of his being Gift. The idea of giving implies both a person who is a giver, and a person who is a receiver; and this applies strikingly to the Holy Spirit as the gift exchanged between the Father and the Son. Thomas continues, 'In addition, Aristotle tells us that, strictly speaking, a gift is something given with no intention of its being returned';[9] on which Thomas comments, 'The reason behind a gratuitous giving is love. we freely give something to someone because we wish their good . . . . And since the Holy Spirit proceeds as love, he proceeds as the first Gift.'[10]

Much of what we have seen Thomas explain above can be summed up in the observation of Wayne J. Hankey, that

> the Spirit has a dual role in the theology of Thomas. His is the procession of will or love. Love is a force impelling to unity, but it also carries the subject out of himself and is an endeavor to attain union beyond the possession already given in knowledge. . . .And so, because the Spirit is love he is the gift by which God bestows his other graces. The movement is outward to creatures from love.[11]

In his magisterial study, *The Trinitarian Theology of Saint Thomas Aquinas*, Gilles Emery makes the important theological point that the central aim of Thomas's enquiry in this section of the *Summa* 'is to elucidate what belongs eternally to the Holy Spirit, in the immanence of the Trinity, *but to do it a way that provides the foundation for understanding his action in creation and salvation*'.[12] In expounding the doctrine of the Trinity, Thomas naturally spends much of his time and attention focusing on God's internal life, so to speak, exploring within the one God the technicalities of interior 'processions', 'spirations' and 'relations' among divine Persons who are identified in Revelation as the Father, the Son, and the Holy Spirit. In addition to this 'immanent' Trinity, however, which is also termed the 'ontological' Trinity and is concerned with seeking the understanding of who the triune God *is*, Christian theology is by definition also profoundly concerned with what this God *does*, in the 'economies' of divine creation and divine salvation. In this context of God's so-called 'external' activity, reference is made to the 'economic Trinity' whose aim and action is to gather up God's human creatures into what has been described as the 'mutual altruism' of Father, Son and Holy Spirit.[13]

## Appropriation

According to Emery, 'The generation of the Word and the procession of love are the source of God's works in the world'.[14] This affinity between characteristics of the divine Persons within the immanent Trinity, on the one hand, and their external actions on and in creatures as the economic Trinity, on the other hand, finds expression in Thomas's teaching on the 'appropriation' of aspects of creation to individual Persons in the Trinity.[15] God cannot be divided in action, of course, and every created effect cannot but result from the one supreme Cause. However, Thomas explains, some created effects appear particularly appropriate to one particular Person of the Trinity, and they thus have an affinity with that Person; as, for instance, what relates to the understanding, such as truth, knowledge, wisdom and law, is appropriated to the Son who proceeds by way of understanding as the Word.[16] Likewise, the themes of created love, impulse, dynamism and, particularly, as we shall see, instigating, or 'prompting' (*instinctus*), are associated with, and appropriated to, the Holy Spirit who is 'spirated' by way of mutual love and gift between Father and Son in the immanent Trinity. On the subject, Torrell quotes the compendious statement of Dondaine, 'Saint Thomas fully and without limit exploits the appropriation of the things of the intellect to the Son, and the things of the will to the Holy Spirit'.[17] Torrell also draws attention to the *Summa* I. 43.5 ad 1, which observes that 'all gifts, as gifts, are attributed to the Holy Spirit, who is the first gift insofar as he is Love; while other gifts have a certain appropriation to the Son, namely, those which relate to the intellect'.[18] In our following section, we shall illustrate from Thomas's Scripture commentaries how the ideas of 'being sent' (mission) and of 'inhabiting' are characteristically appropriated to the Holy Spirit, thus mirroring widespread among creatures, as it were, the corresponding disposition of the Spirit within the divine being itself.[19]

## A BIBLICAL PORTRAIT OF THE HOLY SPIRIT

The briefest reading of what Scripture tells us about the Holy Spirit of God shows how continually he is depicted in terms of dynamic activity, including the influencing of human moral actions. Having in this opening chapter briefly examined the teaching of Aquinas on the Person of the Holy Spirit, we can turn now to examining what Thomas made of the powerful activities of the Spirit, as these are delineated in Scripture; and this provides us with a richly detailed biblical portrait of God's Holy Spirit.

Such an analysis of scriptural concepts and themes was not, of course, original in Thomas's writings, nor in other mediaeval writings, for all the theologians of the Middle Ages drew heavily on the works of the early Fathers in the church who had seen in the rich complexity of scriptural language a continual invitation to penetrate behind the human letter of Scripture in a puny attempt to comprehend at least something of the riches of the reality, the wisdom and the dynamism of God. On Thomas's achievements in this field, Spicq commented that Aquinas was perhaps the mediaeval exegete most careful to clarify the meaning of biblical ideas, and that the exactness of his analyses was so remarkable that it enabled him, for instance, to provide an exegesis of 'the true light' of Jn 1.9 which was 'much better than that of St John Chrysostom and St Augustine'.[20]

In this type of theology the acknowledged master in the Middle Ages was pseudo-Dennis, whose treatise on the names applied to God in Scripture was commented on by Thomas, and from whom Thomas accepted the threefold division of theological discourse into mystical, intelligible and symbolic.[21] The first of these categories, mystical theology (the *via negativa*, or way of negation or 'negative theology' of the mystics) does not concern us here, since it is not used systematically by Thomas; but in his Scripture commentaries, as elsewhere, he continually invokes the other principles of intelligible and symbolic theology, and some understanding of these categories is essential to appreciating his thought.

For Thomas, following pseudo-Dennis, symbolic theology is the analysis of symbols, or metaphors, which Scripture applies to God. Why, for instance, should God be called a rock, or a lion or the sun? What is meant when we sing of God as 'a mighty fortress', or when Scripture describes the Holy Spirit in terms of water, or oil or fire? What do such human images really tell us about the divine reality? Interestingly, at the beginning of Thomas's introduction to theology in the *Summa*, he raises the intriguing question 'should holy Scripture use metaphors'? In defence of such regular scriptural usage, Thomas argues that it is appropriate for sacred Scripture to express divine and spiritual matters to us through bodily similarities. God provides for everything in accordance with its nature, and it is natural for human beings to come to matters of the mind through their senses, since all our knowledge begins from the senses. 'It is fitting, therefore, that in sacred Scripture spiritual matters are expressed to us through bodily metaphors, as pseudo-Dennis explained, "it is impossible for a divine ray of light to get to us unless it is clothed in a variety of sacred veils" .'

Additionally, Thomas continues, it is fitting that in the sacred Scriptures which are meant for everyone, spiritual matters are expressed in the likeness of bodily things, so that they can be grasped even by people who are uneducated, and are incapable of understanding purely intellectual matters.[22]

For Thomas, the study of such creaturely symbols in Scripture is an invitation to enter into the mind of the biblical human writer, and to speculate on what particular aspect of the divine being or activity he was attempting to identify and highlight by this particular choice of words; for obviously we are not intended to remain at the surface level of such expressions.[23] As Thomas observed, 'Sacred Scripture does not propose divine matters to us in sensible terms so that our mind remains there, but so that it may rise from them to the invisible realities.'[24]

A typical example of this symbolic theology in Thomas's Scripture commentaries is to be found in his exegesis of Heb. 12.29 'for our God is a consuming fire'.

> As Dionysus points out, God is called 'fire', not because there is anything material about him, but because intellectual realities are designated by sensible things, among which we find that fire possesses greater nobility, greater clarity, greater activity, a higher natural location, and greater cleansing and consuming power. Hence God is especially called 'fire' because of his clarity, since he 'dwells in unapproachable light' (I Tim. 6.16). He is also most active, 'for indeed all that we have done, you have done for us' (Isa. 26.12). He is located higher than all, 'because he is high above all nations, etc.' (Ps. 113.4). Moreover, he cleanses sins and, as it were, consumes them, 'for he is like a refiner's fire', Mal. 3.2; etc.[25]

This practice of citing Scripture to illuminate Scripture is a general principle in Thomas's Scripture commentaries, but he regards it as of particular importance in explaining scriptural metaphors which refer to God. Moreover, against the objection that Scripture's use of metaphor is unnecessarily clouding the truth rather than revealing it, he points out that what Scripture expresses in one place metaphorically always expresses more clearly elsewhere.[26]

## God as 'Holy Spirit'

We have noted earlier how Thomas justifies the applying of the name 'Holy Spirit' to the third Person of the divine Trinity, but among the several rich terms which are applied by Scripture in describing the Holy Spirit, it could be easy to overlook the associations of the very word 'spirit' itself, *ruach* in Hebrew, *pneuma* in Greek and *spiritus* in Latin. The New Revised Standard Version (NRSV) opens its recital of creation by describing in Gen. 1.2, how 'a wind from God swept over the face of the waters', and it acknowledges alternative understandings of the Hebrew *ruach* here as 'the spirit of God' or 'a mighty wind'.

This idea of spirit, or wind, or breath, continues to be applied graphically throughout the Bible to express, in recognizably inadequate human terms, the being and the attributes of the creating God; and this enabled Thomas to explain, for instance, that, when Jesus in Jn 4. 24 taught the Samaritan woman that 'God is spirit', he was indicating not just that God does not have a body, but also that God is life-giving, 'since our entire life is from God as its effective principle'.[27]

Moreover, Scripture uses this idea of 'spirit' not only to express God's outgoing and creative life-giving breath. It also invokes the same term to refer in a particular way to 'the Holy Spirit', the personification of God that Christians accept as the third Person of the divine Trinity. As Thomas explained of the processions within the Trinity,

> We cannot describe God except in terms of creatures, as explained above (*ST* 1.13.1). And because the sharing of a nature occurs in creatures only by generation, procession in divine matters does not have a proper or a special term apart from 'generation'. And the procession which is not generation has remained without a name, although it can be described as 'spiration', because it is the procession of the Spirit.[28]

To offer some light on the mystery of the interior procession of the third Person of the Trinity, Thomas follows Scripture in finding help in the psychological process of human loving. 'For in bodily matters the word "spirit" seems to convey the idea of impulse and movement (we call breath and the wind "spirit"), and it is the property of love to move and impel the will of a lover towards the beloved'. Moreover, 'in order to signify the divine person that proceeds by way of love, Scripture has adopted the term "Holy Spirit", because among bodily things the term "spirit" seems to mean an impulse and a movement; and it is typical of love to move and impel a lover's will towards the beloved'.[29] Again, this biblical teaching on transferring the Hebrew term 'spirit' (*ruach*) to denote the Holy Spirit of God is explained by Thomas in pointing out, for example, that, as 'spirit' is used of something hidden and invisible, so the Holy Spirit possesses a subtle, or fine, nature, as Jn 3.8 informs us. 'The wind blows where it chooses, and you hear the sound of it, but you do not know where it comes from or where it goes. So it is with everyone who is born of the Spirit.' As Thomas adds, as 'spirit' implies an impulse of some kind, like the wind, so the Spirit shows its power by moving us to act well, citing, as he loved to do, both Rom. 8.14, 'All who are driven by the Spirit of God are children of God', and Ps. 143.10 'let your good spirit lead me on a level path'.[30]

An outstanding factor in Thomas's understanding of the notion of God as 'spirit' is his understanding of spirit as the sign and source of life. As we have seen earlier, John's declaration that 'God is spirit' (4.24) refers not just to God's being incorporeal, but also to his ability to vivify, 'because our whole life is from God as its effective principle', and while the Spirit of God is regarded as the source of natural life in human beings, he is much more frequently seen by Thomas as the source of the spiritual life of grace. 'Just as the body lives with bodily life by the bodily spirit, so the soul lives with spiritual life by the Holy Spirit, as we see in Ps. 104.30, "When you send forth your Spirit, they are created". '[31]

It is this life of the Spirit which the baptized receive as a seed of spiritual life which already contains within itself potentially the whole perfection of eternal life, or beatitude. 'What is born of the Spirit is spirit' (Jn 3.6), that is, Thomas explains, 'spiritual'.[32] And this seed of the spiritual life which germinates in humans and eventually blossoms into eternal life is their very own, given them by the Holy Spirit. This realization, as we shall see in detail later, is fundamental to the understanding of Thomas's teaching on moral behaviour as the behaviour of God's children who are 'driven' (Rom. 8.14) by God's own Spirit. God is 'the life of the soul', as Thomas frequently states following the Vulgate Dt. 30.20, and as the soul is the life of the body, so God vivifies the soul. There is this difference, however, that while the soul vivifies the body as its formal cause, God vivifies the soul as its efficient cause by informing the soul with grace. 'So, it is by bestowing grace on humans that the Holy Spirit imparts spiritual life to them; and as this seed of life grows in humans, they themselves are growing in the life of the grace of the Holy Spirit'.

This truth finds a rich significant expression in Thomas's explanation of the Pauline and Johannine doctrine of 'the spiritual person' that the Holy Spirit in a profound sense 'spiritualizes' God's offspring. ' "That which is born of the Spirit is spirit" (Jn 3.36); that is', Thomas comments, 'what is born by the power of the Spirit is spiritual'; and it is a condition of entry into the kingdom of God that a person is thus made 'spiritual' by the Holy Spirit.[33] While it is true, of course, that we call 'spirit' that part of the human soul which comprises the intellect and will, the theme of the 'spiritual person' implies much more than that. It refers to the person whose spirit is elevated above human nature by the Holy Spirit,[34] whose intellect is illuminated and whose will is inflamed by the Holy Spirit, and who thus has a right judgement in matters of the spirit.[35] This 'spiritual' activity is the natural expression and unfolding in the behaviour of the spiritual person of that spiritual life which they have received from the Spirit of God. Not only are 'spiritual persons' like God in the spiritual life which they receive from the Spirit of God; they also act like God in the actions they perform which manifest the growth of that life within them. And they show themselves as being God's offspring (Rom. 8.14), now and in eternity, in being vivified and driven by God's Spirit.

This doctrine of the 'spiritual' person being progressively 'spiritualized' by the Holy Spirit is fundamental to Thomas's whole moral theology: those who live and act by the Spirit as 'spiritual persons' have good, or right, judgement; that is, they 'discern all things', as Paul explained. Thomas comments that when Paul wrote (1 Cor. 2.15) that 'those who are spiritual discern all things and they are themselves subject to no one else's scrutiny', he meant that 'the person whose mind is illuminated and whose feelings are kept in order by the Holy Spirit has a right judgment on individual matters relating to salvation. On the other hand, the person who is not "spiritual", also has their mind darkened and their feelings disordered about spiritual values; and the "unspiritual" person cannot judge the spiritual person, just as a person awake cannot be judged by someone who is asleep'.[36] As Josef Fuchs expressed it summarily, when writing of 'grace', 'we must see it as power, as the effective activity of the holy Spirit in us. . . . The Spirit of Christ in us overcomes the demand of the flesh, the egoistical concupiscence of the human being under original sin, and forms in its place the spiritual human being.'[37]

## The Holy Spirit as Fire

The most striking of the symbols used by the Bible, and analyzed by Thomas, in referring to the being and activity of the Holy Spirit is the idea of fire. As we have seen earlier, Thomas followed pseudo-Dennis in showing in what sense God can be called fire; and similar treatments are to be found in his commentary on Isaiah where, on Isa. 33. 11 ('your breath is a fire that will consume you'), he observes that God is called fire because he purges, inflames and condemns, citing in each case, as usual, other verses to provide biblical confirmation of his explanation.[38] Charity too is called fire because it illuminates, warms, converts everything into itself, lightens and draws upwards.[39]

And the word of God is called fire because it illuminates, inflames, penetrates, liquefies and consumes.[40] In all of these cases, Thomas quotes other passages of Scripture to show how Scripture itself compares the divine activity with those various aspects or activities of fire which he has distinguished.

So far as the Holy Spirit is concerned, Thomas's general principle can be seen in his commentary on Jn 4. 10 ('he would give you living water'), where he writes, following Chrysostom, that the grace of the Holy Spirit is sometimes called water and sometimes fire, in order to show that in itself it is neither of these things, but that its activity is similar to those of both water and fire. 'For it is called fire because it elevates the heart with fervor and warmth ("Be aglow with the Spirit", Rom. 12.11); and because it consumes sins ("The lamps [of love] are fire and flames", Cant. 8.6)'.[41]

The idea of being aglow, or fervent, with the Spirit (Rom. 12.11) recurs frequently in Thomas's Scripture commentaries, and naturally its fullest explanation is to be found in his commentary on Romans chapter 12, where Thomas explains that fervour proceeds from an abundance of heat, and so, fervour of the spirit implies that the abundance of divine love makes the whole person fervent for God, as Apollo was said to speak 'being fervent in spirit' (Acts 18.25). For we must not 'quench the spirit' (I Thess. 5.19).[42] Not that the Spirit himself can be extinguished or quenched, but, as Thomas explains, the fervour of the Spirit can be quenched, either in oneself or in another, when a good thought or impulse arises. And in this sense, quenching the Spirit is equivalent to 'resisting the spirit' (Acts 7.51).[43]

These and other comments of Thomas on the fervour of the Holy Spirit serve to bring out the effects which the Spirit has on a person when the Spirit 'ignites' them with his own love; when, that is, the spirit of a human being is inflamed by that of God.[44] 'Just as a coal which has caught fire has the properties of fire, so the properties of the Holy Spirit are in the spiritual person.'[45] 'For then we cry Abba, Father, when we are fired with the heat of the Holy Spirit to desire God'.[46]

This idea of warmth, or fire, also lies beneath Thomas's notion of God's benignity, for, according to the etymology of the mediaeval theologians, the Latin *benignitas* derives from '*bona igneitas*', conveying the idea of well-disposed warmth. Thus, in his exposition of the fruits of the Spirit (Gal. 5.22) which include 'kindness' (*benignitas*), Thomas explains that this *bona igneitas* (kindly warmth) makes one flow to help other in their needs. 'Therefore, we should have benignity towards all, which is a sort of *bona igneitas*. For fire melts what is humid and makes it flow; and if the good fire is in you it softens and dissolves whatever is humid in you. This is the work of the Holy Spirit'.[47]

This section on fire as a symbol of the Holy Spirit can close with a consideration of Thomas's two favourite verses of Scripture on the subject. Of the various verses from throughout Scripture which he loves to weave into his exegesis of individual verses concerning the Holy Spirit, one popular reference which can seem initially puzzling is Cant. 8. 6, where Thomas followed the Latin Vulgate *lampades eius lampades ignis et flammarum,* which translates into the Douai-Rheims version as 'the lamps thereof are lamps of fire and flames'.[48] Since we do not possess a commentary on Canticles by Thomas, we have no explicit exegesis of this text, but it seems to have been frequently in his mind, influencing his reflection, and enriching his theological argumentation. Mention of 'lamps' gives the key to much of the patristic and mediaeval interpretation of the verse: the hearts of the faithful are like lamps burning with the fire of love and consequently producing the flame of action, that is, internal devotion to God leads to external love for neighbour.

This dynamic thrust of the interior love of the faithful for God flaming into external actions for their neighbour is shown in other passages where Thomas also cites Cant. 8.6 to support his argument.[49] On Ps. 18 [19].6, 'No one can hide from his heat', Thomas comments succinctly, 'The Holy Spirit gives heat. Cant. 8. his lamps are lamps of fire'.[50]

From the context, then, in which Cant. 8.6 is cited, and from the arguments that it is invoked to support and to illustrate, we can conclude that for Thomas one of the main meanings, if not the predominant meaning, of this verse of Scripture is that fire produces flame, that is, that the love of God is never inactive, whether it be God's own love for us issuing forth in creative or redemptive action, or the creature's love for God issuing forth in deeds influenced and stimulated by the Holy Spirit.

What may be considered as a preparatory stage of this driving of people by the Holy Spirit appears to be a favourite interpretation by Thomas of the other text that he cites frequently, 'I came to cast fire upon the earth' (Lk. 12.49), since it often occurs in the context of the Spirit purifying one's heart from whatever will interiorly hinder the Spirit's dynamic force. At times, Thomas understands Lk. 12.49 of the fire of charity which Christ enkindles,[51] and he also quotes it to show that Christ enkindles this charity in us by giving us the Holy Spirit.[52] But to a great extent, he favours this text as an illustration of the purifying activity of the Holy Spirit, whether this be seen as purifying the creature's pleasure and thoughts from the taints of the flesh[53] or as burning and dissolving one's hardness of heart.[54]

These two favourite quotations of Thomas on the activity of the Spirit in terms of fire bring out much of what this scriptural symbol meant for him, and with them we can conclude this review of his thought on the Holy Spirit as fire. Basically, there appears the idea of the desire on the part of the Spirit for self-communication, since the Holy Spirit seeks to be received by all, and whoever receives the Spirit shares the qualities of the Spirit, as wood or coal which are kindled share the properties of the fire that does the kindling.

This participation by human beings of the Spirit's characteristics is shown by Thomas above all, perhaps, in the ease with which he passes back and forth between the fire of the Spirit and the heat that it generates in humans, illuminating the close dynamic connection between the activity of the Spirit and that of the human being who possesses the Spirit.

It can happen, of course, that a human being is reluctant to receive this self-communication of the Spirit, and so another facet of the Spirit's activity is that of preparing humans by purifying and disposing them to receive the Spirit. But once the person is disposed, the Spirit gives himself in abundance. And finally, just as the self-communication of the Spirit to humans is an act of the dynamism of the Spirit himself, so it has a dynamic effect also on humans. Because of their reception of the Spirit they desire God ardently in affective love, and also exhibit an expansive love of self-giving towards others. It could hardly be otherwise, for the one who receives the Spirit receives also the restless and expanding activity which is so characteristic of the Spirit of God and of fire.

## The Holy Spirit as Living Water

It would be difficult to find a symbol of the Holy Spirit more apparently opposed to fire than that of water, and, as will be remembered, Thomas followed Chrysostom in explaining that these two symbols are chosen in Scripture to represent the grace of the Holy Spirit partly because their contrast shows that neither is to be taken literally, and also because the activity of each of them can nevertheless in some way be transferred to characterize the action of the Spirit. Just as the grace of the Holy Spirit is called fire, Thomas points out, because of the elevating, warming and consuming properties of fire, so it is called water because it cleans from uncleanness, cools from the heat of temptation and quenches the thirst for what is material and transitory.[55]

The idea of washing and cleansing is, of course, inevitably connected by Thomas with the activity of the Holy Spirit at baptism, and on Mt. 3.11 ('I baptize you with water for repentance, but he . . . will baptize you with the Holy Spirit and with fire') he explains that John's baptism which was without the Spirit washed only the body, whereas the flow of the Holy Spirit is required for complete washing.[56] So much so, that the descent of the Holy Spirit on Jesus at his baptism (Mk 1.10) is a sign of this flowing of the Holy Spirit at baptism.[57]

Although at baptism the Spirit cleanses from actual sins as well as original sin,[58] Thomas does not appear in his Scripture commentaries to connect washing by the Spirit with the forgiveness of post-baptismal sins; but he does explain that the fiery thirst for the desires and the concupiscences of the flesh which lead to sin is quenched by the coolness experienced by all who have drunk of the one Spirit (1 Cor. 12.13).[59] Moreover, the water which comes from the Spirit, besides removing this thirst for mundane pleasures, has the additional property of giving one a thirst – and a taste – for the spiritual; and this new thirst for the spiritual is always being satisfied, because the spiritual water which slakes it comes from an ever-flowing source. As Thomas observes, 'Spiritual water has a perpetual source, namely, the Holy Spirit who is the inexhaustible source of life; hence whoever drinks from that fountain will never thirst; just as if someone had a fountain of living water welling up within them, they would never feel thirst'.[60]

For Thomas, in fact, it is not so much the symbol of water itself which characterizes the Spirit, as the symbol of living, or running, water. He follows Augustine in explaining that water separated from its source is dead, like still water gathered in pools, while living water is water which is flowing continually from its source. As he writes,

> The reason for the grace of the Holy Spirit being called 'living' water is because we are given not just the grace of the Holy Spirit, but also the fountain of grace, that is, the actual Holy Spirit. In fact, it is by the Spirit that the grace is given. 'God's love has been poured into our heart through the Holy Spirit that has been given to us' (Rom. 5.5). The Holy Spirit is an inexhaustible spring from which flows all the gifts of graces. 'All these are activated by one and the same Spirit' (1 Cor. 12.11). Hence it is that if anyone has a gift of the Holy Spirit without having the Holy Spirit himself, it is water separated from its source and is dead, not living. 'Faith without works is dead' (Jas 2.20, Vg).[61]

In an illuminating passage of the *Summa theologiae*, we can see more clearly what is in Thomas's mind when he concludes that if anyone has a gift of the Holy Spirit without having the Spirit himself, it is like water separated from its source and is dead, not living. He is considering in the *Summa* whether *fides informis* (unformed faith; that is, belief whose act is not imbued with love) is a gift of God; and he explains that sometimes God will give a person the gift of believing without giving them the gift of charity, 'just as some people are given the gift of prophecy, or the like, without charity'.[62] Even such a gift as faith, then, can be dead, or lifeless, if it is not ever-active through vital contact with the Spirit that is its source;[63] and this connection between virtuous works and the dynamism of the Spirit is an important aspect of what Thomas understands by the scriptural theme of 'living' water. It is the spring of spiritual water within a person which raises them up through good works to eternal life,[64] and without the Spirit, one's good works have no elevating power, because, as Paul wrote, 'the sufferings of this present time are not worth comparing with the glory about to be revealed to us' (Rom. 8.18). But that applies only if we take those sufferings at their own value. If we consider them, however, as being freely accepted for God out of the charity which the Holy Spirit causes in us, then through such sufferings, we merit eternal life appropriately (*ex condigno*), because 'the Holy Spirit is the spring whose waters, that is, whose effects, spring up into eternal life'.[65]

It is interesting to note how in Thomas's teaching on merit, the fundamental importance for him of the Johannine theme of living water issuing from the Holy Spirit is confirmed in an important passage of the *Summa*.

> If we were to speak of a meritorious act insofar as it is one proceeding from the grace of the Holy Spirit, it then merits eternal life appropriately (*ex condigno*). For the value of merit is considered according to the energy of the Holy Spirit as it moves us into eternal life, in accordance with Jn 4.14. 'The water that I will give will become in them a spring of water gushing up into eternal life.'[66]

Again, Thomas's appeal to the living water from the Holy Spirit is central to his exegesis of Jn 7.37–39, where Jesus proclaims that those who are thirsty, and those who believe in him, should come to him and drink, quoting 'out of the believer's heart shall flow rivers of living water', and referring to the Spirit which believers in Jesus were to receive. If anyone thirsts to serve God, they should come to Christ and drink, not just a drop of water, but its source, which is the Holy Spirit. From their heart will then flow the rivers of the different gifts of grace which they hasten to share with others, since they do not drink for themselves alone. As Peter exhorted his readers, 'Serve one another with whatever grace [NRSV 'gift'] each of you has received' (1 Pet. 4.10).[67]

One could condense what we have seen so far of Thomas's understanding of the water symbolism of the Spirit by concluding that Christians are caught up in the flowing stream of the Holy Spirit which is welling up within them. Thomas sees in John's reference to the plural 'rivers' (Jn 7.38) an indication of the abundance which is so characteristic of the activity of the Spirit. 'He says "rivers" to express the abundance of spiritual gifts promised to the faithful. Rivers of this kind are the living waters which are continuous with their origin, namely the indwelling Holy Spirit'. But he also sees in the idea of 'river' in the singular a reference to the torrential power of the Spirit, and to this effect he cites Ps. 47. 6 [46.4] 'There is a river whose force [NRSV. streams] makes glad the city of God'.

Confirming this powerful dynamism of the Spirit, Thomas points to Paul who himself 'was moved by the prompting and fervor of the Holy Spirit, and who observed that the charity of Christ drives us (2 Cor. 5.15) and that the offspring of God are driven by the Spirit of God (Rom. 8.14)'.[68] Elsewhere, in Ps. 46 [45].4 ('There is a river whose streams make glad the city of God'), Thomas described God's consolation as a river; and while this metaphor portrays the outpouring of divine grace in rich abundance, and shows the connection of that grace with the Holy Spirit that is its source, it also shows something of the inexorable power of the grace of the Spirit. 'As a river shifts sand and pebbles, so the Holy Spirit moves the heart to act. "Out of the believer's heart shall flow rivers of living water" (Jn 7.38)'.[69] Again, some rivers are sluggish in movement, but this river of grace is fast-flowing – the psalmist remarks on its force – and this refers to the suddenness with which the Holy Spirit floods the heart, as well as to the impetuous love with which the Spirit moves the heart, as Isaiah confirms, "for he will come like a rushing stream driven by the Spirit of the Lord (59.19)" '.[70]

This examination of how Thomas understood and exploited the scriptural symbol of water as applied to the Holy Spirit would be incomplete without some acknowledgement of the way in which he uses such terms as 'outpouring', 'infusing', 'flowing' and the like, all of which have in his theology a continual Scriptural background and resonance connected with the theme of pouring. It is a general rule of language that metaphors tend to become effete and lose their original force, but the application of this rule to the language of Holy Scripture – the word of God – would have been unthinkable to Thomas. The distinguished sixteenth-century Thomist commentator, Cardinal Cajetan, observed famously that 'Thomas always chooses his words very precisely' (*Thomas semper formalissime loquitur*), and this would apply above all to his handling of the Word of God. When he himself uses words which might be thought to have lost any of the metaphorical force they once possessed in Scripture, he can give them full weight by frequently recharging them, appealing to parallel passages and word associations elsewhere in the Bible in which they are to be found in their freshness. Thus, commenting on the reference in Titus 3.5–6 to the Holy Spirit that God our Saviour 'poured out on us richly (*effudit in nos abunde*)', Thomas explains that this 'effusion' denotes the abundance of grace received at baptism with the full forgiveness of sins as well as the variety of gifts of grace.[71] And enlarging on this in his commentary on Peter's claim that Pentecost was fulfilling the prophecy of Joel 2. 28, 'I will pour out my spirit on all flesh', Thomas explains, 'In the word "pour out" (*effundam*) is to be understood the abundance of the effect of the Holy Spirit, and how it will not remain with one person but will extend to several, and then from them will also flow to others, just as happens with liquids'.[72]

This rich application of the idea of the Spirit being poured out abundantly (*effused*) is balanced in Thomas's exegetical work with the complementary idea of the Holy Spirit's being also *diffused*, that is, being spread out and all-pervasive as well. Expounding Rom. 5.5, on how 'God's love has been poured (*diffusa*) into our hearts through the Holy Spirit that has been given to us', Thomas explains that 'the charity with which we love God is said to be diffused in our hearts, that is, it extends to perfect all the practices and actions of our soul'.[73]

The idea of the totality of human activity being bathed by the love which the Holy Spirit pours into the human heart has an obvious affinity with the expansive generosity which the fire of the Spirit effects in the human heart; and there are other similarities in Thomas's examination of these two symbols of the Spirit. Each of them dynamically in its own way illustrates the inexhaustible generosity of God's love for human beings, whether this be expressed in the 'flaming' forth or in the copious 'outpouring' of that love. Each of them also shows that the love of God will not countenance in humans the presence of anything incompatible with that love, whether this be expressed in the purifying fire or in the cleansing flow of the Spirit. And each of these symbols illustrates how God communicates to humans God's own dynamic characteristics, whether these take the form of fervent and glowing desire for God and the salvation of one's neighbour, or of a thirst and taste for the spiritual, and a flowing current to share with others the gifts one has received from the Spirit.

But there are also differences to be found between these basic scriptural metaphors which may raise theological questions on how to express in inept human terms the work of the Holy Spirit in human lives. Once a coal is ignited, Thomas might say, the original flame can be withdrawn; but for water to remain alive, it must never be cut off from its source, from which it derives all its continuing vitality. It might not be too much of an oversimplification to view the metaphor of fire as stressing more the inflammatory activity communicated by the Spirit, while the metaphor of water shows more the passivity of the human recipient who is being enlivened and carried along by the Spirit. This latter symbol is developed strikingly as the current of the Holy Spirit bearing the recipient along as well as up, through the impetus deriving from the living water springing up within the recipient. It is the current of this water which carries the recipient along, or rather, raises them up or elevates them, to eternal life by means of the creature's good works, which are imbued, as we have seen earlier, by the Johannine living water as the divine element which is essential to all human merit.

It can be suggested, then, that for Thomas, the ideas of fire and of water which scripturally symbolize the activity of the Spirit are richly complementary. While the metaphor of fire expresses more clearly, the way in which the Spirit communicates its dynamism to humans to inflame them, the idea of water, and especially of living water, stresses more the idea of immediate and continual vital contact of the Spirit with humans, as well as the way in which the Spirit maintains the initiative and directive force in all human behaviour.

## The Holy Spirit as Oil

A third major symbol of the Holy Spirit and his power which Thomas finds in Scripture is that of oil, and his richest explanation of this symbol occurs in his exegesis of Ps. 45.7, 'Therefore God, your God, has anointed you with the oil of gladness beyond your companions'. He writes,

> The Holy Spirit is called oil because, as oil floats above all liquids, so the Holy Spirit is over all creatures. 'The Spirit of God was moving over the face of the waters' (Gen. 1.2);[74] that is, it ought to be above everything in human hearts, because it is the love of God. Secondly, the Holy Spirit is called oil because of its soothing qualities. Mercy and all gentleness of the mind comes from the Holy Spirit. '(by) forbearance, kindness, the Holy Spirit . . . (2 Cor. 6.6)'.[75] Thirdly, as oil spreads out, so the Holy Spirit communicates: 'the communion of the Holy Spirit be with all of you' (2 Cor 13.13); 'God's love has been poured into our hearts through the Holy Spirit that has been given to us' (Rom. 5.5). Again, oil foments fire and heat, and the Holy Spirit foments and nourishes the heat of love in us. 'The lamps thereof are lamps of fire' (Song 8.6).[76] And as oil provides illumination, so also does the Holy Spirit. 'The inspiration of the Almighty gives understanding' (Job 32.8).[77]

In Thomas's scripture commentaries, there are further occasional references to all these points of comparison between oil and the Holy Spirit, notably within the context of anointing with oil and especially in developing the theology of the 'Christ' as the one anointed with oil. He explains, 'The Hebrew "*Messiah*", which in Greek is "*Christ*", is in Latin "*Unctus*" (anointed), because he was specially anointed with invisible oil, that is, the Holy Spirit. Hence, he is called that especially. "Therefore, God your God has anointed you with the oil of gladness above your fellows" (Ps. 45.7), that is, above all the saints: for all the saints are anointed with that oil; but he is especially anointed, and is especially holy'. Thomas favours this verse of the psalm to show what may be called the *intensive* abundance of the presence of the Holy Spirit within the human Jesus. He also appeals to Ps. 132 (133) 2, referring to the precious ointment which ran down Aaron's beard to reach the skirt of his garment, as highlighting the *extensive* abundance of the communication of the Holy Spirit through Christ, seeing in this verse a reference to the Spirit proceeding without measure from the divinity to the humanity of Christ, and thence overflowing to enter all Christians.[78] ' "His fellows" are said to be anointed, because whatever is possessed of that oil, that is, of the grace of the Holy Spirit, overflows from Christ. "From his fullness have we all received" (Jn 1.16); "the precious ointment on the head, etc." (Ps. 132.2)'.[79]

Again, expounding the verse in Heb. (1.2) which quotes from Ps. 45.7 ('God, your God, has anointed you with the oil of gladness above all your companions'), Thomas remarks that being anointed by God had the purpose of equipping Christ for his triple messianic office of king, prophet and priest. This anointing with the oil of sanctification was the one that God ordered should be conducted by Israel (Ex. 30) on sacred vessels and also on priests and kings, and prophets;[80] an anointing, Thomas adds, which applies to Christians also, who derive their anointing from Christ. 'For they are kings and priests' and, he adds, 'they also have the Holy Spirit that is the spirit of prophecy, as shown in Joel 2.28. "I will pour out my spirit on all flesh; your sons and daughters shall prophesy". Moreover, all were anointed with an invisible anointing . . . "you have been anointed by the Holy One, and all of you have knowledge" (1 Jn 2.20)'.[81]

It appears, then, that a new scriptural characteristic of the Spirit which emerges from the metaphor of anointing with oil is that it shows the Spirit capacitating his recipients for a particular role or activity in a community. Although both fire and oil can symbolize the self-communication of the Spirit to human beings, fire more suitably expresses the active participation of some people in the further communication of the Spirit flaming forth to others; and further, anointing with oil, which is a fuel for fire, appears more suitably to express the reception of the Spirit by those others, a receptivity, be it noted, which is itself a power and which likewise proceeds from the Spirit.

## The Holy Spirit as the Finger of God

While the metaphors of fire, water and oil which we have been examining are for Thomas the major scriptural symbols which contribute to a biblical portrait of the Holy Spirit, there are other minor ones which receive some treatment in his commentaries, and it will be of interest, in closing this portrait, to consider what significance for Thomas was contained by those verses of Scripture which describe the Spirit in terms of being the finger of God, of being 'sent', of being a dove and of being new wine.

Comparing Mt 12.28, 'if it is by the *Spirit* of God that I cast out demons', with Lk 11.20, 'if it is by the *finger* of God', Thomas concludes in his commentary on Matthew that the Holy Spirit is the finger of God, and he follows patristic tradition in seeing the parts of God's finger as a symbol of that multiplicity of giving which we have come to recognize as for Thomas a characteristic of the Spirit. Yet he also seems to see the symbol of the indicating finger as expressing something of a distance between God and God's handiwork. The law of Moses, he explains, is called 'spiritual' by Paul in Rom. 7.14, because it was given by the Holy Spirit, being written, according to Ex 31.18, on the 'tablets of stone written with the finger of God'; that is, by the Holy Spirit. If this is the case, however, for the Mosaic Law, how can Paul in Rom. 8.2 then call the New Law the 'law of the Spirit'? Thomas's answer is a typically Pauline a fortiori argument, explaining that 'the new law is called not just a "spiritual" law (7.14) but the "law of the Spirit" (8.2) because the law was not just given, or passed on, by the Holy Spirit (Ex 31.18); the Holy Spirit actually imprints it in the heart in which it dwells'.[82]

Thus Thomas appears to follow Paul in seeing in this idea of the Spirit as the finger of God a contrast between God's activity from a distance, as it were, whether in history or in place, and the fuller and richer activity resulting now from God's 'closer' and more immediate presence; while it also expresses the continuity between both Laws, since it is the same Spirit that is progressively at work in history and has been approaching ever closer, until his climactic and definitive presence in Jesus. In fact, this aspect of the progressive presence of the Holy Spirit in salvation history is to be seen in Thomas's interesting comment on Jesus's casting out devils 'by the finger of God' (Lk 11.20). As he explains, if the demons are now beginning to be trodden underfoot, then the Kingdom, that is, the dominion, of God has now drawn close, and Jesus's adversaries should not be defying the inauguration of that kingdom.[83]

Overall, then, for Thomas, the idea of the Holy Spirit as the finger of God does not express the abundance and richness of the Spirit's self-communication which is to be found in the major scriptural symbols of the Spirit that we have been examining. And yet, in an interesting way, it does that, because it is a symbol of the *promised abundance* which was in the process of being realized, and which is for Thomas fully realized in the New Law. the presence of the Spirit in the human heart which was prepared for and promised by the Old Law, the one written down for humanity in anticipation by the finger of God.

## The Holy Spirit as Being 'Sent'

The self-communication of the Spirit which we have been examining in its symbolic expressions is also described by Scripture as a 'mission', or a sending of the Spirit, although, as Thomas points out, this cannot imply any actual change occurring in the divine Spirit. It is true, of course, that the idea of being sent normally implies the idea of local movement, but mission can be understood in two ways, Thomas explains. 'One implies local movement, as with inferior beings. But mission can also refer to bringing about a new effect in a creature, which is how the Son and the Spirit are "sent". '[84] So, when Jesus spoke of the Spirit being 'sent' to his disciples by the Father in Jesus's name (Jn 14.26), 'he was dealing with the Spirit's "mission". This should not be understood as the Spirit coming to us by a movement in space; he must be within us in a new way which he was not previously. Ps 103.30, "when you send forth your Spirit, they are created", namely, in "spiritual existence". '[85] Thomas explains the repetition of Jesus's promise to 'send' the Spirit in Jn 15.26 more succinctly when he observes. 'We should understand the Spirit being sent, not as its changing location, since "the Spirit of the Lord has filled the whole world", according to Wis 1.7; but because the Spirit begins to live in a new way through grace in those whom he is building up as a temple, as 1 Cor 3.16 notes, "You are God's temple, and God's Spirit dwells in you". '[86] More generally, as Thomas explained in his commentary on Job, 'God is said in Scripture to come to human beings when God imparts benefits to them, either illuminating their minds, or inflaming their feelings, or benefiting them in any way. Likewise, God is said to depart from human beings when God withdraws benefits or protection from them.'[87]

In other words, for Thomas the sending, or the coming, of the Spirit to human beings is a new manifestation of the power of the Spirit within them; and for him, this phenomenon was eminently illustrated in the significance of Pentecost for the disciples. 'A visible mission is always the sign of an invisible mission, and it signifies either the grace of God newly received, or an increase of grace. Thus, in the case of the Apostles, when the Holy Spirit appeared in tongues this signified an increase in grace.'[88] The sending, then, or the inhabiting, of the Spirit in humans is intended to show a new effect in them of the power and activity of God's Spirit. Traditionally, for Thomas, God '*is*' in everything in three ways, by the divine presence, the divine power and the divine essence; but, as he goes on, God is said to '*inhabit*' only the saints through grace.

> The reason for this is that God is in all things by divine action, as giving them being and conserving them in existence. But God is in the saints by their own operation through which they attain to God and somehow possess God; that is, they love and know God, since loving and knowing subjects are said to possess within themselves whatever they know and love.[89]

The 'mission' of the Spirit, then, like the Spirit's 'indwelling', is an operative and dynamic coming and presence which implies a gradual change in the human recipient. But this change in the human creature is no more static than are the 'coming' and 'indwelling' of the Holy Spirit. They result in activity on the part of the recipient under the influence of the Spirit, and this in turn leads to a further 'mission' of the Spirit, that is, a more profound presence and active influence of the Spirit. This progressive manifestation of the power of the Spirit in us, and its cyclic and cumulative character, is more prosaically, but equally profoundly expressed by Thomas when he explains, 'God is said to come to us, not because he is moved towards us, but because we are moved towards God'.[90]

## The Spirit as Dove

Patristic tradition was rich, not to say ingenious, in the variety of ways in which it explained the significance of the Holy Spirit as the dove which all three Synoptic gospels describe descending on Jesus at his baptism (Mk 1.10 et par.); and in his explanation of this symbol, Thomas relies heavily on that tradition. The particular aptness of this symbol to represent the Holy Spirit arises, of course, from the qualities peculiar to the dove, and these qualities are similar to those which the Spirit produces in all the baptized, following Jesus.

Thus, the simplicity of the dove, which Jesus commended to his disciples (Mt 10.16), represents the innocence and the simple regard for God which the Holy Spirit brings about, and shows also the genuine simplicity of intention which is required of those who are approaching baptism;[91] while the moaning of doves is expressive of the 'sighs too deep for words' (Rom. 8.26) with which the Holy Spirit intercedes for us, the sighs for the things of heaven which are as yet deferred; or it could resemble 'moaning like doves' (Nahum 2.7) in regret for our sins.[92] Moreover, the bonding of love which is typical of the dove symbolizes the charity with which the Holy Spirit unites the church, the only gift of the spirit which cannot be counterfeited by the unclean spirit; while the fecundity of the dove is symbolic of the rich multiplication of spiritual grace within the church.[93]

The dove as a symbol of the Holy Spirit also for Thomas corresponds to the type of Noah's dove in Gen. 8.8–12, for 'Just as the dove bringing the branch of green olive-tree showed a sign of God's clemency to those who had survived the waters of the flood, so also in baptism, the Holy Spirit coming in the form of a dove shows the sign of the divine clemency which forgives the baptized their sins and confers grace on them'.[94]

### The Spirit as New Wine

Perhaps no other symbol in Scripture so graphically portrays the lively effects of God on human beings as that of wine, especially new wine; and Thomas is not slow in following Scripture in developing this symbol to illustrate the activity of anyone who is 'under the influence' of divine love, or of the Holy Spirit of God. Thus, he sees the chalice with which the psalmist is inebriated (Ps. 22 (23). 5) as a symbol of the gift of divine love which so takes the psalmist under its control that he speaks as God does, being in ecstasy. When the psalmist speaks, we might say in the popular idiom, it is the wine, or the love of God, which is speaking in him, and he can speak or think only of God, so deep is the draught of divine love which has been offered to him.[95]

It is not surprising, then, observes Thomas, that the Apostles should have been accused of being drunk when they spoke in tongues at Pentecost! They had partaken of the new wine of the New Law, and Jesus himself had warned his listeners of the effect of putting new wine into old wine skins.[96] It was, of course, this new wine which Jesus came to give, and which was symbolized by his miracle at Cana. Before the Incarnation, the wine of justice and wisdom, as also of charity or grace, was lacking, because under the old law, they had received only the spirit of slavery in fear (Rom. 8.15). 'But Christ turned the water of fear into the wine of charity when he gave the Spirit of adoption of sons, in whom we cry, Abba, Father (Rom. 8.15), and when God's love was poured out in our hearts (Rom. 5.5)'.[97]

Again, when Paul exhorts the Ephesians to rid themselves of their old vices and be renewed in the spirit (Eph. 4.22–23), he refers to drunkenness as a source of vice and tells them to be filled with the Spirit rather than with wine (Eph. 5.18). A fitting comparison, explains Thomas, because, just as wine generates liveliness and makes people talkative, so the Holy Spirit generates the warmth of devotion (cf. 'ardent in spirit', Rom 12.11), as well as spiritual happiness and joy; and the Spirit also makes people speak out boldly, which is why those who heard the Apostles speaking after receiving the Spirit thought that they were drunk.[98]

## CONCLUSION

In this survey of Thomas's analysis of the descriptive symbols of the Holy Spirit which are provided by Scripture we have been able to see how he regards them as so many picturesque and informative attempts on the part of the sacred writers to convey the diverse facets of the one divine reality. That reality is the Holy Spirit of God, as he relates to human creatures, or, to express the same thing in other terms, the power of God's Spirit in its various manifestations and effects within and through created humanity; and each symbol is seen as having its own specific contribution to offer in expressing or confirming some aspect of that power.

While, for example, all the symbols portray the abundance – one might say the whole-heartedness – with which the Holy Spirit gives himself, his reaction to human resistance and even human opposition to its self-giving is best expressed by the cleansing power of water, by the refining and melting power of fire, and perhaps also by the promise contained in the idea of the finger of God. While, too, the resulting simplicity of the human being's regard for God is conveyed mainly by the symbol of the dove and by the theme of self-forgetting inebriation, it appears that the all-pervasive influence of the Spirit, in both its intensive abundance and its extensive expanse, is most effectively conveyed by the symbol of oil, as well as that of mission. On the other hand, the oil metaphor conveys less for Thomas of that urgent dynamism of the Spirit that he finds aptly and diversely expressed by the themes of fire, whose abundance creates the fervour of love, and of wine, with its effects of ecstatic alienation from the things of earth; and, perhaps most of all, by the torrential outpouring of living water.

Yet the metaphor of oil seems to emphasize more aptly something of the passivity and receptivity of human beings before the Holy Spirit which we have also seen in the water symbol, in which a key idea is that of one being carried along, and upwards, by the stream of the Spirit. Anointing by the Spirit renders one receptive, not only to the teaching of the Apostles but also to the teaching of the Holy Spirit himself, whose anointing will teach one all things, as is promised by 1 Jn 2.20. Perhaps, however, it is the theme of the new wine which most strikingly expresses this idea of being totally under the influence of the Holy Spirit, whether being taken out of oneself in rapture, and made to speak of the things of God, or of being emboldened, having the biblical *parrhesia*, to teach and preach these things to others.

Thomas's reflections on the theme of living water constitute for him an important expression of the progressive and continuous nature of the spiritualizing activity of the Holy Spirit which he brings about within God's children. Becoming more and more spiritualized, they acquire a growing thirst for spiritual realities, and also a growing taste and affinity for them – Thomas would say, connaturality with them – through the charity that they receive in growing measure from God's Spirit. Spiritual realities drive out one's thirst for temporal realities and cause a thirst for themselves to be possessed fully. Our soul's thirst for the living God (Ps. 42. 2) is unsatisfied in this life because of our imperfection, but it is moved to be fully satisfied in the life of glory. And Thomas cites aptly, ' "Blessed are those who thirst for righteousness" (Mt. 5.6) in this life, for they shall have their fill in the life of glory'.[99]

Each symbol too, in its own way, shows how the power of the Spirit affects human beings in their relations not only with God but also with their fellows. If one is fired by the Spirit in love for God, one's heart is also kindled and melted to go to the aid of others. If one is caught up in the water springing up to eternal life one also hastens to share the gifts of the Spirit with others. And if the dove causes people to voice their longing for God and their sorrow for sins, it also symbolizes the unity among men and women which the Spirit effects in the church. Again, if Jesus drives out evil spirits by the finger of God so that God's kingdom may spread, it is for our benefit; and if he is anointed with the oil of gladness, it is so that his unction will overflow to all those who belong to him.

We have seen Thomas explain how God's being described as moving towards us really means that we are being moved towards God.[100] He expands this theologically when he further explains that 'our being given the Holy Spirit, that is, the love of the Father and the Son, is our being brought (*adduci*) to share in the love which is the Holy Spirit'.[101] The theme of our participating personally in some way in the Spirit of God, or in the love of God given to us, constitutes the basis for Thomas's immensely rich unpacking of the Pauline and Johannine idea of 'the spiritual person (*homo spiritualis*)', as we have seen.

It is difficult to concentrate all that the scriptural symbols of the Holy Spirit convey in Thomas without losing much of their individual vividness and richness, even their beauty and poetry, and also without losing many of the nuances of Thomas's own thought, as one after another he piles up his parallel texts, with a remarkable array of associations, to compose a varied kaleidoscope portraying the Spirit of God and the Spirit's activity in God's sons and daughters. For it should by now be evident to what an extent his familiarity with these varied symbols and metaphors which Revelation contains enriched and penetrated Thomas's entire theology of the Holy Spirit of God, including that Spirit's dynamic influence on God's children, whether this influence is seen in his intimate analyses of the symbols in his scripture commentaries and elsewhere, or in the regular allusions and cross-references to his favourite verses across all his works, as these invoke or evoke the Spirit.

Concentration brings its own richness, as we attempt to penetrate the inadequate luxuriance of scriptural language, aspiring to come face to face with the inexhaustible depth of the reality which that language is striving to express. If the symbols of the Spirit taken together convey any one thing to Thomas, it is above all the inexhaustible divine *dunamis*, the drive of the Holy Spirit, in all his manifestations and, above all, in the abundance and urgency of the Spirit's self-giving to Jesus, with all that this entails through him for his fellow humans as these are bonded by the Spirit to the risen Christ. This restless love which has been poured out in our hearts, as Thomas never tires of pointing out, commenting – naturally – on Paul's epistle to the Romans, whether it be God's initiative of love for us or our reciprocation to God and our neighbour, is *the* manifestation of the Spirit's power; for as Thomas expounds in one of his finest and most scriptural passages, on Rom. 5.5.

> The love of God can be understood in two ways, either as the love with which God loves us ('I have loved you with an everlasting love' Jer. 31.3), or as the love with which we love God ('I am convinced that neither death, nor life, . . . will be able to separate us from the love of God', Rom. 8.38–39); and each of these loves of God is poured out in our hearts by the Holy Spirit who has been given to us.

Our being given the Holy Spirit, who is the love of the Father and the Son, is our being led to share in the love which is the Holy Spirit. By that participation, we are made lovers of God. And the fact that we love God is a sign that God loves us. 'I love those who love me' (Prov. 8.17). 'Not that we [first] loved God, but that God first loved us. . . . We love because God first loved us (1 Jn 4. 10, 19)'.[102]

## 'THE GRACE OF THE HOLY SPIRIT'

In the prelude in the *Summa*, in the passage in which Thomas sets the environment for his systematic treatment of the subject of grace, Thomas explained,

> We must now consider the outer principles of actions. The principle which exteriorly inclines us to do bad is the devil, on whose temptations we have dealt with above. The principle which exteriorly inclines us to good is God, who both instructs us through law and helps us through grace (*qui et nos instruit per legem, et iuvat per gratiam*). So, first we should speak of law, and then of grace.[103]

In the treatise on grace, which significantly provides the climax to his treatment of law,[104] 'Thomas', according to Torrell, 'regularly calls grace "the grace of the Holy Spirit" (*gratia Spiritus Sancti*) – with the two possible meanings of the Latin expression, the grace that is the Holy Spirit, or the grace given by the Holy Spirit'.[105] The philosopher, John Macquarrie, had the happy thought of describing the Holy Spirit as 'God in his closeness to us', a phrase which Emery echoes in concluding his listing of the different forms which the grace of the Spirit can take in people's lives and actions. He writes of

> the absolute priority of uncreated grace in relation to created gifts, the latter being participations (dispositions, or helps in action and expression) of the uncreated Gift who is the Holy Spirit. It is thus through the Holy Spirit that all other gifts are given; beginning with gifts of the natural order (not forgetting creation itself, for the first gift of all is to be); the charisms which come after it, given for the common good and the building up of the Church; and above all the gifts in which the |Holy Spirit is given in person, to wit, the gifts of sanctifying grace, and, at the summit of the life of grace, the gift of charity. In sum 'the Holy Spirit is the pattern of all gifts'.[106] He is also, in this sense, the divine person 'closest to us', so to speak, the one who is most intimate with us, because he is given to us.[107]

Thomas's general statement, quoted earlier, that God 'teaches us by law and helps us by grace' might appear to imply that the Holy Spirit's regular influence affects only our wills, or conative powers, in accordance with Rom. 8.14 ('*driven* by the Spirit', Latin *aguntur*, Greek *agontai*). It very quickly becomes clear, however, as we shall see in detail in chapter 3, that the law, particularly the new law of the Gospel, is for Thomas equally the grace of the Holy Spirit, and, indeed, is primarily the very presence of the Holy Spirit in the hearts of believers. This is more than confirmed by Thomas's other favourite biblical quotation concerning the Spirit, 'Let your good Spirit enlighten me' (Ps. 143.10), describing the action of the Holy Spirit, this time on our cognitive powers, our mind or intellect, and inspiring God's children on how and when to act. Indeed, Thomas's first two questions in considering the human need for grace cover the human mind as well as the human will: 'Can a person *know* anything true without grace?', and 'Can a person *will* and do good without grace?' The nub of his answer to the first question comments on a favourite maxim from Ambrosiaster that 'every truth, no matter who utters it, is from the Holy Spirit' (*omne verum, a quocumque dicatur, est a Spiritu Sancto*):

> This comes about by the Holy Spirit imparting the natural light of intelligence, and moving a person to understand and speak the truth; not by the Spirit's indwelling through sanctifying grace, or by his imparting some habitual gift over and above nature. This latter occurs only in the case of knowing and expressing some truths, especially those relating to faith, as Paul exemplifies in writing 'No one can say "Jesus is Lord", except by the Holy Spirit'. (1 Cor. 12.3)[108]

In other words, according to Thomas, God need not give people a special grace each time to enable them to know something, but he can do so on some special occasions. More particularly, some truths are beyond our natural capacity, and we can come to know and voice these only with the additional help of God's grace.

Answering his second question, can human beings will or do anything without the help of grace, Thomas says that this depends on whether we are considering human nature before the Fall of Adam, or as it has been since the Fall. At all times, he distinguishes, people need God's help, as their first cause, to will and to do anything good. In addition, however, 'in the state of healthy nature, humans need the adding of grace freely bestowed to their natural resources for only one purpose, namely, to will and perform the good of a supernatural act. By contrast, in the state of corrupt nature, two things are needed. First, to be healed (*ut sanetur*), and secondly to perform a good act of supernatural virtue'.[109] From these preliminary questions, it is clear that Thomas viewed additional grace from God as necessary at times with regard to people's minds, as well as to their wills. As he observes in countering a quote from Aristotle, 'humans cannot even know the truth without divine help, as was said above (art. 1), although human nature was corrupted by sin more as concerns desiring the good than as concerns knowing the truth'.[110]

Moreover, in referring above to the 'healing' role of grace, Thomas has in mind the strong Augustinian tradition that the original sin of disobedience committed by humanity's protoparents wreaked devastating effects on their relationship with God, and consequently within themselves. As Haight explains, 'Since Augustine, the notion of grace as a medicinal force, as a sanative power of God releasing us from an internal bondage, especially of sin, has been a permanent fixture in the Christian language about grace'.[111] Clearly, Thomas subscribed to this tradition, but he also witnessed to the development of a vastly richer understanding of God's grace than it's simply being curative, with the scholastic appropriation of Aristotle and the growing appreciation of the 'supernatural'.[112] Awareness of this resulted from the realization that the being and activity of God infinitely transcend the level of created human nature and action, and are utterly unattainable to God's human creatures. However, God is able to 'raise' humanity 'above' its natural stratum of existence and operation, and to equip it to act and behave 'supernaturally' at God's 'higher' level, by communicating to human creatures what is termed 'elevating' grace; leading Haight to observe that 'grace in Aquinas is before all else *elevating*'.[113]

In developing his theology of grace, Aquinas also deploys other distinctions besides this major one between healing grace and elevating grace, as may be seen in Emery's list shown above, and as further shown in Thomas's treatise on grace in the *Summa*.[114] The multiple classes and subclasses of grace are also made abundantly clear by John M. Meinert in his detailed study of the connection between grace and the Gifts of the Holy Spirit, in which he itemizes and analyses all of the different types of graces which can be used by Thomas, whether habitual or actual, or the divisions of actual grace into operative and cooperative, prevenient and subsequent, efficacious and sufficient, even healing and elevating actual grace, and exciting or helping,[115] not to mention habitual or transient, regular or occasional, personal or charismatic, cognitive or conative. All of these can be seen as so many created impressions, or dispositions, effected in the souls of God's children as these are being driven by the Spirit of God (Rom. 8.14), to quote one of Thomas's favourite verses describing the Spirit's characteristic activity. Deriving as they all do from the divine impact which theology appropriates to the Holy Spirit, they can all be also described, simply, and generically, as they frequently are by Thomas, as 'the grace of the Holy Spirit'. In the following two chapters, we shall be considering the multiform dynamics of the grace-conferring Holy Spirit, as he characteristically pervades human moral action, first, in and through the wills of God's human creatures, and then as he works also in their intellects and minds.

## NOTES

1. Aquinas, *Summa Theologiae (ST), Prologus.*
2. *ST* I, 2, introduction.
3. Matthew Levering, *Scripture and Metaphysics. Aquinas and the Renewal of Trinitarian Theology* (Oxford: Blackwell, 2004, 185–96). Jean-Pierre Torrell, *Saint Thomas Aquinas, 2. Spiritual Master* (Washington D.C.: Catholic University of America, 2003,153–224); Gilles Emery, *The Trinitarian Theology of St Thomas Aquinas* (Oxford: Oxford University Press, 2007, chaps 10–15).
4. 1 Jn 5.7 according to some authorities, accepted by Thomas in *ST* I.36.1 *sed contra,* and *corpus articuli.*
5. *ST* I.36.1. Augustine *de Trin* xv, 19, *PL* 42, 1086.
6. *ST* I.36.1.
7. *ST* I.37.1 sed contra and corp. Gregory *Hom in Evang* II, 30; *PL* 76, 1220.
8. *ST* I.37.1 ad 3.
9. Aristotle, *Topica* IV,4. 125a18.
10. *ST* I,38.2.
11. W. J. Hankey, *God in Himself. Aquinas' Doctrine of God as expounded in the* Summa Theologiae (Oxford: Oxford University Press, 1987, 121–2).
12. Gilles Emery, *The Trinitarian Theology of Saint Thomas Aquinas* (Oxford: Oxford University Press, 2007), 219, emphasis added.
13. J. Mahoney, *Christianity in Evolution. An Exploration* (Washington, D.C.: Georgetown University Press, 2011, 43–5). On immanent and economic Trinity, see Emery, pp. 40–4.
14. Emery, 42.
15. See Torrell, 2, pp. 158–61.
16. *ST* I, 39, 8. Cf Emery, *Trinitarian,* p. 335.
17. Torrell, 2, 161 quoting H.-F. Dondaine, *La Trinité (Summa,* I, 27–43)*,* Paris; Revue des Jeunes, 1946, vol 2, p. 418, note.
18. Torrell, 2, 161–2, n. 27.
19. See below, pp 36–37. See also, Emery, *Trinitarian,* ch 15. Missions.
20. C. Spicq, *Esquisse d'une histoire de l'exégèse latine au moyen age* (Paris, 1944, 253). Cf pp 253–5.
21. Thomas, *In librum Beati Dionysii de Divinis Nominibus Expositio,* edd. Pera et al. (Turin: Marietti, 1950) (*Div Nom*) 1, 3 (M 104).
22. *ST* I,1.9. Pseudo-Dennis, *de Cel Hierarch* I, 2 *PG* 3, 121.
23. Thomas, *Div Nom.*, Proëm (M 1007). For a fuller treatment of the use of metaphors in Scripture, see *St. Thomas Aquinas. Summa Theologiae,* vol 3 (I, 12–13). Knowing and Naming God, Edited and translated by Herbert McCabe (London: Eyre and Spottiswoode, 1964, xxx–xxxi); Franz Mussner, 'Thomas von Aquin uber die Entmythologisierung', *Catholica,* Munster, no. 3, 1965.
24. Thomas, *Expositio super librum Boethii de Trinitate,* in Vol 2, *Opuscula theologica,* ed. R. Spiazzi and M. Calcaterra (Turin: Marietti, 1954), 6, 2 ad 1.
25. *In Heb.* 12. 29 (M725).

26. *ST* I.1.9 obj 2 et ad 2, 'ea quae in uno loco Scripturae traduntur sub metaphoris in aliis locis expressius exponuntur.'
27. *In Joann.* 4, lect. 2, 14 (M 615).
28. *ST* I.27.4 ad 3.
29. *ST* I.36.1.
30. *In Joann.* 14, lect. 4, 3 (M 1916).
31. *In Joann.* 6, lect. 8, 5 (M 993).
32. *In Matt 3*, lect. 2 (M 299). P.M. Kimball, *Commentary on the Gospel of Saint Matthew*, trans. (Bristol, Dolorosa Press, 2012, 107). On Kimball, see above, Introduction, p. xv.
33. *In 1 Cor.* 2, lect. 3 (M 117).
34. *In Joann.* 3, lect. 1, 5 (M 477).
35. *In Rom.* 8, lect. 1 (M 616).
36. *In 1 Cor.* 2, lect. 3 (M 117–8).
37. Josef Fuchs, *Human Values and Christian Morality* (Dublin: Gill and Macmillan 1970), 82.
38. *In Is.*, cap. 33. For a similar but much more elaborate treatment by Thomas, cf. *In Is.*, cap 10.
39. *In Is.*,30.
40. *In Jer.* 5, lect. 8.
41. *In Joan,* 4, lect. 2, 1 (M 77).
42. *In Rom.* 12 lect. 2 (M 988).
43. *In 1 Thess.* 5, lect. 2 (M 133).
44. Cf. *In 1 Cor.* 2, lect. 3 (M 117).
45. *In Joan.* 3, lect. 2, 1 (M 456).
46. *In Gal.* 4, lect. 3 (M 215).
47. *In Col.* 3, lect. 3 (M 160).
48. The NRSV translates it as Song 8.6, '[Set me as a seal upon your heart, as a seal upon your arm; for love is strong as death, passion fierce as the grave.] Its flashes are flashes of fire, a raging flame'.
49. See *In 2 Cor.* 5, lect. 3 (M 181).
50. *In Ps.* 18, 6.
51. *In Is*, 26.
52. *In Rom.* 8, lect. 7 (M 733).
53. *In Ps.* 25, lect. 1. Cf *In 2 Cor.* 11, lect. 6 (M 433–4).
54. *In Ps.* 45, lect. 7.
55. *In Joann.* 4, lect. 2, 1 (M 577).
56. *In Matt.* 3, lect. 1 (M 275, 282). See Kimball, 101.
57. *In Matth.* 3, lect. 2 (M 299). Kimball, 106.
58. *In Hebr.* 10, lect. 2 (M 506).
59. *In 1 Cor.* 12, lect. 3 (M 734).
60. *In Joan.* 4, lect. 2, 3 (M 586).
61. *In Joan.* 4, lect. 2, 1 (M 577). NRSV 'faith without works is barren'.
62. *ST* II-II.6.2 ad 3.
63. *In Rom.* 8, lect. 4 (M655).

64. *In Joan.* 4, lect. 2, 4 (M 587).
65. *In Rom.* 8, 4 (M 655). Cf *In Ps.* 1, lect. 2.
66. *ST* I-II.114.3.
67. *In Joan* 7, lect. 5, 2 (M 1090).
68. Ibid.
69. *In Ps.* 45, lect. 1–3.
70. *In Ps.* 35, lect. 4. (NRSV 'like a pent-up stream that the wind of the Lord drives on'.)
71. *In Tit,* 3, lect. 1 (M 93).
72. *SG* 4, 23.
73. *In Rom* 5., lect. 1 (M 392).
74. NRSV 'a wind from God swept over the face of the waters.'
75. NRSV 'holiness of spirit'.
76. NRSV 'Its flashes are flashes of fire'. On the mediaeval significance of the verse, see above, p. 13.
77. NRSV 'the breath of the Almighty that makes for understanding.' *In Ps.* 44, lect. 5.
78. *In Joann.* 17, lect. 4, 3 (M 2231).
79. *In Ps.* 44, lect. 3. Cf *In Hebr.* 1, lect. 4 (M 63–65).
80. *In Hebr.* 1, lect. 4 (M 63).
81. *In Hebr.* 1, lect. 4 (M 64).
82. *In Rom.* 7, lect. 3 (M 557). See below, chapter 3.
83. *In Matth.* 12, lect. 3. Kimball, 437.
84. *In Heb.* 1, lect. 6 (M 87). Cf *ST* I.43.2 ad 2.
85. *In Joan.* 14, lect. 6, 6 (M 1956).
86. *In Joan* 15, lect. 5, 7 (M 2061).
87. *In Job* 9, lect. 3.
88. *In Math.* 3, lect. 2 (M 301). Kimball 107–8.
89. *In 2 Cor.* 6, lect. 3 (M 240). Cf *ST* I, 43, 3.
90. *In Joan.* 14, lect. 6, 3 (M 1944).
91. See *ST* III. 39.6 ad 4.
92. *In Joan.* 1, lect. 14, 4 (M 272). Cf *In Rom.* 8, lect., 5 (M 693); *In Matth.* 3, lect. 2 (M 300).
93. *In Joan.* 1, lect. 14, 4 (M 272). Cf *In Matth.* 3, lect. 2 (M301), Kimball 107–8.
94. *In Joan.*, ibid.
95. *In Ps.* 22, lect. 2; *Ps.* 35, lect. 4.
96. *In Matth.* 9, lect. 3 (M 772), Kimball, 347.
97. *In Joan.* 2, lect. 1, 3 (M 347).
98. *In Eph.* 5, lect. 7 (M 306, 308).
99. *In Joan.* 4, lect. 2, 3 (M 586).
100. Cf above, p. xx.
101. *In Rom.* 5, lect. 1 (M 392).
102. *In Rom.* 5, lect. 1 (M 392).
103. *ST* I-II, q.90, prologue.
104. *ST* I-II, qq. 90–114, including, on grace, qq 109–114.

105. Torrell, 2,155.
106. *1 Sent.* d.18, q.1, a.3.
107. Emery, *Trinitarian*, 257–8.
108. *ST* I-II.109.1 ad 1. Emphasis added.
109. *ST* I-II, 109, 2.
110. *ST* I-II, 109, 2 ad 3.
111. Roger Haight, *The Experience and Language of Grace* (Dublin: Gill & Macmillan, 1979), 50–1. On this Augustinian medicinal tradition, see further Haight, 56–61. On the consequences for Catholic moral theology, see J. Mahoney, *The Making of Moral Theology. A Study of the Roman Catholic Tradition* (Oxford: Oxford University Press, 1987), chapter 2, The Legacy of Augustine, pp. 37–71.
112. Haight, 58–61.
113. Haight, 61. Emphasis in original.
114. See pp. 36–7; also *ST* I-II, q 111.
115. Meinert, John M, *The Love of God Poured Out: Grace and the Gifts of the Holy Spirit in St Thomas Aquinas* (Stebenville: Emmaus Academic, 2018), 9–30.

*Chapter 2*

# The 'Prompting' of the Holy Spirit

In our opening chapter, we saw how, for Thomas Aquinas, the language which the Bible uses to describe the Holy Spirit provides us with a rich portrait of the Spirit, with his dominant characteristics of loving self-communication, and abundant and impetuous power; and we also saw how, for Thomas, participating in the power of God's Spirit is a major feature of the 'spiritual' person. We now propose to examine in detail the influence of the Holy Spirit on the process of human moral action, and to show how for Thomas, this influence of the Spirit on human behaviour is viewed predominantly as a growing manifestation in them of the power of the Spirit, as he interiorly enlightens people's minds, and stimulates their wills, thus enabling them to act as God's sons and daughters, and achieve their divinely willed fulfilment as such.

Thomas's favourite biblical verse in connection with the influence of the Holy Spirit on moral behaviour is Rom. 8.14, which the New RSV translates, 'For all who are led by the Spirit of God are children of God (*quicumque enim spiritu Dei aguntur, ii sunt filii Dei*)';[1] and in his writings, Thomas frequently and closely links this verse with the idea of the 'prompting' of the Holy Spirit (*instinctus Spiritus Sancti*), 'a phrase dear to Thomas', as Valsecchi has remarked.[2] How Thomas understood this 'prompting' of the Holy Spirit seems to have undergone some enrichment for him, accompanied by what appears to have been a deepened insight into the content and meaning of Rom. 8.14. This chapter begins, then, with an examination of Thomas's mature exegesis of this key verse of Paul.

### THE TEACHING OF THE COMMENTARY ON ROMANS

What first strikes English-speaking readers of Thomas's exegesis of Rom. 8.14 is that the verb which is most frequently used in translation, 'those who are *led* by the Spirit', is much too weak to convey what Thomas understood by this verse: it does not sufficiently express that all-embracing dynamism of the Spirit which Thomas considered that Paul had in mind here. The Latin verb (*aguntur*; Greek *agontai*) is crucial; and in order to catch something of the contrast which Thomas and his sources made between the active and passive voices of this verb in their discussion of its precise significance, it will be helpful to translate those forms by the admittedly cumbersome English active and passive equivalents of 'to act' or 'to be active' (*agere*) and 'to be acted upon' (*agi*).

The Interlinear Gloss of the Bible, which is a collection of synonyms composed in the twelfth century by Anselm of Laon and placed, literally, 'between the lines' of the Latin Vulgate version, offers on the Pauline *aguntur* the laconic comment '*reguntur*', so that the sense of Rom. 8.14 becomes 'those who are *ruled*, or *directed*, by the Spirit of God are God's children'.[3] By contrast, the Ordinary Gloss on the Bible, which is a running commentary on the Vulgate text composed in the ninth century by Strabo, and providing authoritative patristic and other excerpts,[4] offered on Rom. 8.14 no less an authority than Augustine as objecting that 'being acted on is more than being ruled or directed' (*plus est agi quam regi*). In his original anti-Pelagian text, from which this quotation is taken by the Gloss, Augustine had objected

> Pelagius said that 'everyone is ruled (*regi*) by their own will', as if God actually directs nobody, and as if Psalm 28.9 [Vg] is meaningless when it asks God to 'save your people and bless your heritage; and rule them and raise them for ever', in case, if they are 'ruled by their own will without God', they remain 'like sheep without a shepherd (Mk 6.34)'. Far be that from us, for undoubtedly, being acted upon (*agi*) is more than being ruled (*regi*) (*procul dubio plus est agi quam regi*). Those who are being *directed* are *active* in being directed to act rightly; but those who are being *acted upon* are not considered to be themselves active. Yet our Savior's grace provides so much to our wills that Paul has no hesitation in saying that 'those who are acted upon by God's Spirit are God's children'.[5]

The major premise of Augustine's argument, *plus est agi quam regi* (being acted on is more than being directed), was taken up, as Zoltan Alszeghy remarks, by a surprising number of scholastic exegetes.[6] Possibly they felt the need to correct the Interlinear Gloss's equating *agi* (being acted on) with *regi* (being directed), as we have seen earlier, by citing the phrase from Augustine of which they were aware from the Ordinary Gloss. The two views appear in the exegesis of Rom. 8.14 by the twelfth-century Peter Lombard; and we find there too an echo of Augustine's *de gratia Christi* when Lombard explains that a person is made more a good child of God the more abundantly the Father bestows on them his Holy or good Spirit by whom they are acted upon (*agitur*) and by whom they act (*agit*). 'Thus, they act well who are acted upon by the good one.'[7] As Augustine himself had written, 'Of those of whom it is written that "those who are acted upon by the Spirit of God are God's children", in order that they are active in doing what is good, they are acted upon by the one who is good'.[8]

When Thomas came to explain Rom. 8.14, he was well aware of this traditional contrast between, on the one hand, being directed, or instructed, and on the other hand, being acted upon (*agi*) by the Holy Spirit; and while his exegesis is dependent on the traditional explanation, he sought at the same time to penetrate further into the sense of Paul's words.

'It is true', he explains, 'that God's children are led by God's Spirit in the sense that they are directed (*reguntur*) by the Spirit acting as their leader and guide, illuminating their minds interiorly on what actions they ought to perform; as the Psalmist remarks, "Let your good Spirit lead (*deducet*) me on a level path (Ps. 143.10)". However, Thomas continues crucially, the Holy Spirit is more than a guide, philosopher and friend who presents us with reasons or motives for acting, but who cannot in the last analysis directly affect our autonomy or our initiative for action. As he went on, 'The spiritual person is not only instructed by the Holy Spirit what to do; their heart is also moved by the Holy Spirit, so there is more to be understood in "those who are acted upon, etc." than just receiving directions from the Holy Spirit'.[9]

In other words, the spiritual person is not just 'led'. We cannot shrink from saying that for Thomas, they are *driven* by the Spirit acting on their will, as well as on their mind. As Thomas remarks in the *Summa*, referring to this verse of Romans, 'the acts of the person who is acted upon *(agitur)* by the Holy Spirit are said to be more the acts of the Holy Spirit than the acts of that person'.[10]

Thus far in his exegesis of Rom 8.14, Thomas has done little more than elaborate the traditional teaching which derived from Augustine, that 'being acted on is more than being directed', but Thomas is of a more metaphysical mind than Augustine. In a few phrases, he now sketches in a whole new dimension which will throw light on what he considers the deeper meaning of Paul's words.

> Those things are said to be acted upon (*agi*) which are moved by a higher prompting. We say of animals that they do not act but are acted upon, because they are moved to their actions by their nature, and not by their own movement. Likewise, spiritual persons are inclined to act in some way, not principally by the movement of their own will, but by a prompting of the Holy Spirit, in accordance with Isaiah 59.19 (Vg), 'when he comes like a rushing river whom the Spirit of God compels (*cogit*)', and Lk 4.1 (Vg), that 'Christ was acted upon (*agebatur*) by the Spirit in the desert'.[11]

Some idea of the dynamic impetus of the Holy Spirit which is in the background of this explanation by Thomas of Rom. 8.14 can be grasped when we recall the significance for him of the powerful 'living water' symbol of the Holy Spirit in Scripture, including his comment on Isa. 59.11 that 'as a river moves sand and pebbles, so the Holy Spirit moves the heart to act'.[12] But even this appeal to the inexorable power of a river in spate to illustrate Paul's words pales before the theological implications which must have been in Thomas's mind when he here also invoked Lk 4.1 to describe Jesus as being 'acted upon by the Spirit'. This Christological verse forms the climax to Thomas's exegesis of Rom 8.14, and he has chosen it well, to show how among God's children, the Holy Spirit was in the habit (the verb is in the imperfect tense) of acting upon *the* Son of God par excellence before being active on God's adopted children. And not just 'in the desert'; for, as Thomas points out elsewhere, 'it is obvious that the soul of Christ was moved (*movebatur*) by the Holy Spirit in the most perfect way, as Lk 4.1 shows'.[13] The parallel verse in Matthew (4.1) reads that Jesus 'was led (*ductus*) by the Spirit' into the desert, and in this theological content, this is precisely what Thomas does not mean, for it would imply only that Jesus was guided, or even invited, into the desert. It contains nothing of the thrust which Thomas sees in the Pauline *aguntur*, and which he elsewhere explains in terms of repeated excitement or agitation (*agitantur*).[14] As Emery explains, 'both verbs involve the idea of "putting into action", the second emphasizing the intensity of the motivation given us by the Holy Spirit'.[15]

The Holy Spirit is not just a teacher, then, giving direction, but a continuing vital force in the conduct of all God's children, as he was in that of Jesus; and this is what Rom. 8.14 means for Thomas. Not being 'led by the Spirit', then, but much more strongly, being 'driven by the Spirit' is what Thomas understood Paul to teach. As we have seen Thomas explain this, just as an animal is driven interiorly to act by the prompting of its nature, so the spiritual person is driven interiorly to act by the prompting of the Holy Spirit.

## AN INNER PROMPTING

In comparing the spiritual person's being driven by the Holy Spirit with an animal's being driven to act by its inner nature, Thomas in both cases ascribes the activity to an 'impulse', or a 'prompting' (*instinctus*), a Latin term which comes from the verb *instinguere*, meaning 'to incite or to impel'. The term obviously provides the derivation for the common English term 'instinct', and this connection has had the unfortunate consequence of misleading some scholars to obfuscate Thomas's regular use of the term *instinctus*, by making it refer to some sort of reified pneumatological 'instinct' located within the human agent, which is spiritually equivalent and analogous to the innate and dormant animal drive found within animals, equipping them to react in a certain way under the appropriate stimulus. As a result of this, such writers at times express Thomas's teaching on *instinctus* elaborately in terms of 'instinct' in English, and its equivalent in other languages, rather than simply as referring to the Holy Spirit's 'instigation'.

Thomas's teaching on 'natural prompting' (*naturalis instinctus*) was studied in detail by Max Seckler, who saw an important connection between Thomas's understanding of this phrase and his teaching on the role in the act of faith of the 'inner prompting' (*instinctus interior*) and the 'prompting of faith' (*instinctus fidei*); and the importance of this connection was also explored by Juan Alfaro exploring the act of faith and its properties.[16] When it comes to the *instinctus* at least of the Holy Spirit, however, Thomas's understanding of it, and his use of it, does not appear to be as complicated, nor as quasi-mystical, as Seckler and Alfaro appeared to claim. This seems to apply equally to recent writers, including O'Meara and Bouchard, who launch from Thomas's growing liking for the term *instinctus* a whole pattern of 'instinctive' knowledge and 'instinctive' action, issuing apparently from some interior human Spirit-created 'instinct', which is equivalent to an animal's biological 'instinct'.[17] Likewise, Lecuyer, in his article '*Docilité au S. Esprit*', seems to be captivated by this association when he writes that 'certain external actions ... will therefore be *quasi-instinctive* for those who let themselves be directed by grace (*ex instinctu gratiae producuntur*), ST I-II, 108.1)'.[18]

A much simpler, and preferable, approach to the Latin *instinctus* as used by Thomas is expressed by Pinsent, when he observes that 'the connotations evoked by the modern word "instinct" are unhelpful, given the association of the word with the behaviour of animals rather than the union of persons'.[19] In the latest contribution to the discussion, John Meinert, in his 2018 study exploring the relationship of the Gifts of the Holy Spirit to grace, surveys various approaches to the use and meaning of *instinctus* in Thomas. He introduces this by observing that Thomas claims that the Gifts 'make the believer proportionate to the *instinctus Spiritus Sancti*', and adds 'This, at least, is very clear. What is less clear is what Aquinas means by *instinctus* or *instinctus Spiritus Sancti*'.[20] On *instinctus*, he continues, 'the term ... could indicate almost any *cause,* direct or indirect', and proceeds to analyze in detail its major contexts and applications in Thomas, concluding that the primary meaning of *instinctus* for Thomas is simply that of 'motion', emanating from a variety of agents, whether natural or supernatural.[21] As he concludes later, after analyzing actual grace in Thomas as a help (*auxilium*), 'Aquinas's account of *instinctus* ... particularizes the general account of *auxilium* as motion'.

Following Meinert, then, we should be quite clear that the Latin term *instinctus*, or 'prompting' or 'impulse', applied to the Holy Spirit, does not refer to any human 'instinct' in the human recipient.[22] It denotes a transient initiative, or, literally, an 'instigation', on the part of the Spirit in action, and it is accurately translated as a temporary impulse or a prompting or a prodding, and certainly not as an interior agency which produces 'instinctive' actions. We would do well to remember, also, that as well as being familiar with *instinctus* as a fairly common term in classical writers, Thomas was aware that 'that movement of the Spirit is called *instinctus* according to Augustine',[23] and, highly significantly, he also adopted the term from his revered Aristotle, 'the Philosopher', who wrote variously and appositely of a 'divine prompting' and an 'interior prompting', which we shall examine further.[24] In spite of Bouchard's express disapproval, Edward D. O'Connor was correct in concluding, after an examination of the way that Thomas uses the term, that *instinctus* was chosen by him in order 'not to specify in any way whatsoever the nature of *the Holy Spirit's action*', not the recipient's.[25] Legge rightly observes that Thomas is arguing that humans are not moved by the Spirit 'from outside. Man is moved *within*, by a movement fully consistent with his freedom but that surpasses his reason without contradicting or opposing it'.[26] Finally, the simple sense of 'prompting' is clear in Thomas's treatment in the *Summa* of the question whether the Gifts of the Holy Spirit differ from the virtues, when he refers to a person's being given by God a 'special prompting', as well as simply equating the 'prompting' of the Spirit with his 'movement' (*instinctus et motio Spiritus Sancti*).[27]

## 'ACTED UPON, YET ACTIVE'

As we noted earlier, Thomas draws an analogy between animal behaviour and that of the spiritual person responding to a 'prompting', whether in the one case of nature or in the other of the Holy Spirit; and this illustrates well how in a person's activity all initiative lies with the higher principle which is continually instigating the human individual's reaction to each situation. It is, however, only an analogy and there are obvious qualifications to be made. The most obvious is that whereas the animal must always of necessity follow the promptings of its nature, the spiritual person is, and remains, free under the prompting of the Holy Spirit. This difference, however, which at first sight might appear to make nonsense of Thomas's whole comparison, is not so great as one might think, because, as Thomas points out, the initiative and dynamism of the Holy Spirit transcend the dichotomy between a person's necessary acts and their free acts, so that, even in the case of the human's free acts, it is still the Holy Spirit who causes the movement of the will and the free choice in the human being. As Thomas comments,

> This does not exclude spiritual persons from working through their will and their free choice, because the Holy Spirit causes the very movement of the will and free choice in them, in accordance with Phil. 2.13, 'it is God who is at work in you, enabling you both to will and to complete [NRSV, work]'.

What is to be noted, however, as of central significance is that Thomas carefully adds in explanation that the spiritual person 'is inclined to act, not *principally* by the movement of their own will, but by the prompting of the Holy Spirit'.[28] This simple adverb, 'principally', introduces a significant qualification into Thomas's teaching on the influence of the Holy Spirit on the behaviour of the spiritual person: namely, that such influence does not supplant, nor coerce, the use of reason or of free choice on the part of that person. As is reported in the Basel Matthew, Thomas comments on Jesus's promise to his disciples that 'it is not you who speak, but the Spirit of your Father speaking' (Mt. 10.20),

> the prophets and the apostles are moved in such a way that they retain the use of their reason, and they are acted upon in such a way that they also are active (*ita aguntur quod agunt*), because those who are acted upon by the Spirit of God are God's children, that is, they are free.[29]

In fact, Thomas expands, when a person's reason is disturbed or deranged, as it can be by the spirit of the devil, then that person is completely acted upon (*totaliter agitur*); whereas, by contrast, those who are acted upon by the Holy Spirit are acted on in such a way that they too are active (*ita aguntur quod agunt*), freely exercising their own rational and volitional powers. In other words, although an animal's internal nature drives the animal to act directly and immediately, the driving influence of the Holy Spirit on human action is mediated through the human's own intellect and will.

In this way, we find Thomas aware of the limitations of the similarity which he had drawn from animal behaviour to illustrate the 'acted upon' (*aguntur*) of Rom. 8.14. He had been drawing upon a favourite source, the Syrian John of Damascus (CE 696–749), 'the Greek who foreshadowed Aquinas', according to David Knowles,[30] who drew a contrast between animals without free choice, which are acted upon by their nature rather than being active, and rational humans, who act upon their nature more than being acted on by it.[31]

This contrast had originated with Augustine, whom we have already met campaigning against Pelagius in preferring to see the children of God being 'acted upon' by the Spirit rather than just being 'directed' by the Spirit. Yet

Augustine was also at pains to point out that the force of 'acted upon' in Rom. 8.14 does not reduce the spiritual person to the status of a moral robot, bereft of their own reason and free will. This consideration led Augustine first, typically, to ask the question, 'if they are acted upon, how can they themselves be active' (*si aguntur, quomodo agant?*); and this led him to coin the paradox, 'they are acted upon so that they act' (*ita aguntur ut agant*). As he tried to explain, 'if they are God's children, they should understand that they are acted upon by God's Spirit to act as they should act, and, after they have acted, they should thank Him by whom they act. For they are acted upon so that they should act, not so that they themselves do not act'.[32]

Augustine's rhetorical dexterity cannot conceal the fact that in the long run he can only explain the dilemma by suggesting lamely that when God's children act, the Holy Spirit is a 'help' to them.

> Someone will object, 'So we are acted upon; we are not active'. My reply is that, in fact, you are acted upon, and you also act; and that you act well if you are acted upon by the good God. For the Spirit of God which acts upon you, helps you in your acting. . . . And if the Spirit is lacking, you will not be able to do anything good.[33]

Thomas Aquinas, however, was more metaphysically equipped than Augustine to address the paradox which baffled the latter, which he did by invoking the Greek philosopher Aristotle's doctrine of causality. In explaining Thomas's understanding and expansive application of Aristotle's teaching on 'the four causes', Nicholas Austin remarks that the Aristotelian causes 'are put to theological work to understand things in heaven and on earth undreamt of by the philosopher'.[34] Distinguishing causality first into the four causes: formal, material, final and efficient, Thomas further distinguished within efficient causality (or what actually produces the effect) between primary and secondary causes, and applied this latter distinction by analogy to God's own divine activity. In this way, in any divine prompting, Thomas analyzed God as the primary cause, and all other created causes which contribute to the effect as the secondary, subordinate, subsidiary or instrumental causes, brought into action by God.[35] We have seen this already hinted at in Thomas's careful explanation that the spiritual person 'is inclined to act not *principally* by the movement of their own will but by the prompting of the Holy Spirit'.[36] He explains this in commenting on Jesus's promise to his disciples that, when they are under pressure, it is the Holy Spirit who would speak through them (Mt. 10.20):

> It should be noted that every action which is caused by two things, of which one is the principal agent, and the other the instrumental, ought to be ascribed to the

more principal. [The disciples] were acting instrumentally, and the Holy Spirit principally, so the whole action should be ascribed to the Holy Spirit.[37]

Appealing yet again to Rom. 8.14, Thomas expands his teaching:

> An action is always attributed more to the principal agent than to the secondary, as when we say that it is not the axe that makes the box, but the carpenter through the axe. Now, the human being's will is moved to good by God, since 'those who are acted upon by God's Spirit are God's children' (Rom 8.14). Therefore, the interior operation of human beings is to be attributed, not principally to them, but to God.[38]

Both the Holy Spirit's and the human being's operations are respected by this principle of primary and secondary causality. On the one hand, Thomas is able to assert that in every action of the spiritual person, it is the initiative of the Holy Spirit which is the source and principle of the action, and that God's children are truly acted upon (*aguntur*, that is, driven) by God's Spirit. At the same time, he can use the Augustinian formula, that they are acted upon in such a way that they themselves act (*ita aguntur quod agunt*), by locating it within the context of principal and instrumental causality, as Augustine did not; and he is thus enabled to safeguard the real activity of the spiritual person, along with that of the Spirit, but in subordination to that of the Spirit.

For Thomas, the theorem of instrumental causality does not deny, nor derogate from, the activity of the spiritual person; it puts that activity firmly in its true created perspective as real, yet at the same time completely dependent on the activity of God's Spirit. Thomas had too profound a respect for God's creatures to deny their inherent dignity of being and power for action, especially humanity's, and he refused to countenance the philosophy of occasionalism: that is, of ascribing activity to God alone, and of conceiving all other apparent causality as only providing the 'occasion' for God alone to act.[39] It might be characteristic of Satan to act on human beings by blinding their reason, Thomas points out, but such an attitude is inconceivable on the part of God who has given humans their reason as their unique distinction in creation. It was this respect of God for God's own handiwork that led Thomas to assert that God moves everything, but each always in accordance with its nature; and in the case of humans, this is in accordance with their free will, although God is the principal agent.[40] Putting it very concisely in his response to an objection in the *Summa* that the person 'acted upon' by the Spirit is a mere instrument of the Spirit, Thomas observed that the human is not the sort of instrument that is acted upon but not itself active: 'they are so driven by the Spirit as to be still active insofar as they have free choice';[41] a clarification he repeats elsewhere: 'The children of God are acted on by the Spirit of God in their own way, namely, respecting their free choice, which is the exercise of will and reason'.[42]

The outstanding instance of Thomas's theological application of this widely applied principle of instrumental causality must be in his analysis of the Incarnation, where we can observe him identify and move between the two planes of causality, principal and instrumental, in his commentary on Heb. 9.14 which describes how Christ 'through the Eternal Spirit offered himself'. As Thomas explains, 'The cause why Christ shed his blood was the Holy Spirit, by whose movement and prompting, namely, by the love of God and his neighbour, he did this.' And he powerfully invokes the biblical symbol of living water to add that, 'he will come like a rushing stream driven by the Spirit of the Lord (Isa. 59.19)'.[43] Clearly, Thomas is referring to the one act of Jesus, but he is adducing two distinct agents of that act, the Holy Spirit, and the created virtue of charity in Jesus's soul; and we can conclude that this act of *the* Son of God, like all the acts of the children of God who are acted upon by the Spirit of God, 'comes not principally from the movement of his own will, but from the prompting of the Holy Spirit'.[44]

Behind the human actions even of Jesus, then, Thomas discerns the Augustinian formula, 'they are acted on in such a way as to act' (*ita aguntur quod agunt*), but now in the sense of instrumental causality which Thomas has given it, reversing the phrase neatly in the *Summa*, to observe that Jesus's humanity was 'an instrument animated by a rational soul which acts in such as a way as being also acted upon (*ita agit quod etiam agitur*)'.[45] However, his clearest expression of the two interacting planes of activity which are implied in this principle is Thomas's remark on the behaviour of God's children that 'the movement and prompting of the Holy Spirit who is in them is their own prompting, since charity thus inclines them';[46] further explained by Thomas's observation elsewhere that the Holy Spirit, which is 'the most powerful of movers', so moves a person to love that the Spirit also induces in that person the virtue of charity.[47]

## UNDERSTANDING DIVINE CAUSALITY

Aquinas's application of a distinction between primary and secondary efficient causality to throw light on how the children of God can really act at the Holy Spirit's prompting of their minds and wills, and yet at the same time be acting completely freely, implies an understanding of divine causality, and, indeed, of the overall Aristotelian and Thomist understanding of causation, which has long been considered alien to modern scientific thought. As Michael Dodds has shown, from the Renaissance onwards, the striking development and success of empirical science through measurement resulted, first, in the disregard, and then the formal rejection, of Aristotle's formal, material and final causality.[48]

As a result, the only causation recognized, so far as science was concerned, was reduced to efficient causality. As Dodds observed, 'Potentiality, form, and finality are types of causality that are not measurable and so do not come directly under the microscope.'[49] Even efficient causality, however, became contracted to 'the one unique type of causality to be found in the cosmos: the efficient causality of the energy that moves the atoms',[50] before even that last metaphysical trace of causation was ousted by Hume and Heisenberg.[51]

For the most part, scientists considered, then, that the cosmos was dominated and determined by laws of observable measurement, with only one vestigial form of efficient causality to be taken into account, that of physical force; and the result was that 'the methodological assumption that the laws of science apply uniformly throughout the cosmos became a metaphysical assertion that such laws formed a closed causal nexus that cannot be violated'.[52] Any attempt, then, to introduce and apply the idea of continuous divine causality must be explained away as illusory or imaginary, like occasionalism, or it must be rejected as an unacceptable intervention which breaches and disrupts the regularities to be found in the material world's 'closed causal nexus'.[53]

Since the development of Newtonian physics, Christian theologians have been maintaining a sustained defence of divine causality in the world; and one of the most recent is the study by Dodds, quoted earlier, *Unlocking Divine Action*.[54] Two particular features of this study are its approach from the viewpoint and writings of Thomas Aquinas, and its argument that, in some respects, modern science is retreating from its impoverished view of causality, and beginning to accept a broader understanding of it through modern scientific developments. The limited purpose of this study does not lend itself to considering a modern scientific rapprochement with causality, nor Dodd's statement that 'contemporary developments in science have opened new ways of thinking about causality beyond the constricted views of classical Newtonian physics'.[55] We must restrict ourselves to considering the thinking of Thomas Aquinas and, where necessary, to defending from unjustified attack his views on divine causality and the role of the Holy Spirit in moral actions.[56] Our defence depends on a double counterattack: one being Thomas's sustained distinction between primary and secondary, or instrumental, efficient causality, as we have seen; and the other relying upon the traditional theological doctrine of analogical predication, based on the analogy of being, to which we may now turn.

## ACKNOWLEDGING ANALOGY

We saw in the previous chapter, in introducing Thomas's portrayal of the Holy Spirit in terms of symbolic, or metaphorical, theology, that he drew heavily on the work of pseudo-Dennis.[57] It is now worth noting further, that, for the latter, describing God by the use of metaphor was only one, and that the lesser way, in which we can attempt to describe God. As Thomas explained, 'Dionysius points out that, so far as is possible to us, in knowing divine matters we use appropriate signs of two kinds: signs which are perfections that proceed from God to creatures; and metaphors which are transferred from creatures to God because of some similarity between them.'[58]

The way of enlisting 'perfections that proceed from God to creatures' to express our knowledge of God is termed intelligible theology by pseudo-Dennis, and it has become central to classical theological reflection as the doctrine of analogical predication, which recognizes in human creatures qualities which are the effects in them of God's creative action, and then re-applies these to an outstanding degree ('eminently') to God as their cause. It was with this type of theology, as it is found in Scripture, that pseudo-Dennis was concerned, in discussing the sense in which we can properly and positively apply to God such terms as 'being', 'living', 'wisdom', 'justice', 'power', and so on, which we first experience in creation but come to recognize as deriving from the creator God.[59] In a study of *Aquinas and Analogy*, Ralph McInerny pertinently asked, 'How is it possible to name God otherwise than from creatures?', and he pointed out how this is a two-way process, combining both 'the order of naming and the order of being'.[60] As Thomas explained, 'when it is said that "God is good", . . . it means that what we call goodness in creatures exists first in God, and, in fact, in a higher manner . . . . It is because he is good that he imparts goodness to things.'[61]

In using such terms in naming God, then, we are now not merely speaking in metaphors. We realize that some terms are signposts pointing over the horizon in a Godward direction, and it is with the proper reading of such signposts that intelligible theology concerns itself. God, of course, is classically believed to be supremely simple, and so all our signposts point along roads which must converge; but the point at which they converge is out of our sight, over the horizon. Thus, it may be said that the very richness of Scripture in speaking of God is also a demonstration of Scripture's inherent incapacity to comprehend God. In other words, it is the abiding paradox of Christian theology, this side eternity, that the God of many names is also the God who is ultimately unnamable.[62]

It is only in imperfect ways, then, that humans (and therefore the Bible) can speak and write of God, limited as they are by a language which is drawn solely from their experience as, and of, creatures, and which is radically incapable of fully transcending the horizon of creaturehood. In other words, the human terms starting from creatures and pointing back to God have the liability of being inherently ambiguous in their use, that is, of being partly true yet partly false, especially when we agree with Emery on the basic difference between 'the perfection signified' and its 'mode of signification'.[63] The terms we apply are true as far as they go; but they do not go far enough. Thomas makes this clear at the start of his *Summa* when he completely rejects the possibility of using human language univocally about God, that is, identically, in transferring it from creatures to their prime cause,[64] the transcendent God 'whose essence is above what we understand of God and can express in word'.[65] Augustine himself was compelled to concede, as he began his famous commentary on John's sublime Gospel, that in divine matters 'Whoever speaks, says what he can. For who can say it as it is?' Disarmingly he added, 'Brothers, I presume to say that perhaps not even John himself said it as it is, but even he only as he was able to say it'.[66] And tradition could only agree.

The possibility, and the very nature, of analogical predication thus unavoidably exposes theologians to the continual danger of forgetting, or of coming to ignore or to disregard, the inherent limitation of human language when it is applied to God. This danger will accompany all our exploration in this study, as we shall have cause to repeat. Writing, for instance, of the term 'person' as applied to God, Emery makes a comment which should never be allowed to be lost sight of, 'As with all analogous attribution, one has to be aware of the fact that one is in the presence of a perfection which God possesses in a way unique to him'.[67] Even from the very beginning, just to describe the godhead as 'a being' can be woefully misleading: it appears to locate God in a genus on the same level as all non-divine, and therefore finite, beings. Yet, as Thomas explained early in his *Summa*, 'It is denied of God that he is in the same genus as other good things, not because he is in some other genus, but because he is outside genus and is the source of every genus'.[68]

In addition, within the terrain of our being limited to expressing divine reality in purely human terms, a particular minefield is encountered in our attempts to grasp and express the whole idea of God as a 'cause'. Battista Mondin concluded of Thomas's teaching on analogy that 'the ontological ground of the analogy between God and other beings is the relation of efficient causality of these beings with God'.[69] It appears, then, that second only to the risk of erroneously identifying God as a 'being' must lie attempts to portray God as an 'efficient cause', that is, somewhat like a being which produces further entities.

Thomas was thoroughly familiar with what Philipp Rosemann names the 'principle of causal similarity' which the latter considers 'the linchpin of Scholastic thought'; namely, the scholastic axiom that 'every agent produces a likeness of itself' (*omne agens agit sibi simile*).[70] Consequently, it seems we must conclude, if the being of the so-called divine agent is totally immersed in mystery, then all its activity must also partake of that mystery, so that even created effects which emanate from the divine reality are themselves located in the foothills of mystery, bearing some trace of their mysterious origin within them. It follows that, as the divine origin of all created being is essentially incomprehensible and mysterious, so also, in some degree, must be its every created effect, up to – and culminating in – human beings. As the question is famously asked, why should anything exist? And how little we know about what does, far less are we able to express it truly, and comprehensively. All this existential incoherence, which finds its fullness in negative theology, must be continually borne in mind whenever questions are raised, not only about God's activity, but also even about every divine creature.[71]

Hence, the definitive theological response to science's rejection of divine causality is to point out that God is not 'a cause' just like any other cause, and simply must, and may, never be treated as such. As Dodds comments, 'This is the exercise of faith seeking understanding. We grope for some sort of action or activity in the creaturely sphere to use as a model or analog to help us to penetrate – however inadequately – the mystery of God's action.'[72]

Further, importantly, the systematic use of analogical predication in referring to God, as we have described it, relies on a more fundamental theological doctrine, that of the 'analogy of being', as Pesch showed.[73] According to this, God as the supreme being imparts to all non-divine beings, in creating them, likenesses of the supreme being in varying ways and degrees (*omne agens agit sibi simile*). What makes it possible for us to use and apply to God our experience and terminology drawn from created realities is not only that God made these non-divine realities, and that all effects resemble their cause, but that in doing so, God shared the divine being with them variously. This is particularly the case, as Genesis narrates (1.26), in God's creating human beings in the 'image and likeness' of God.[74] To the tragic loss of post-Enlightenment thought, 'Causality', according to Rosemann, 'is the "cement" which holds the medieval universe together, linking all its elements in a great chain of being ordered according to their respective degrees of (dis)similarity to the first Cause'.[75] Although, then, 'all that is actually accessible to us in the present world are the effects of agent forces (and of the Agent Force) and *not* the agent forces in themselves, the law of similarity guarantees that these effects are possessed of a real revelatory quality'.[76] They point back to God as their origin. The second letter of Peter, 1.4, describes believers as being 'participants of the divine nature', and to some degree this sharing, or emanation, of sheer existence from the Divine Existent applies to each created non-being in its own particular way, that is, in accordance with its inherent nature, as this is determinedly and providentially given it by God.

Moreover, this participation applies not only to God's existence, but also to God's attributes (Pseudo-Dennis's 'Divine Names'), that is, God's wisdom, love, patience, freedom, concern for creatures and the like. Inexhaustible in themselves, such divine qualities are to be found mirrored and imaged in God's human creatures, inevitably in a limited way; and it is insofar as these qualities are identified as such in creatures that they are able to be traced back and transferred 'eminently', that is, to a supreme degree, to their infinitely perfect originator. As we have seen Thomas points out, 'when it is said that "God is good" . . . it means that "what we call goodness in creatures exists first in God", and, in fact, in a higher manner . . . .It is because he is good that he imparts goodness to things.'[77]

Such an incredibly rich God thus embraces all non-divine reality, being ever active to create and continually to sustain it, in its being and its native activity. As Moses asserts in Deuteronomy (33.27), 'Beneath are the everlasting arms'. If divine causality is such, then it simply cannot be conceived of, nor 'scaled down', as neighbouring, or existing alongside, earthly causality, and somehow as raising a problem of 'intervention', or of how divine causality interacts with the 'closed causal nexus' which science has come to perceive in the cosmos, as we mentioned earlier. God and the world are not in competitive tension; they are not like tectonic plates jostling against each other, struggling to gain ground one over the other in inverse proportion, so that the success of one indicates a failure of the other. The Catholic belief to the contrary was put in forthright terms by the bishops of the Second Vatican Council (1962–1965) when they stated:

> Far from thinking that the works produced by humanity's own talent and energy are in opposition to God's power and that the rational creature exists as a kind of rival to the Creator, Christians are convinced that the triumphs of the human race are a sign of God's greatness and the flowering of God's own mysterious design.[78]

It is interesting to contrast this conciliar statement with the conclusion which Dodds quotes from Taede Smedes, as the latter comments on the views even of some contemporary Christian theologian-scientists: 'though they are aware of the peculiar character of God-language, they still talk about God in competition-terms, as if God's action is similar to creaturely, causal and/or intentional action, including the limitations inherent to the creaturely condition'.[79]

The way, then, in which divine and non-divine being can successfully be understood to coexist, including as causes, is by realizing that non-divine being does not rival divine being but originates from it, and depends on it; and that the latter does not oppose created being, but embraces and sustains it. In other words, they do not act on the same level, or on the same plane, of being or of action, but on different levels, in a relationship of primary and secondary causality, as we saw Thomas richly develop this earlier in the chapter. As Dodds explains it, 'One may speak of God as the "First Cause" whose action pervades the world in and through natural causes, which may now be viewed as "secondary" or "instrumental" causes'.[80] Moreover, if reality is viewed through this double-layered principle, it remains entirely possible for science to devote itself simply and solely to the considering of all the world's secondary causes as constituting among themselves, at their own level, a 'closed causal nexus'. They each retain their own proper God-given and God-actuated causality, all within the brackets, as it were, of the existence and all-pervading activity of the supreme First Cause of all.

It is essential, therefore, to be continually sensitive to acknowledging, even at the risk of boredom, that the very idea even of 'causality', or of being a 'cause', cannot be used univocally of God and creatures, but only analogically and, therefore, ultimately, in God's case, opaquely, so far as humans are concerned. This is perhaps most evidently the case when we consider how a secondary human cause, endowed with a nature characterized by the power of reason and of free choice, can be understood to be activated by the primary cause to operate spontaneously and freely, that is, be 'prompted' in all its good actions by the Holy Spirit. It seems true that if both actions existed in the same order or on the same level and with similar 'purchasing power', they must inevitably conflict and contradict each other, but the fact that they must be understood to exist and interact at different levels of being, and, moreover, to do so analogically, allows for the first cause to transcend and embrace the activity proper to the secondary, instrumental cause, while at the same time respecting the limited unique effect of which the latter is innately capable by divine design.

Moreover, if it is the case that the analogy of being can help to explain how God can share God's own attributes with humans, as explained earlier, this will include their participating as human creatures not just in the divine justice, the divine love and the like; but also, perhaps almost unbelievably, in the divine *freedom*, that is, humans actually participating in God's own sovereign power of initiative. The suggestion here is not that God gives up his freedom, the kenotic self-'emptying' of Phil. 2.6–11, or the 'process theology' move adopted by some theologians to have God either choose, by a self-denying ordinance, or even necessarily to concede, a divine limitation in God's own causal activity. Such moves are evidently contrived to leave room in reality, as it were, for human creatures to exercise their own causality quite independently of God.[81] To the contrary, the thought here is not that of God on occasion *abandoning* or *surrendering* God's power and freedom of action over creatures, a move which implies univocity.[82] Rather, it is one of God positively *sharing* the divine power of choice with God's human creatures creatively and lovingly, and in this way respecting and making use of the nature endowed with reason and free will with which God had privileged them in creating them. In a remarkable passage which links God's supreme guiding providence with genuine creaturely initiative, Thomas explains that the rational creature is 'subject to divine providence in a more excellent manner than other creatures, insofar as it is made *a sharer in providence, taking foresight for itself and for others*' (fit providentiae particeps, sibi ipsi et aliis providens).[83]

This consideration helps to confirm the need to stress, as Silva does, that 'underlying Aquinas' understanding of causality is the idea that this is an analogical notion; it is therefore appropriate that it should be used to account for creaturely actions as well as God's action',[84] provided, we should add, that when God is described analogically as a 'cause', the term is not transparent, but is opaque, shrouded in transcendent mystery.[85] Dodds regularly finds it necessary to repeat the objection to modern scientific approaches to divine action, that 'despite their occasional protestations to the contrary, they all tend to treat God as a univocal cause alongside of natural causes'.[86] And this is the basic flaw in modern science's view of divine causality.

> How God manages to do this [act in the world] without interfering with creaturely causes is often viewed as the fundamental problem. Two solutions are generally proposed.... Both of these solutions, however, presuppose a univocal understanding of divine causality. Absent such an understanding, the problem itself does not arise.[87]

Analogical predication relating to God is not simply a matter of introducing a few cautionary qualifications when applying a human term to its prime analogate; that is no way to allow for God's infinity and eternity! It might be helpful to think of someone born and brought up in a country with a permanently overcast atmosphere, where people never have any sight of the sun. All that they regularly experience under a cloudy sky is a prevailing greyish light and a regularly median temperature; and they have a notion that these phenomena must have some sort of explanation somewhere up there. If, one day the ceiling of clouds were to open, and reveal the sun, the inhabitants would be utterly astonished, and rendered speechless at what they beheld: a gigantic orb of blazing incandescent fire suspended in the sky high above them, much too bright for them to gaze at and far too hot for them to be exposed to. No wonder some people adored it. To describe this just as the cause of the little light and warmth that filter regularly through the clouds to the earth far below would fall unbelievably short of an adequate description of the sun and its activity.

There is a tradition about Thomas Aquinas which was repeated at his canonization process and which is often, in the writer's view, misunderstood: that once, after receiving a divine vision, he decided to stop writing theology; and when he was asked to explain this decision, he described all that he had written in his life as 'so much straw'. Far from Thomas in these words repudiating his life's work as valueless, he was far more likely to be making the deep theological point that, compared to what he had personally experienced in his vision, everything else that he had done so far was completely inadequate. Torrell comments, 'These words have sometimes been interpreted as Thomas's dismissal of his work as theologian. This is highly improbable. Elevated by a special grace to contemplate the reality itself, Thomas had good reason to feel detached from the words he had employed until then, but this does not imply that he considered his work worthless. Simply, from that moment on, he had passed beyond it.'[88] To which we can add, that Thomas's remark can be taken as providing a dramatic confirmation of the permanent need for the human analogical approach whenever God and godly matters are being considered.

## 'DISPOSING ALL THINGS SMOOTHLY'

Under God, then, the children of God are really and truly active. In producing their acts, God uses as a medium the nature, or the inherent principle of action, with which God has endowed them. And, far from impairing those principles of action, of thought and of will, God is bringing them to perfection in their operation, with the result that God's daughters and sons are enabled – and ennobled – to perform the acts which God wills them and causes them to perform.

Just as the nature of creatures, Thomas explains, is in one sense the end-product of God's operation, and yet is in another sense the principle of the operations which God proceeds to effect in those creatures, so also the created habit of grace by which God re-creates humans is related to the Holy Spirit, partly as the end-product of the Spirit's operation, but also partly as the medium of the Spirit's further operation.[89] It was Peter Lombard's error that, although he held rightly that humans are moved by the Holy Spirit to love God and their neighbour, he denied that there is in humans a created habit by which their will is perfected to perform this kind of loving acts.[90] In Thomas's view, an act of charity produced in a person by the Holy Spirit, without the medium of a created supernatural habit within them, would do violence to the human nature which God had given humans. It could not be called the person's own act, nor a voluntary act, nor a meritorious act.[91]

Nature and its faculties, grace and the virtues and gifts: they are all in one sense the completion of God's creative activity, and they are possessed of a dignity and beauty in the static order as various perfections of God's human creature deriving from and dependent on divine reality. In another sense, however, in the active sense, they are only a means or instrument to a further manifestation of God's activity in and through his human creatures. It is worth recalling here what we observed in analyzing Thomas's theology of grace,[92] that it is essential to our understanding of Thomas's dynamic and holistic view of created reality to realize that underlying what we conceptually distinguish and classify as strata, or layers, in the created effects in us of God's uncreated act: graces, virtues, gifts and so on, there are also to be discerned an existential unity and an overall purpose which manifest the pervading wisdom and power of the Spirit. If we haul a salmon out of a river and place it on a slab, we can examine it in detail and observe much to admire about it. But we should continually bear in mind that it is a fish out of water. Only when we replace it in its natural environment and observe it resume its darting natural course do we begin fully to appreciate what it is, and observe its beauty of function, and its elegant grace of movement, all of which enhance and fulfil the promise and the demand which we could observe only dimly in its static perfection. A salmon's swimming is what it's all for: as Thomas put it succinctly, 'purpose is the cause of causes' (*finis est causa causarum*).[93]

So it is with the spiritual person who is borne along by the living stream of the Spirit, as our study of the Spirit as living water indicated.[94] Analysis and examination of the endowments which God has given, whether in nature or in supernature, in intellect or in will, are of obvious importance; but the spiritual person can begin to be judged adequately only when seen in action, like the salmon as viewed from the bank and not just on it. From that dynamic vantage point, all that God has given are seen to be perfections, but they are perfections with a purpose: endowments and adaptations which the Spirit has developed in spiritual persons, in order that they may feel, and act, at home in the element into which the Spirit has plunged them, and in which the current of the Holy Spirit carries them along knowingly and freely.

This continuity and cumulative purpose of God is clearly shown by Aquinas in his consideration of God's resting on the seventh day of creation (Gen. 2.2–3). God's work was completed and finished on the seventh day, Thomas points out, insofar as creation was perfect, in one respect. But there were further perfections to come, namely the perfection of activity leading to, and consummated by, the ultimate perfection of the beatitude of the saints. 'There is a double perfection. The first is the existence of something, and the second is its operating, which is greater.'[95] The forms and faculties with which humans have been endowed are thus perfections with a purpose; and towards that purpose, they have a natural affinity and inclination, a built-in tendency, which disposes humans to that activity which will realize their further, and eventually their ultimate, God-given purpose. This is what Thomas meant when he wrote in the *Summa Contra Gentes*:

> For someone to arrive at the happiness of that enjoyment of God which belongs naturally to God, they must first be made like God by spiritual perfections, then

act according to those perfections, and so at length they will achieve that happiness. Now, as we have seen, it is by the Holy Spirit that gifts are given to us; and thus it is by the Holy Spirit that we are configured to God; it is by the Spirit that we are able to act well; and it is likewise by the Spirit that the way to happiness is being prepared for us.[96]

Acting according to the perfections which the Spirit has given us means acting in accordance with the dynamism latent in these perfections; and in particular, it means acting in accordance with that inclination and predisposition which is part of the virtue of charity, since, as Thomas explains, 'no virtue has so great an inclination to its act as charity does'.[97] This does not mean, however, that the internal activity and initiative of the Holy Spirit are thereby dispensed with.[98] The 'spiritual gifts' which the Spirit has bestowed on humans remain only a medium of the Spirit's activity, but they do show how divine wisdom 'orders all thing well' (Wis 8.1) or, as an earlier translation has it, 'disposes all things smoothly', insofar as God provides every creature with the forms and virtues by which they are disposed to do what God is moving them to do and wishes them to do. The result is that when the creature proceeds to act at God's or the Spirit's initiative, it does so effortlessly and not, as it were, reluctantly. And not only is the wisdom of God manifested by God's thus predisposing creatures, but so also, paradoxically, is God's power displayed. It is a sign of greater power, Thomas explains, when a cause not only moves something to act, but also imprints on it a form through which it itself acts. Hence the Holy Spirit, which is 'the most powerful of movers', so moves a person to love that the Spirit also induces in that person the very virtue, or capability, of loving.[99]

Yet, however exalted the ontological perfections which the Spirit imparts to humans, and however powerful the inclinations and predispositions to act which those perfections possess, and however refined the person's activity is by these perfections and dispositions, the human being is still only the instrument of God, attendant on the initiative and the prompting of that superior principle of all human activity. A principle which Thomas regularly observes is that 'no habit proceeds to act spontaneously; it needs to be aroused by some agent'.[100] This was why Paul could write to the Corinthians that through God's grace, he had been enabled to work harder than any of the Apostles; and yet it was not himself, he added, but the grace of God which was with him (1 Cor. 15.10). On which Thomas comments that God had poured into Paul the grace by which his acts were made pleasing and meritorious. But God did more than that, in also moving Paul himself to use that grace well. And this was why Paul said that it was not he alone who worked, but the grace of God moving his will to work. The success of Paul's apostolate, Thomas stresses, came 'not from himself alone but from the prompting and help of the Holy

Spirit'.[101] We see this confirmed in Thomas's commentary on Eph. 3.7, where he explains that the help in the ministry which Paul received from God was twofold; namely, the ability to act, and also the very activity itself. 'God gives the ability by pouring in the power and the grace which enable and fit one to act; but God also confers the act itself, insofar as God acts in us, moving and prompting us interiorly to good'.[102]

## THE GIFTS OF THE HOLY SPIRIT

These cumulative and complementary perfections of being and of activity which the Holy Spirit effects in and through God's children are seen by Thomas at their most refined in his mature teaching on the role of the seven gifts of the Holy Spirit as sensitivities within God's sons and daughters to the continuous promptings of the Holy Spirit.[103] Meinert concluded, at the end of his thorough study of grace and the Gifts in Thomas, that for him 'the gifts are the heart and height of the moral life, a life led under the influence of the Holy Spirit';[104] and Michael Sherwin, in his study of charity's relation to knowledge in Aquinas, equally recognizes that Thomas 'assigns the gifts a central place in the moral life'.[105] Moreover, as O'Connor observed of them, 'Thomas's work was, on the one hand, deeply rooted in tradition and, on the other hand, so original that it revolutionized the theological approach to the Gifts'.[106]

What was to become the classical doctrine of the seven gifts of the Holy Spirit with which all believers are endowed at baptism, alongside the gifts of sanctifying grace and the theological and moral virtues, found its origin in the passage in the Old Testament book of Isaiah which foretold that the promised Saviour of Israel would be especially equipped for this role by the Spirit of God: 'The spirit of the Lord shall rest on him, the spirit of wisdom and understanding, the spirit of counsel and might, the spirit of knowledge and the fear of the Lord. His delight shall be in the fear of the Lord' (Isa. 11.2). In fact, only six 'spirits' are listed in the Hebrew text of Isaiah, with 'the fear of the Lord' repeated; but the first of these occurrences was translated by the Greek Septuagint translation as *eusebeia*, 'piety' and thence into the Latin Vulgate as *pietas* (piety), thus culminating in what became for the church fathers, and subsequently, the traditional list of the seven Gifts of the Spirit with which Thomas was familiar: wisdom, understanding, counsel, fortitude, knowledge, piety and fear of the Lord.[107] The later references in the Book of Revelations to 'the seven spirits of God' (Rev. 3.1, 4.5, 5.6) may be seen as so many symbols of the Holy Spirit.

Ambrose Gardeil shows, in his classic article on the Gifts in the *Dictionnaire de Théologie Catholique*, that the fathers of the church, especially the Latins

Augustine and Gregory, were not slow in linking the messianic prophecy of Isaiah 11 with other passages in the Old Testament which refer to the Spirit of God, and with the various New Testament references to the Holy Spirit, and to the Spirit's action on Jesus (e.g. Mk 1.10).[108] They extended the Spirit's influence beyond Jesus to cover his disciples also, who were 'baptized' and 'filled' with the Holy Spirit (Acts 1.5; 2.4). In time, the gift, and gifts, of the Spirit came to be applied as a standard baptismal endowment conferred on all believers who are being sacramentally identified with Christ,[109] the Vulgate numbering of 'seven' additionally symbolizing multiplicity and abundance, as often in Scripture, and in this case the loving generosity associated with God's Spirit.[110]

Inheriting and developing this patristic doctrine, the scholastic and university theologians from the twelfth century onwards, in their typical fascination with categorizing and classifying, set out to systematize the Holy Spirit's Gifts, and we find Thomas in his early commentary on Isai. 11.2–3, explaining that the seven gifts itemized there are, precisely as 'gifts', all ascribed to the Holy Spirit 'who is the first gift, in whom all gifts are given'. He raises the standard question of the day, how the 'gifts of the Spirit' relate to the theological and moral virtues; and he answers that the gifts are given as a help to the virtues, by conferring on their recipients a more exalted capacity for action (a 'higher habit') than the 'human manner' with which the virtues perfect the powers of the soul to act.[111] As the early Thomas explains,

> A virtue is defective in two ways; one, in being possessed inadequately by someone, and this can be remedied by an increase in that virtue. The other defect can apply to the virtue itself, as faith is imperfect in its possessor, in being mysterious. That deficiency can be removed by a higher disposition (habit), which is called a 'gift' because it is given by God as if to surpass the degree of human activity; as, for instance, the gift of understanding somehow makes matters of faith lucid and clear.[112]

In repeating this explanation in more detail in his equally early *Commentary on the Sentences* of Peter Lombard, where Thomas treated of Lombard's own authoritative teaching on the Gifts, the early Thomas reviewed, and discarded, several current theological explanations of the Gifts of the Holy Spirit, before accepting the one which held that 'the gifts are given for acts which are more exalted (higher) than those produced by the virtues'.

'A virtue, or power', he had explained. 'is a capacity in everything enabling it to operate as it should do successfully; as, in moral matters, human virtue perfects a person to behave well as a human being. Human activity can thus be considered characteristically human in its operating in accordance with reason.

But if a person engages in human matters in a more than human manner, the activity will not be simply human, but divine in some way. Aristotle distinguished simple virtue from 'heroic' virtue which he called 'divine', since through outstanding virtue one is made like God.[113] This is why I say that the gifts differ from the virtues, because the virtues perfect one to act in a human manner, whereas the gifts perfect one to operate beyond the human manner, as is obvious in the case of the virtue of faith and the corresponding gift of understanding. The manner connatural to human nature is to perceive divine matters only through the mirror of creatures and the obscurity of similitudes; and the virtue of faith perfects one to perceive such divine matters in this way. But the Gift of understanding, as Gregory explains, enlightens the mind on what is heard, so that even in this life one receives a glimpse of future manifestation.[114]

Thus the early Thomas. It is striking, however, that later in his career, in writing on the Gifts of the Spirit in his comprehensive *Summa* of Theology, Thomas adopts a completely different line of theological approach from the one we have just seen him take in his commentary on the *Sentences*. In examining again the basic question of how the gifts differ from the virtues, and after again reviewing and rejecting several current theological explanations, Thomas now directs his reader's attention back to the originating passage in Isaiah 11, where, he now points out, the text does not, in fact, mention 'gifts' at all; it actually writes of 'spirits'. 'From which it is obvious', he concludes

> that the seven things listed there as 'spirits' are within us by divine inspiration, which implies some movement coming from outside us. We have to realise that in every person there is a double moving principle: one interior, which is their reason; and the other exterior, which is God, as explained above,[115] and by Aristotle in a chapter in *The Good Luck Book*.[116]

Warming to his subject, Thomas continues,

> Everything that is being moved has to be proportionate to what is moving it, and the perfection of anything that is being moved, precisely as movable, is its aptitude to be moved well. The more exalted the mover, the more need there is for what is being moved to be proportioned to it with a more perfect aptitude, just as we see that a student must be more perfectly equipped to understand advanced teaching.
>
> Clearly, human virtues perfect people in accordance with their nature to be moved by reason in what they do interiorly or exteriorly. To be disposed to be moved by God, therefore, people must have higher dispositions in them. Those perfections are called 'gifts', not only because they are infused by God, but also because people are disposed by them to become promptly movable by a

divine inspiration, as Isaiah said, 'The Lord God has opened my ear, and I do not resist'. (50.5)

In a crucial new insight, Thomas continues,

> Aristotle also says in a chapter in *The Good Luck Book* that those people who are moved by a divine prompting do not need to have recourse to human reason, but they follow an interior prompting: they are moved by a principle better than human reason. And this is why some say that the gifts perfect people to more exalted actions than acts of the virtues.[117]

In short, for Aquinas in his mature teaching, the Gifts of the Holy Spirit are not now just ways of acting virtuously in a heightened mode of activity. They are now, he explains in more explicitly theological terms, 'human endowments which enable one to follow the prompting of the Holy Spirit',[118] creating a heightened docility, or susceptibility, to the Spirit's activity and influence. Garrigou-Lagrange expresses the role of the gifts well when he follows the famous elegant simile of John of St Thomas, in describing the Gifts as habitual capacities within a person to receive inspirations from above, like the sails which equip a boat to respond to the wind, in contrast to the laborious rowing of the crew.[119] A more contemporary comparison could be that of seeing the Gifts as fine tuning in the recipient enabling them to receive divine transmissions with more fidelity and fewer distortions.

In exploring Thomas's teaching on the act of faith, Seckler usefully brought out, according to Schillebeeckx, how Thomas became aware of the church's condemnation of semi-Pelagian views on the act of faith, and how this had the effect of his toning down the human contribution and highlighting the divine, so that 'the movement of God, the *motio divina*, came to occupy a central place'[120] For the same reason, it seems that Thomas's views on the dynamics of the Gifts of the Holy Spirit were now also tilted more towards the divine initiative, but he was even more influenced now, by having access to a striking new Aristotelian source which would favour even more the highlighting of the divine, rather than the human – even the 'super'-human – element in human acts: the source which we know as the *Liber de Bona Fortuna*, which we prefer to translate more pertinently as the 'Good Luck Book'.[121]

This short treatise consisted of a painfully literal Latin translation of a chapter of Aristotle's *Eudemian Ethics* and another of his *Magna Moralia*.[122] As part of his deep metaphysical interest in causality, Aristotle was philosophically intrigued by the phenomenon of chance, and of good and bad luck; and the *Liber* excerpted in Latin his teaching on these subjects, no doubt as being of particular concern to Christian theologians in the light of their belief in divine providence.[123] It appears that Thomas first made its acquaintance in

Italy, shortly after he had completed his first years of teaching at Paris. From that time, he refers regularly to a short passage of the *Liber*, some fifteen lines of the manuscript which Deman edited in his classic article.[124] Cornelio Fabro comments that it was a 'bold and typical' move on Thomas's part to adopt Aristotle's 'divine prompting' of lucky people and apply it to the working of the Holy Spirit's Gifts within Christians at the apex of their spiritual life.[125] In editing Thomas's treatise on the Gifts of the Spirit, in the modern Dominican translation of the *Summa*, O'Connor devotes an appendix to Thomas's use of the *De Bona Fortuna*, in which he explains that modern versions of the Latin text are unreliably descended from the very literal Latin translation of the original fragmentary Greek, so for interest's sake, he includes in English translation the original relevant chapters which were excerpted from Aristotle.[126]

The gist of Aristotle's teaching is that there is something godly in each of us, which is the origin of all our thinking and decision-making. Traditionally, fortunate people were considered to be those who follow an impulse and are successful without using their reason. They have no need to deliberate, because they have within them a principle which is higher than their understanding and deliberation. Other people, who follow their reason, do not have this internal principle nor any divine promptings. The result is that one type of good fortune consists in being directed by god and divine prompting.[127] In his *Summa*, in referring to the *Liber*, Thomas cites the edition available to him, notably the following passage, as we have seen: 'Aristotle also says in a chapter in *The Good Luck Book* that those people who are moved by a divine prompting do not need to have recourse to human reason, but follow an interior prompting: they are moved by a better principle than human reason'.[128]

Such, in brief, is Thomas's mature teaching on the Gifts of the Holy Spirit, a teaching which progressed from seeing the Gifts as enabling a person to act in a manner more exalted than that which characterizes virtuous activity, to seeing the Gifts as rendering a person sensitive to the inspirations and promptings of the Holy Spirit. Whereas in the *Sentences*, it is human beings who occupy the centre of our attention, in the *Summa*, they yield to the presence and pervading activity of the Holy Spirit. Now the Gifts are seen as the most refined instance of the power and wisdom of God in the cumulative and complementary perfection of endowment and behaviour in people which manifest that power and wisdom. It is now the initiative and dynamism of the Spirit and human receptivity rather than human activity, even 'heroic' human activity, which are more in evidence, just as the divine wisdom too is more evidently manifested in equipping people by the Gifts to follow smoothly and, as it were, effortlessly, the promptings of the Holy Spirit. Fabro had no hesitation in concluding that 'Thomas's acceptance and deepening of the *Liber de Bona Fortuna* seemed to suggest a deeper and original mode of the causality and active presence of God in the human soul'.[129] It also enabled Thomas in a striking passage to explain the primacy of the Spirit's Gifts within all the graded spiritual dispositions with which he considers God's sons and daughters have been equipped:

> The theological virtues are those by which the human mind is joined to God; the intellectual virtues are those by which human reasoning is perfected; the moral virtues are those by which our appetites are perfected to obey our reason; and the Gifts of the Holy Spirit dispose the powers of the soul to be subject to divine movements.[130]

In this theological setting of the Spirit's Gifts, the significance for Thomas of the interior prompting of the Holy Spirit could not be greater, nor its role more exalted. As he concluded, 'People are not perfected towards their final end by the theological and moral virtues without their always needing to be moved by a higher prompting of the Holy Spirit'.[131] Further, in the light of all the above on the seven gifts of the Holy Spirit, it is not surprising to find Emery observing in an informative article on the Holy Spirit in Thomas's *Summa* of Theology, that 'the structure of virtues developed by Aquinas accords a central place to the seven gifts of the Holy Spirit'.[132]

We have seen Gardeil's tracing of the history of the development of the church's doctrine on the Gifts, from which he concluded candidly that 'we can only admit that the doctrine of the seven gifts ... is a pure construction of theological speculation built on a base of vaguely revealed data'. In defence of its later authority, he proposed that it seemed to be like a case of the development of doctrine, such as Newman had conceived this.[133]

If one accepts Gardeil's proposal that the doctrine of the seven gifts of the Holy Spirit, as we traditionally have it today, fulfils Newman's criteria for the development of a doctrine within the church under the continuing influence of the Holy Spirit of God, then there appears to be no intrinsic difficulty in accepting belief in the doctrine of the seven gifts of the Holy Spirit as an entirely appropriate – Thomas would say *conveniens* – way of associating all God's loving and intimate giving to his children particularly with the Holy Spirit of love and truth who is drawing us ever closer to the Father, The traditional significance of what the mediaeval hymn, *Veni, sancte Spiritus*, called the Spirit's 'septiform gift' is recognized by Farrell and Hughes when they write that although 'it is not a solemnly declared dogma, it is a part of tradition to which liturgical usage and the ordinary teaching authority of the Church give ample witness'.[134] The belief is more formally and technically expressed in the modern *Catechism of the Catholic Church*, in the passage on the Gifts, where the influence of Thomas's treatment is obvious, including reference to his two favourite scriptural verses which describe the influence of the Spirit in human moral action. The Catechism teaches:

> The moral life of the Christian is sustained by the gifts of the Holy Spirit. These are permanent dispositions which make one docile in following the promptings of the Holy Spirit. The seven gifts of the Holy Spirit are wisdom, understanding, counsel, fortitude, knowledge, piety and fear of the Lord. They belong in their fullness to Christ, the son of David (Cf Is. 11.1–2). They complete and perfect the virtues of those who receive them. They make the faithful docile in readily obeying divine inspirations. 'Let your good spirit lead me on a level path' (Ps 143.10); 'those who are led by the Spirit of God are [children] of God'. (Rom. 8.14)[135]

By way of conclusion, this chapter on 'the prompting of the Holy Spirit' has aimed to show how Thomas understood the phrase, and how his recourse to it, and his understanding of it, developed in the course of his study and writing, from his early use, following Augustine and others, until he came under the influence of the Aristotelian *Good Luck Book*. With this went a fuller appreciation of Rom. 8.14 and of the influence of the Holy Spirit in 'driving', and not just leading, God's children. Much of this is well summed up in the following passage from Thomas's *Summa contra Gentes* 4, 22:

> Since it is through the Holy Spirit that we are made lovers of God, it is also through the Spirit that we are somehow driven (*agimur*) to observe God's commands, according to Rom 8.14, 'those who are driven by the Spirit of God are God's children'. But it should be considered that God's children are driven by God's Spirit not as enslaved, but as free. Since people who are free have control over themselves, we do freely what we do by ourselves, that is, what we do of our own will; whereas what we do against our will, we do not freely, but as slaves. . . . The Holy Spirit inclines us to act in such a way as to make us act voluntarily insofar as he makes us lovers of God. Therefore, God's children are driven freely by the Holy Spirit out of love, not out of fear, as slaves. (Rom. 8.15)[136]

## NOTES

1. On the author's preference for translating this famous verse as 'children' of God rather than the literal 'sons', see p. 17 of this book.

2. A. Valsecchi, *La 'Legge Nuova' del Cristiano secondo san Tommaso d' Aquino*, Varese, 1963.

3. Nicolas of Lyra, *glosa ordinaria cum expositione Lyre litterali et morali, necnon additionibus ac Replicis*, tt 6 (Basileae, 1506–1508), VI, 18v. Cf. J. P. Green, ed., *The interlinear Hebrew-Greek English Bible* (Peabody, MA: Hendrickson, 2005).

4. Migne *PL*, vols. 113–4.
5. Augustine, *de gestis Pelagii*, III, 5 (*PL* 44, 323).
6. Z. Alszeghy, *Nova Creatura. La nozione della grazia nei commentari medievali di S. Paolo* (Romae: Analecta Gregoriana 81, 1956), 130–1.
7. Migne *PL* 191, 1439. Cf Augustine, *de gratia Christ*i, XXV, 26 (*PL* 44, 373).
8. Augustine, *de correptione et gratia*, cap 2 (*PL* 44, 918).
9. *In Rom.* 8, lect. 3 (M 635).
10. *ST* II-II.93.6 ad 1. Cf *In 2 Cor.* 13, lect. 2 (M 520).
11. *In Rom.* 8, lect. 3 (M 635).
12. Supra, pp. 29–32, especially 32.
13. *ST* III.7.5.
14. *In 2 Cor.* 5, lect. 3 (M 181).
15. Emery, *Trinitarian*, p. 263, n. 183.
16. See Max Seckler, *Instinkt und Glaubenswille nach Thomas von Aquin* (Mains, 1961); Juan Alfaro, 'Supernaturalitas fidei iuxta S. Thomam', *Gregorianum* 44 (1963), 501–42, 731–87.
17. Charles E. Bouchard, 'Recovering the Gifts of the Holy Spirit in Moral Theology', *TS* 63 (2002) 550–1; T. F. O'Meara, 'Virtues in the Theology of Thomas Aquinas', *TS* 58 (1997, 276 n. 59, quoting S. Pinckaers, *The Sources of Christian Ethics* (Washington, D.C.: The Catholic |University of America Press, 1995).
18. J Lecuyer, 'Docilité au S. Esprit', *DSp* III (Paris: Beauchesne, 1967), col. 1488, emphasis added.
19. Pinsent, *The Second-Person Perspective in Aquinas's Ethics. Virtues and Gifts* (New York: Routledge, 2012), 38, referring for support to the review of Seckler by Edward Schillebeeckx in *RSPT,* 1964, 393.
20. John M, Meinert, *The Love of God Poured Out. Grace and the Gifts of the Holy Spirit in St. Thomas Aquinas* (Steubenville, OH: Emmaeus Academic, 2018), p. 88.
21. Meinart, 89–113.
22. Meinart 197.
23. *In Hebr.* 11, lect. 7.
24. *ST* I-II.68.1. Cf. below, p. 71, endnote 127.
25. Edward. D. O'Connor, St Thomas Aquinas, *Summa theologiae*, vol 24 (London: Eyre & Spottiswoode, 1974), 131–2, emphasis added. See also 136–41. Bouchard, 551, n. 44.
26. Dominic Legge, *The Trinitarian Theology of St Thomas Aquinas* (Oxford: Oxford University Press, 2017), 206.
27. *ST* I-II, 68.1.
28. *In Rom.* 8, lect. 3 (M 635), emphasis added.
29. *In Matth* 10 (*Ms B V 12*, f 93 ra 32-b9). On the Basel Matthew, see above p. 5.
30. David Knowles, *The Evolution of Mediaeval Thought* (London: Longmans, 1962), 180.
31. John Damascene, *de fide orthodox*, 2, 27 (Migne *PG* 94, 960–1).
32. Augustine, *de corr. et gratia,* cap 2 *(PL* 44, 918).

33. Augustine, *Serm* 156, cap 10–11 (*PL* 38, 855–6). Cf *de gratia Christi*, 25, 26 (*PL* 44, 373).

34. Nicholas Austin, *Aquinas on Virtue. A Causal Reading* (Washington, D.C.: Georgetown University Press, 2017), 64–5.

35. Cf B. Lonergan, 'St Thomas' Theory of Operation', *Theological Studies* 3 (1942) 373–402.

36. *In Rom.* 8, lect. 3 (M 635) (emphasis added).

37. *In Matth* 10, lect. 2 (M 849). Kimball, 378.

38. *In Rom.* 9, lect. 3 (M 777).

39. Ignacio Silva, 'Thomas Aquinas Holds Fast: Objections to Aquinas Within Today's Debate on Divine Action', *Heythrop Journal*, 54 (2013) 658–67.

40. *In Rom.* 9, lect. 3 (M 778).

41. *ST* I-II.68.3 ad 2.

42. *ST* II-II.52.1 ad 3.

43. *In Hebr.* 9, lect. 3 (M 444).

44. *In Rom.* 8, lect. 3 (M 635).

45. *ST* III,7,1.

46. *In Gal.* 5, lect. 5 (M 318).

47. *De car*, 1 ad 2.

48. Michael J. Dodds, *Unlocking Divine Action. Contemporary Science and Thomas Aquinas* (Washington, D.C.: The Catholic University of America, 2012), 48–53.

49. Dodds, 97.

50. Dodds, 52–3.

51. Dodds 65–6, 186.

52. Dodds, 51.

53. Dodds, 106–7. On occasionalism, see Dodds 210–11.

54. See endnote 48.

55. Dodds, 179.

56. See also Ignacio Silva, 'Thomas Aquinas Holds Fast: Objections to Aquinas Within Today's Debate on Divine Action', *Heythrop Journal*, 54 (2013) 658–67.

57. Above, see pp. 22–23.

58. Thomas, *In Div Nom* 1, 2 (M 69).

59. Thomas, *In Div Nom* 1, 3 (M 104); cf 9.2 (M 823).

60. Ralph McInerny, *Aquinas and Analogy* (Washington, D.C.: Catholic University of America, 1996), 158. On Thomas's use of analogy, see also Battista Mondin, *The Principle of Analogy in Protestant and Catholic Theology* (The Hague: M. Nijhoff, 1963).

61. *ST* I.13.2. Cf. McInerny, 161.

62. Cf *In Div Nom* 1, 3 (M 98).

63. Emery, *Trinitarian*, pp. 107–08.

64. *ST* I.13.1 ad 1.

65. *ST* I.13.5.

66. Augustine, *In Joannis Evangelium tractatus CXXIV*, tr. 1, 1. Migne, *PL* 39, 1379.

67. Emery, *Trinitarian Theology*, 107.
68. *ST* I.6.2 ad 3.
69. Mondin, 34.
70. Rosemann, Philipp W., '*Omne agens agit sibi simile*: a "repetition" of Scholastic metaphysics' (Leuven: Leuven University Press, 1996), 11. Cf, for example, *ST* I.115.1; 110.2.

See also Mondin, pp. 86–98, who provides, p. 86, the neat translation of *omne agens* and so forth that we have used earlier in the text.

71. On negative theology, see above p. 22.
72. Dodds, 177.
73. Pesch 209–14. See also Thomas J. White, ed., *The Analogy of Being: Invention of the Antichrist or the Wisdom of God?* (Grand Rapids, MI: Erdmans, 2011).
74. See Stephen J. Pope, 'Theological Anthropology, Science, and Human Flourishing', in Lieven Boeve, Yves De Maeseneer, and Ellen Van Stichel, edd., *Questioning the Human. Towards a Theological Anthropology for the Twenty-First Century* (New York: Fordham University Press, 2014) 13–30.
75. Rosemann, 23.
76. Rosemann, 341.
77. *ST* I.13.2, above, p. 43. Cf. McInerny, *Aquinas and Analogy*, 161.
78. The Second Vatican Council, *Pastoral Constitution on the Church in the World (Gaudium et spes)*, par 34; in Walter M. Abbott, *The Documents of Vatican II* (London: Chapman, 1965), 232.
79. Taede A. Smedes, *Chaos, Complexity and God: Divine Action and Scientism* (Leuven: Peters, 2004), 207, in Dodds, 156.
80. Dodds, 188.
81. Cf. C Stephen Evans, ed., *Exploring Kenotic Theology: The Self-Emptying of God* (Vancouver, B.C.: Regent College Publishing, 2009); and B. G. Epperly, *Process Theology. A Guide for the Perplexed* (London: T & T Clarke, 2011).
82. Dodds, 114–18, 211–12.
83. *ST* I-II.91.2. Emphasis added.
84. Silva, 665.
85. Cf Dodds, 107–9.
86. Dodds, 153.
87. Dodds, 186.
88. J.-P. Torrell, *Christ and Spirituality in St Thomas Aquinas* (Washington, D.C.: The Catholic University of America Press, 2011), 19–20.
89. *In I Sent.*, d 17, q 1, a 1 ad 3.
90. *De caritate*, a. 12.
91. *ST* II-II.23.1.
92. See above, pp. 44.
93. *ST* I.5.2 ad 1.
94. See above, pp. 30–31.
95. *ST* I.73.1.
96. *CG* 4.21.

97. *ST* II-II.23.2.
98. Wis 8.1. RSV 'orders all things well'.
99. *De car.* 1 ad 2.
100. *De virt.* 1 ad 14.
101. *In 1 Cor.* 15, lect. 1 (M 909).
102. *In Eph* 3, lect. 2 (M 145).
103. See Yves Congar, *I Believe in the Holy Spirit*, 3 vols. (New York: Seabury Press, 1983), especially vol 2, 134–41.
104. Meinart, p. 276.
105. Michael S. Sherwin, *By Knowledge and by Love. Charity and Knowledge in the Moral Theology of St Thomas Aquinas* (Washington, D.C.: The Catholic University of America Press, 2005), 164.
106. Edward. D. O'Connor, St Thomas Aquinas, *Summa theologiae*, vol 24, *The Gifts of the Spirit* (London: Eyre & Spottiswoode, 1974), 88.
107. *ST* I-II. q. 68.
108. Ambrose Gardeil, 'Dons du Saint-Esprit', *DTC*, 4/2, coll. 1728–81.
109. O'Connor, Appendices I-II, pp 80–98. See, *Catechism of the Catholic Church* (London: Burns & Oates, 2000), par 1830–1.
110. Gardeil, Dons, col 1751. Cf Rev. 1.4, and so on.
111. *In Is.* 11.
112. *In Is.* 11.
113. Aristotle, *Ethics*, VII, 1; Aristotle *Ethics*, Penguin Classics, 1976, p. 226.
114. *Comm in Sent*, Lib III, 34, 1, 1. On 'more than human' acts, see O. Lottin, 'A propos de la formule "ultra humanum modum" de saint Thomas d'Aquin', *RTAM* 30 (1963) 289; and more recently, Klooster, Anton ten, *Thomas Aquinas on the Beatitudes* (Leuven: Peeters, 2018), 136–40.
115. *ST* I-II, 9, 4 and 6.
116. *ST* I-II.68.1.
117. ST I-II.68.1.
118. *ST* I-II.68.3.
119. R. Garrigou-Lagrange, *Perfection chrétienne et contemplation*, t. 1, (Saint-Maximin 1923), 349, quoted in J. Lecuyer, 'Docilité au S. Esprit', *DSp* III (Paris: Beauchesne, 1967), col 1487. See also Bouchard, 'Recovering' 555.
120. Edward Schillebeeckx, *Revelation and Theology* (New York: Sheed and Ward, 1968), vol 2, 35–6, quoted in Michael Sherwin, *By Knowledge and By Love. Charity and Knowledge in the Moral Theology of St Thomas Aquinas* (Washington, D.C.: The Catholic University of America Press, 2005), 140–1, On Semi-Pelagianism, see Rebecca Harden Weaver, *Divine Grace and Human Agency a Study of the Semi-Pelagian Controversy* (Macon, GA: Mercer University Press, 2003).
121. Thomas Deman, Le "Liber de Bona Fortuna" dans la théologie de saint Thomas d'Aquin, *RSPT* 17(1928), 38–9. Cf H. Bouillard, *Conversion et grâce chez s. Thomas d'Aquin* (Paris: Aubier, 1944), 124–6.
122. *Magna Moralia*, 1206 b 30–1207 b 19; *Eth. Eud.* 1246 b 37–1248 b 11. See Deman, 38, n. 1.
123. Deman, 38–9.

124. Deman, 39–40, 42.

125. Cornelio Fabri, Le "Liber de Bona Fortuna" de l'Éthique à Eudème d'Aristote et la dialectique de la divine Providence chez saint Thomas, *RevThom*, 88 (4) (1988), 564.

126. O'Connor, Appendix 6, pp 142–7. The pertinent Latin passage is also included in Sherwin, *By Knowledge and By Love*, 141–2.

127. Deman, 40; Fabro, 559; O'Connor; 144.

128. *ST* I-II.68.1, p. 67 of this book. The crucial Latin sentence is 'Et consiliari non expedit ipsis: habent enim principium tale quod melius intellectu et consilio. Qui autem rationem, hoc autem non habent neque divinos instinctus, hoc non possunt; sine ratione enim existentes adipiscuntur', Sherwin, pp 141–2, n.97.

129. Fabro, 570.

130. *ST* I-II.68.8.

131. ST 1I-II.68.2 ad 2.

132. Gilles Emery, 'Holy Spirit', in McCosker & Turner, 135.

133. Gardeil, Dons, col 1766. Cf. Newman, John Henry (1801–1890), *Essay on the development of Christian doctrine* (London; New York: Sheed and Ward, 1960).

134. Hughes, D., 'Grace and the Gifts', in Walter Farrell & Dominic Hughes, 11.

135. *CCC* 1830–1, 1845; cf 1266, 1299.

136. *CG* IV, 22.

*Chapter 3*

# 'The Law of the Spirit of Life' (Rom. 8.2)

It is evident from the previous chapter that the loving dynamism of the Holy Spirit which is manifested in and through the moral acts of God's children in instigating, or 'prompting', them to act, cannot be limited to the Spirit's influence just on their minds; and for that reason, as we saw, Thomas realized that Rom. 8.14 implies much more than that the children of God are 'led', or simply instructed, by God's Holy Spirit. Such an interpretation would imply that the Spirit's only internal influence is that of a guide and leader enlightening people interiorly on what they ought to do; whereas spiritual people are not just instructed by the Holy Spirit, Thomas strongly maintains. In addition, they decide, or their will is actually moved by the Spirit, to act on that instruction. In the previous chapter, we have examined how Thomas explained this movement of people's wills by God's Spirit as the Spirit's 'driving' them freely without coercing them (Rom. 8.14). In this chapter, our aim is to examine Thomas's teaching on the other element of the Spirit's influence: namely, how the Spirit is also active precisely on the minds of God's children, in connection with which Thomas loves to quote Ps. 143.10: 'Let your good Spirit lead me.'

The Spirit's influence on human moral reflection and deliberation was seen by Thomas as pre-eminently manifested in his systematic expounding of what Paul called 'the law of the Spirit of life' (Rom. 8.2), and what Thomas himself termed 'The Law of the Gospel, called the New Law', which in many respects is his richest and most fruitful unfolding of the loving moral dynamism of the Holy Spirit.[1] Josef Mausbach rightly described this section of the *Summa* as unsurpassed for its evangelical spirit.[2] And J. Lecuyer, in his article on 'docility' to the Holy Spirit, or sensitivity to being taught by the Spirit, judged that

> one would not be able to explain in any depth Thomas's thought on docility to the Holy Spirit without taking into account his teaching on the New Law, which

is too little known. For if docility to the Holy Spirit consists in allowing oneself not just to be instructed, but to be guided by the Spirit, this profound activity of the Spirit has nowhere been better brought to light than in Questions 106–108 of the *Prima Secundae* on the New Law.[3]

For Thomas, who has been described by Edouard Hamel as 'the theologian of the New Law',[4] that law, according to William Van Roo, is 'the very presence of the Holy Spirit and the effects He produces in the soul: grace and the virtues and gifts, and all the actual graces enlightening man's reason and moving his will'.[5]

In his introductory article on the New Law in the *Summa*, Thomas addresses the question of 'whether the new law is a written law', and in his reply, he introduces a fundamental distinction of the utmost significance for understanding his entire approach to moral theology, according, as it does, a central and predominant role to the inner presence and influence of the Holy Spirit within the believer's mind and heart. Thomas's reply to the question is as follows:

> Aristotle tells us that everything is seen to be whatever is predominant in it. And what is predominant in the law of the New Testament, in which all its power (*virtus*) consists, is the grace of the Holy Spirit given through faith in Christ. Therefore, the New Law is principally the very grace of the Holy Spirit which is given to Christ's faithful. This appears obvious from Rom. 3.27, where Paul writes, 'By what law? By that of works? No, but by *the law of faith*', thus calling the very grace of faith a 'law'. More clearly, Rom. 8.2 says 'For the *law of the Spirit of life* in Christ Jesus has set you free from the law of sin and of death'. That is why Augustine writes in his *de Spiritu et Littera* [24; *PL* 44,225; 17; *PL* 44,218] that 'just as the law of deeds was written on tablets of stone, so *the law of faith* was written in the hearts of the faithful'. And elsewhere in the same book [26; *PL* 44, 222;] he writes, 'What are the laws of God written on hearts by God's own self but the very presence of the Holy Spirit?'[6]

Having established this internal presence and grace of the Holy Spirit within the believer as what is first and most important of all in the New Law, Thomas then proceeds to identify the function of what by comparison he then calls the New Law's secondary element:

> But the New Law contains some things which dispose people to *receive* the grace of the Holy Spirit, and some things which pertain to *the use* of that grace: things which are secondary, so to speak, in the New Law. On these Christ's faithful had to be instructed orally and in writing about what they should believe, as well as how they should behave. So, [in answer to the question] we should say that the New Law is principally an interiorly inscribed law and only secondarily a written law.[7]

What emerges strikingly from this fundamental distinction which Thomas introduced is that the written element of the New Law, its secondary external expression, is instrumental, being either conducive to receiving God's grace, or directive to putting God's grace into effect, but it can no more impart the dynamism to fulfil what it decrees than a signpost can impart the power to reach the destination towards which it is pointing. Josef Fuchs sums it up well:

> Christian morality will prove to be the Spirit of the Lord, a spirit which works primarily from within, where it lives as the gift of the Lord, and secondarily finds expression in the prescriptions and commandments which concern men and women who are called in Christ; both together, the Spirit of Christ, living and working in us, and he same Spirit, expressed in prescriptions and commandments, constitute the law of Christ.[8]

Even the institutional church Thomas considered only a secondary or instrumental, while still significant, expression of the New Law of the Spirit, and, as we shall see later, he considered it richly and characteristically the 'Church of the Holy Spirit'.[9] From this teaching, Pesch drew the logical conclusion that 'St Thomas was able to combine his very unambiguous partisanship for the form of the western church, with the papacy at its head, with an equally unambiguous, almost Lutheran way of viewing all the institutional aspects of the Church as a pure means of God's grace'.[10] Nevertheless, although only secondary to the very presence and activity of the Spirit within the believer, this written law of the Gospel is still of the utmost significance, as being a constituent part of the New Law; and it is importantly, as Thomas explained, a way of instructing God's faithful 'on what they should believe as well as how they should behave'. The question then arises, however, what is the role of the Holy Spirit in this instructing of Christ's faithful through the written text of the Gospel, or, indeed, through the expressed teaching of the church.

## THE SPIRIT AS INTERNAL TEACHER

In his Scripture commentaries, particularly, Thomas refers often and strikingly to the role of the Holy Spirit as an internal teacher and moral guide, instructing Christians on how they should behave. We see him explain this in his commentary on Romans 8:

> The Holy Spirit, inhabiting our minds, does not just teach us what ought to be done by enlightening our mind on what we should do; he also inclines our

desires (*affectus*) to act rightly, as Jn 14.26 says, 'The Advocate, the Holy Spirit whom the Father will send in my name, will teach you everything (as regards the first) and remind you of all that I have said to you (as regards the second)'.[11]

Likewise, when the Galatians are instructed to 'walk in the Spirit', according to the Vulgate Latin (Gal. 5.16), this is, Thomas explains, 'through the Holy Spirit directing and leading, whom we should follow as showing us the way'.[12]

This internal teaching by the Holy Spirit for Thomas is clearly a characteristic of the New Testament, as contrasted with the Old. When he is discussing the difference between the New and the Old Testaments, he points out that there are two ways of passing something on:

> One is through something exterior, such as speaking words to inform someone. A human being can do this, and this is how the Old Testament was handed on. Another way is by operating internally, as is proper to God, as Job 32.8 says: 'truly it is the spirit in a mortal, the breath of the Almighty, that makes for understanding'. This is the way in which the New Testament was given, because it consists in the infusion of the Holy Spirit who instructs interiorly. But it is not enough just to know; action is required. And therefore, first he enlightens the mind in order to know; which is why it says 'I will put my laws in their minds'. (Heb. 8.10)[13]

The same is echoed in the classic article on the New Law in the *Summa* when Thomas replies to an objection by explaining that 'the New Law is engraved [internally] on human beings, not just indicating what should be done, but also helping them to do it'.[14] We may say, in fact, that although Thomas came in his later teaching to emphasize that the Spirit is active in the believer in every act of their will, he writes no less frequently and strikingly of the influence which the Spirit also exercises interiorly on the believer's mind. This too has its part to play under the Spirit, whose influence is in no sense a suppression of the mind but, rather, an enhancement or perfection of it. It was this profound respect for the human being's intellect, which, it may be suggested, led Thomas to make an important modification in his application of the Aristotelian *Liber de Bona Fortuna*, the 'Good Luck Book', which we met in the previous chapter.[15]

Although Thomas accepts the principle of the *Liber* that all initiative in the process of deliberation comes from God, he does not seem to accept the further statement that in the case of some people, namely, the lucky ones, God bypasses this process of deliberation, and simply prompts them to act without any deliberation. Such a view would imply a certain non-rationality in people's acts; and, as we have already seen, Thomas regards the exclusion of rational activity as characteristic of the spirit of the devil on occasion, not of the Spirit of God.[16] What Thomas does draw from Aristotle, however, is that, over and above the normal human process of deliberation and willing which God always initiates in humans, God also prompts spiritual persons to act in accordance with the divine reasoning, in such a way that, instead of taking counsel with themselves or of other humans, they actually take counsel of God, and follow that counsel. As he argues, 'The movement of reason is not enough, unless there is present from above the prompting and movement of the Holy Spirit.'[17] Although the *Liber* had said that those who are moved by a divine prompting have no need to deliberate, Thomas, the Christian theologian, overwrites this by adding, as emphasized, 'Aristotle says in a chapter of *de bona Fortuna* that those who are moved by a divine prompting have no need to deliberate *according to human reason;* they follow an interior prompting, *because they are moved by a principle better than human reason.*[18]

In other words, even when spiritual persons are following the advice or counsel of God, and for this purpose receive the Gift of counsel from the Holy Spirit, their deliberative faculty is not suppressed; rather, it is enhanced, in order to benefit from that divine counsel, and to apprehend the fuller truth. Thus, in dealing specifically in the *Summa* with the Gift of counsel, Thomas faces the objection that if God's children are in fact driven by the Spirit of God as Paul writes (Rom. 8.14) they surely have no need of counsel. Not at all, replies Thomas: 'God's children are driven by the Holy Spirit in their own manner, namely preserving their free choice, which is the faculty of the will and the reason'.[19] Indeed, as Thomas had explained in the body of the article, 'God moves everything in accordance with its manner of being moved .... It is characteristic of a rational creature that it is moved to do something by rational enquiry, and this enquiry is called "counsel". So, the Holy Spirit moves the rational creature by way of counsel.'[20] In other words, the Spirit does not work by blind impulses[21] but moves people in an advisory manner, 'the moving of a mind receiving counsel by another giving counsel'.[22]

## THE LAW AS EXTERNAL TEACHER

If the Holy Spirit is so intimately active in the Christian's process of thinking and deliberating, and if he enlightens God's children interiorly on what they have to do in terms of belief and behaviour, it is natural to ask how Thomas relates this internal influence of the Spirit to the external written law of the New Testament. We saw earlier how Thomas prefaces his treatment of the New Law by explaining that 'God instructs us by law, and helps us by grace'.[23] Where, then, does the Holy Spirit fit in, in this divine legal instruction?

There is no doubt, of course, that Thomas does regard the written Gospel as a law, and the precepts which it contains as having the obligatory force of law. It is true that not everyone is constrained by, or 'under', the law, as an external compelling principle, but nevertheless everyone is *obliged* by the law, in the sense that they must do what the law commands, even if they do so freely and ungrudgingly, and not under constraint.[24] This 'freedom from the law' that is enjoyed by God's children is most succinctly expressed by Thomas in his remark that 'just as the law teaches virtuous acts from the outside, so the Spirit moves us to them from the inside'.[25] But in what sense is the law a teacher, and how is it related to the internal teaching which Thomas tells us comes from the Spirit?

Interestingly, it is in his commentary on Paul's teaching on prayer in Romans 8 that Thomas offers his clearest explanation on how we can relate precepts that come to us from outside with the personal guidance that comes to us internally from the Spirit. In writing to the Romans, Paul had observed that 'we do not know how to pray as we ought' and his solution was that 'the Spirit himself intercedes for us' (Rom. 8.28). In his commentary, Thomas asks, but surely, we know how to pray as we ought, when Jesus gave us the perfect prayer in the 'Our Father'? 'Speaking generally', Thomas replies, 'we can know what suitable prayer is, yet we cannot know this in particular situations'. We can ask that God's will be done on earth and in heaven, and yet it may not be God's will that we perform a work of virtue that we want to perform, because it is not suitable for this or that person. 'If a person can usefully make progress by a virtuous action, quiet contemplation will not be suitable for them, even if this is an act of virtue. And vice versa.' Or we can pray for some temporal benefit to preserve our life, which is asking for 'our daily bread', but it could become a mortal risk for us: 'Many have perished through riches,' he warns. Or one could ask to be delivered from some temptation, yet this turns out to be good for their humility, as Paul resignedly concluded in his own case (2 Cor. 12.7–10).[26]

Again, Thomas continues, Paul seems to say that not only do we not know *what* we should pray for, but that we do not know how we should pray. But, again, do we not know from James 1.6 that we should 'ask in faith, never doubting'? Again, this is true, Thomas replies, but only in general; for we cannot always discern our true motive in praying. We may be asking for something out of anger, instead of from genuine zeal for God, just as the sons of Zebedee seemed to be asking for a share in God's glory, yet they were asking for it for their own vainglory (Mt. 20.20).[27] However, Thomas continues, in our perplexity over what we should ask for in a particular situation, and with what intention we should ask for it, the Holy Spirit comes to our aid, and makes us ask for the right thing in the right way by putting the right thoughts into our minds and causing the right desires in us.

The Holy Spirit makes us 'ask', insofar as he causes the right desires in us. For asking is the unfolding of desires. Right desires proceed from the love of charity which the Spirit creates in us . . . . With the Holy Spirit directing and prompting our hearts, our desires also cannot but be profitable for us; for, as Isaiah writes (48.17): 'I am the Lord your God, who teaches you for your own good, who leads you in the way you should go'.[28]

In the case of prayerful activity, then, people know from the written Gospel the general principles of how God wishes them to pray, and in what manner; but how those principles are to be applied in particular instances or cases believers do not know: only the Spirit can internally teach them that.

This examination of Thomas's analysis of Paul's teaching on prayer affords a highly instructive example of the sharp contrast which we have seen Thomas draw earlier between the primary and the secondary elements of the New Law, for the prayer given us by the Lord belongs to the 'letter' of the New Law, while the intellectual guidance given interiorly by the Holy Spirit on applying it in specific situations is part of the whole complex internal 'grace of the Holy Spirit', which constitutes the newness of the New Law as its primary component. In fact, this particular teaching of Thomas appears to give us his most explicit account of the relationship which exists between the external written Gospel and the internal illumination of the Spirit, those two sources of moral knowledge; for although Thomas distinguishes sharply between the two elements of the New Law in his formal treatise on it in the *Summa*, he does not write at any length of the actual relationship or connection between the two. He explains, of course, that the role of the written law in the new dispensation is to provide us with information on two counts: how to receive the grace of the Holy Spirit, as well as how to exercise that grace. But he says little more on this functional or instrumental aspect of the written law and, in fact, he is more concerned with discussing its inadequacies, and its content, than with explaining its modus operandi under the Spirit. This lacuna, however, is helpfully filled by his teaching on prayer which we have considered, and it does not appear unreasonable to apply what he writes on that subject to the rest of the written New Law.

We have spoken of the external written Gospel and the internal illumination by the Spirit as two sources of moral knowledge, one external and general and the other more particular and personal; and Thomas does distinguish significantly between them as the two differing elements of the New Law. But it is important to bear in mind that they are two elements of the one New Law which is the 'law of the Spirit', and we can be helped to appreciate the import of this if we recall the remark of Augustine which Thomas invokes several times in his writings, that the statements and precepts of Sacred Scripture can be interpreted and understood from the deeds of the 'saints', 'since it was the same Holy Spirit who inspired the prophets and the other authors of Sacred Scripture who also moved the "saints" to act'.[29] In confirmation of this identity of the Spirit who influences both parties Thomas explains on the one hand that in prophecy 'men and women moved by the Holy Spirit spoke from God' (2 Pet. 1.21), and on the other hand that 'Those who are driven by the Holy Spirit are God's children' (Rom. 8.14), with the final comment that 'thus Holy Scripture is to be understood according as Christ and the other "saints" observed it'.[30] In other words, when the Spirit inspired the men and women of the New Testament to behave as they did, he was also showing us how to read the Scriptures which the Spirit himself had inspired; and, we might add, the Spirit was helping them to read and interpret the inspired word of God which they in their turn possessed, either in the Law and the Prophets, or in the reported words of Jesus himself.

What this means in our present context is that, rather than considering the external written law and the inner enlightenment of the Spirit as two distinct sources of moral knowledge, we should consider them as two complementary ways in which the one divine Spirit influences the individual person. In itself, the letter of the Gospel is insufficient, either for justification, or for instruction on how to behave in the diversity of particular situations and choices which confront a person, as Thomas's remarks on Paul's teaching on prayer have shown. Moreover, the necessarily general and universal way in which laws and commands are formulated requires, as we shall examine later, that they be specifically applied to particular reality. As Thomas observed in introducing the *Secunda Secundae* volume of his *Summa*, which is the one concerned largely with moral matters, 'general moral remarks are less useful, since actions are concerned with particulars'.[31] It is in this process of individualization and of personal determination of the general law in a particular situation that the direct influence of the Holy Spirit on the spiritual person's mind is seen in its true and normal perspective. Lecuyer observes, 'if the New Law has an aspect which makes it exterior, this aspect remains secondary and is of real value only if it is lived under the action of interior grace and charity'.[32]

By holding such a view of the complementary relationship between the influences of the letter and of the Spirit, Thomas was able to respect the reality and source of the written law, and also the reality and value of the human natural process of acquiring information and formulating a moral decision. As we have already seen in the case of the human will, Thomas there sees two principles at work influencing the will to act: the human mind and the Holy Spirit; and the prompting of the will by the Spirit does not render the prompting which comes from the mind redundant or irrelevant. In a similar way, it appears, when the Spirit directly influences the human intellect, he does so, in Thomas's view, in such a way as to respect, and to perfect, the natural manner in which the human intellect operates, namely, by drawing upon the external world and by rationally assimilating, understanding and judging upon the information thus acquired.

Thus, the direct influence of the Spirit on the intellect does not render superfluous the existence and the influence of an external Gospel, but rather perfects the human mind to apply that law in relation to the diverse situations in which a person finds themselves. The Spirit thus influences the human mind in two ways, indirectly by the letter of the law, and directly by helping the subject to discern the spirit of the law, or rather, the Spirit in the law. It is the Spirit who helps us to read the Law, and indeed, to read all of Scripture, and to discern its relevance to our present situation. The Gospel *sine glossa*, or without glosses, was advocated to his brethren by Francis of Assisi; that is, the gospel 'without footnotes' which might too easily explain *away* its strict moral demands; and this is an ideal which has haunted Christians in many generations. Chenu ascribed to the evangelical movement of the twelfth- and thirteenth-century 'faith in the power of the Spirit guaranteed by baldly accepting the letter of the Gospel'.[33] Yet this fundamentalist tendency has to be qualified by accepting from Augustine and Thomas, as we have seen, that there are in fact glosses, or interpretations, which may come to Christians from the same Spirit who inspired the original written Gospel.

We have written that, according to Thomas, the Spirit helps us to discern the relevance of the general command to our present situation, and this appears to be Thomas's teaching. But there is more to be considered. The command or law is possibly itself a constituent factor of the present situation, and so it seems that we can be helped by the Spirit to read this law only if we are enabled by him to read the total situation of which the law is a part. We cannot know how to personalize the law in this situation unless we know what the situation truly is in its entirety, and here too we are reliant on the power of the Spirit. The guidance which Christians receive from the Spirit, then, enables them to give precision and relevance to the written law within the insight which the Spirit gives to the total situation, and to discern within the total situation, the invitation which is being offered here and now by the Holy Spirit to this individual child of God.[34]

How believers are enabled to grasp mentally in their present total situation what God's will is for them is explained basically by the charity which the Spirit imparts to them, and more precisely by the Christian discerning wisdom which is the result and effect of that charity. It is appropriate, then, to consider Thomas's teaching on wisdom now, in order to see what light this may throw on the relationship between the primary and the secondary elements of the New Law, that is, the external general written text of the Gospel and the internal intimate personal guidance of the Holy Spirit.

## THE WISDOM OF THE HOLY SPIRIT

The fundamental basis of the orientation of all creatures to God as their final end is for Thomas the eternal law, or 'God's universal directing wisdom';[35] and partial knowledge of this eternal law is mediated to humans through other laws: the natural law, the divine law and human laws. Natural law, Thomas explains, or what he sometimes prefers to call 'the law of nature' (*lex naturae*), is nothing other than a conscious participation in God's eternal law on the part of rational creatures as they reflect on their God-given nature. Divine law, that is, the Old and the New Laws, is added to natural law as a special revelation from God which confirms natural law, and spells out further participation in the eternal law; and human laws apply and determine the principles of the natural law for a society, and as such are also a part of God's eternal law.[36] Behind all law, then, whether in its archetypal ground which is God's eternal law, or in its various created participations, or refractions, which constitute the natural, divine and human laws, Thomas discerns one wisdom, the infinite wisdom of a provident loving God. This is the ground of all creation, as well as of the ordering and coordinating of all creatures to their fulfilment in God's design. It is a godly attribute which is reflected by God's Spirit throughout creation, and which is especially imparted to God's human creatures in their minds and their wills, within the human analogical category of law.

Yet, however wise the formulations of the derived natural, divine and human laws are, they cannot encompass the originating eternal law, that is, the divine wisdom in its entirety and in all its implications at every moment for each individual creature. As Thomas explains:

> No one can know the eternal law in itself, except the blessed, who see the divine essence. But every rational creature knows some radiation from it, to a greater or less degree. For all knowledge of truth is a sort of radiation and sharing in the eternal law, which is unchangeable truth, as Augustine says. Everyone knows truth to some degree, at least so far as concerns the principles of the natural law. In other matters, some share more and some less in knowing the truth, and to this degree they know the eternal law to a greater or less degree.[37]

Since, according to Thomas, people must thus be content on the whole in this life with knowing only general principles and statements of law, it is here that for him another wisdom enters upon the scene, the wisdom which does not have to do with expressing and formulating law, but which now has to do with its application and its observance. This wisdom, too, like legislative wisdom, is a partial sharing in the eternal wisdom of the supreme Legislator, and because of this, its role is to bring completely home to each individual what is the eternal law for them precisely at this moment of their lives in these particular individual circumstances. In other words, with this personal wisdom, the individual is enabled to take up where the formulator of natural, divine and human law necessarily left off, at the general level, and to complement and personally complete those formulations in order to meet individual situations which involve them personally.

The significance of this personal complementary wisdom is explained by Thomas in an important passage, where he explains that

> since wisdom is the knowledge of divine matters, we understand it differently from the philosophers. Because for us life is ordered to our enjoyment of God, and to participating in the divine nature by grace, then, according to us, wisdom is not only a matter of *knowing about God*, as with the philosophers. For us it is also a matter of *giving direction to human life*, which is directed not only by human considerations but also by godly considerations, as is clear in Augustine XII on the *Trinity*.[38]

This wisdom, which enables humans individually to be perfectly subject to the eternal law, is a knowledge of the highest causes, of course, such as the Greek and Roman philosophers contemplated. But, whereas, for those philosophers, wisdom was thus speculative and concerned with ultimate principles, for the children of God by contrast, that ultimate origin of everything, which is God, is also the ultimate destination and goal towards which they are all being 'ordered', or directed – or, for Thomas following Paul, being actually 'driven' by the Holy Spirit (Rom. 8.14). In other words, Christian wisdom is not just speculative; it is also creative and dynamic. Eleanor Stump acknowledges the importance of this teaching of Thomas on the behavioural role of wisdom when she sees him locate it, not in the intellectual virtue of wisdom, but in the Gift of wisdom which is imparted to God's children by the Holy Spirit.

> Considered as an intellectual virtue, wisdom is an excellence only of the speculative intellect. It is a sort of super *scientia*; it grasps the highest cause or causes of everything (*ST* II-II 45.1; I-II 57.2). Considered as a gift of the Holy Spirit, however, and on Aquinas's view of the highest cause as God, wisdom enables a person not only to know the highest cause of everything but also to make decisive judgments about the way in which other things, such as human actions, are related to that highest cause. Since God is perfect goodness, judging human acts in relation to the highest cause is a matter of distinguishing good or right actions from bad or wrong actions. For this reason, wisdom as a gift is a disposition informing both the speculative and the practical intellect.[39]

It is relevant in this context to recall how, in discussing the Decalogue, Thomas explains that there are three different grades of moral precepts contained in Scripture. Some are so certain that they did not require statement in the list of commandments, and these are the commands to love God and to love one's neighbour. Others are more determined in form and can be easily grasped by anyone, although in some few cases, human judgement can be distorted concerning them, so they require explicit statement; and these are the ten precepts of the Decalogue. Thirdly, 'some precepts are not so obvious to everyone but only to the wise, and these are the moral precepts added to the Decalogue and given to the people by Moses and Aaron'.[40]

What Thomas has to say about what we have identified as complementary personal wisdom is stated more strikingly in his teaching on the wisdom which is one of the traditional seven Gifts of the Holy Spirit, to which Stump referred earlier.[41] Wisdom is clearly a gift of God's Spirit, Thomas explains, because the judgement by which a person can judge and order everything by godly rules is given them by the Spirit who 'searches everything, even the depths of God' (1 Cor 2.10).[42] By this gift, a person's mind can be moved promptly by the Holy Spirit in relation to what pertains to wisdom.[43] Moreover, the Spirit's Gift of wisdom exceeds the intellectual virtue of wisdom because 'it gets us closer to God'.[44]

How the Spirit's Gift of wisdom actually works within God's children is explained in the article in the *Summa* where Thomas asks whether the Gift of wisdom is located in the mind or in the will. In his response, he offers a striking distinction between wisdom which is operative in the mind, and its origin which is to be found in the will, in charity. He writes,

> Wisdom brings a rightness in judgement in accordance with divine principles. Rightness of judgment, however, can come about in two ways, either by the perfect use of reason or because of a sort of connaturality with what is being judged upon. . . . In what pertains to God, a right judgement by the investigation of reason applies to the wisdom which is a virtue of the intellect. But to form a right judgement in this matter through a connaturality with it applies to the wisdom which is a gift of the Holy Spirit. . . . Hence, the cause of the wisdom which is a Gift of the Holy Spirit, namely, charity, is in the will; while the essence of the Gift is in the intellect., whose act is to judge rightly.[45]

Pinsent observes that in this passage, 'Aquinas observes that the intellectual virtue of wisdom involves a judgement being made after reason has made its enquiry, underlining how the virtue of wisdom has a discursive and demonstrative aspect. The gift of wisdom, by contrast, enables judgments of divine things on account of a "sympathy" or "connaturality" for them . . . [which] is the result of a kind of "union" with God.'⁴⁶ For his part, Sherwin notes how here

> Aquinas establishes a balanced parallel between wisdom and love. As he states elsewhere, God's grace 'both perfects the intellect by the gift of wisdom, and softens the affections by the fire of charity' [*ST* 1–2, 79.3]. Wisdom and charity have these two interlaced roles in human action.⁴⁷

The practical aspect of this movement by the Spirit is frequently stressed by Thomas in his remarks on the Gift of wisdom, where his teaching can be summed up in his statement that through wisdom the higher part of the mind not only *contemplates* divine principles, but also *consults* them, insofar as it judges the human by the divine, and thus directs human moral behaviour by divine rules. 'So', in reply to the question whether wisdom is just speculative or is also practical, he importantly concludes in the *Summa* that 'wisdom, *as a Gift*, is not just speculative, but also practical'.⁴⁸ In this, Thomas is simply stating more strongly what he had already concluded in his commentary on the *Sentences*, that 'the action of the Gift of wisdom appears aimed here and in the future at contemplating divine realities that are loved, and through them at judging other matters, that is, not only speculative, but also practical matters to be undertaken, where the judgement depends [ultimately] on finality.'⁴⁹

Of course, for Thomas, the Gift of wisdom is 'first of all, concerned with the contemplation of divine matters, and only then with the directing of human acts *according to divine considerations*', as Conley shows in *A Theology of Wisdom*.⁵⁰ Yet, for Thomas, 'practical' wisdom in moral matters is a highly significant part of the Holy Spirit's Gift of wisdom, and it seems to have been partly disregard for this teaching which has led to the fashionable, but misleading and regrettable, practice of regularly using the English term 'practical wisdom' to translate the classical term 'prudence' (*prudentia*), in order to avoid the misleading associations which the term 'prudence' has, either with financial stinginess or with the ultra-cautious Puritan decorum traditionally ascribed to young women of that name. The verbal decline may have set in with Rackham's influential Loeb translation of Aristotle's *Nichomachean Ethics,* in which, throughout the text, Rackham faithfully translated the Greek *phrónēsis* (Latin *prudentia*) as 'prudence', but he also took the unfortunate step at the beginning of his treatment of adding in the margin the gloss, 'Prudence or Practical Wisdom'.⁵¹ The English Thomist scholar, Thomas Gilby, casually conceded in his translation of the treatise on *prudentia* in the Blackfriars multi-volume translation of the *Summa* that 'it is better called practical wisdom if "prudence" has a mean and grudging ring'.⁵² His fellow Dominican, Herbert McCabe, went further in declaring sweepingly that '*prudentia* does not mean what we call prudence,' explaining that 'prudence suggests to us a certain caution and canniness whereas *prudentia* is much nearer to wisdom, practical wisdom'. McCabe himself did not settle for this 'practical wisdom' as a regular equivalent for *prudentia*, expressing a preference for Jane Austen's term 'good sense'.[53] However, as the acceptance of the term 'practical wisdom' to translate *prudentia* has become widespread, and is now regrettably almost universal, this dysfunctional and quite unnecessary usage of turning prudence into a species of wisdom, or one virtue into a subspecies of another, has served to confuse and dislocate the delicate structure of Thomas's interlocking theory of the virtues.

Yet, despite its exalted nature and function, the Spirit's Gift of wisdom is not the peak of Christian moral activity: as we have already noticed in another context, the Gift of wisdom is the consequence of loving God.

> Wisdom implies a rightness of judgement according to godly reasons, and this rightness of judgement can happen in two ways: one through the perfect use of human reason; the other on account of some connaturality with what is being judged. . . . Having a right judgement on divine matters by rational enquiry is a matter for the wisdom which is an intellectual virtue; whereas having a right judgement on divine matters rising from connaturality with them is a matter for the wisdom which is a gift of the Holy Spirit; and this sympathy, or connaturality, with divine matters is the result of charity, which unites us to God, as 1 Cor 6.17 puts it, 'anyone united to the Lord becomes one spirit with him'. So, the gift of wisdom has its cause, charity, in the will, but its essence in the mind, whose act is to judge rightly.[54]

In short, when a person is united with God through charity, and becomes 'one spirit' (1 Cor. 7.17) with God, having an affinity, or connaturality, with God, he/she is wise according to God's lights. Thus, we return to the Pauline and Thomist doctrine of the spiritual person.[55] As Thomas wrote in a key statement, 'it is from the habit of charity that the spiritual person has an inclination to judge rightly on everything in accordance with godly rules, from which he gives a judgement by the gift of wisdom; just as a just person gives a judgement from the rules of law through the virtue of prudence'.[56]

The charity which is poured out in our hearts by the Spirit unites us to God and makes us in some sense one with God. And from this 'connaturality, or union', we share not only in God's being (cf 2 Pet. 1.4), but also, in some mysterious way, in God's very activity. We become not only one with God, but one 'spirit' with God, participating in the power of God's Holy Spirit, and sharing the intimate secrets of God, those which only the Spirit knows fully, but which to some extent the Spirit communicates to 'spiritual' persons in wisdom.[57] And because, as spiritual persons, we share God's own viewpoint, we 'savor', or have a taste for, the things that are above, not those that are below (Col 3.2).[58] In commenting on this verse of Colossians, Thomas could not ignore the obvious word connection between the Latin 'savor' (*sapite*) and *sapientia* (wisdom), clearly referring to someone 'ordering their life in accordance with heavenly considerations, and judging everything by them. As James 3.17 pointed out, "This is the wisdom from above . . . ". '[59] It appears, then, that all these themes of charity, union, connaturality and wisdom are presupposed and telescoped together by Thomas when he writes simply of the teaching and illuminating function of charity as follows:

> Charity causes enlightenment of the heart. 'We are all wrapped up in darkness', as Job says (37.19); and frequently we do not know what is to be done or wanted. But charity teaches everything that is needed for salvation. This is what is meant by 'his anointing teaches you about everything' (1 Jn 2.27). And the reason for this is because where there is charity, there is the Holy Spirit, who knows everything, and who leads us into the right path, as Ps. 143.10 says. That is why Ecclesiasticus says (Sir 2.10), 'Those who fear the Lord, love him, and your hearts will be illuminated', namely, to know what is necessary for salvation.[60]

And finally, over all the spiritual person's actions, over all the virtues and Gifts and the wisdom which directs them, over even the charity from which wisdom springs to order all things, there presides the eternal wisdom of God which alone gives meaning and content and value to the Christian's wisdom. As Thomas observes, 'Reason is not the rule of charity as it is of human virtues. *Charity is ruled by God's wisdom and goes beyond the rule of human reasoning*, as shown in Eph. 3.19 on "the love of Christ that surpasses knowledge". '[61] It is that one infinite wisdom of God that, on the one hand, rules the charity which pervades the whole supernatural and internal organism of the spiritual person, and that, on the other hand, is the wisdom reflected to humans by external law in its varying manifestations and determinations. The wisdom which the children of God possess interiorly thus enables them to personalize and to embrace in love that wisdom which is refracted in the law proposed to them exteriorly by God.

However, this external law is inherently incomplete, because its reflections of the divine wisdom are universal and general in terms, whereas the divine wisdom which is the eternal law is all-embracing, comprehensive and particular to the utmost degree. Hence, there is need to introduce a further determination of the eternal law, which is what the wisdom of God asks God's sons and daughters to undertake in the here and now; and this specification comes especially from the virtue and the Gift of wisdom within God's children, enabling them to judge the present situation, including the law, in the light of 'divine principles' and to relate it to their goal in the light of those same principles. The wisdom thus imparted to the children of God enables them to give the final determination to the eternal law in this particular case, and to discover and incarnate in their behaviour the very wisdom of God for the present situation.

The wisdom which is enshrined in the law and the wisdom which is possessed by the Christian are each in their own way an expression of the eternal wisdom, and they cannot but be in harmony. But they are not co-terminous. Where the wisdom of the law necessarily stops because of its general and universal character, the personal Spirit-endowed wisdom of the individual Christian takes over, to discern the wisdom *in* the law and to respond in affinity and connaturality to 'what pertains to wisdom' in the law so far as the current situation is concerned.

In a letter he once wrote to a Jesuit confessor who was asking for guidance on how to instruct a penitent in a particular matter of conscience, Ignatius Loyola, the founder of the Jesuit Order, instructed his man to 'see what the *Summae* [Confession manuals] say, and then in particular cases act as God will inspire you'.[62] Basically, that advice exemplifies the teaching of Aquinas (to whose teaching we know that Ignatius was committed) on how God's children are led by God's Holy Spirit externally cum internally: one should consider all the external evidence that the Holy Spirit provides, and then follow the Spirit's intimate personal prompting.

## LAW ETHICS OR VIRTUE ETHICS?

Examining the role of external law in moral matters inevitably raises today the issue of whether an approach to moral behaviour is better served by way of invoking the Aristotelian and later system of virtues, rather than by concentrating on compliance with moral law and rules; and it has become fashionable in theological ethics in recent years to stress the idea of 'virtue ethics,' and to develop and apply this approach across the whole range of moral behaviour. Moreover, particularly relevant to our purpose, Fergus Kerr writes of 'the remarkable revival of interest in "virtue ethics", increasingly engaging with Thomas'.[63]

This recovery of an important feature of Aristotelian ethics was due to the English philosopher, Elizabeth Anscombe, and her penetrating article, 'Modern Moral Philosophy'.[64] In this, she exposed what she considered the two prevailing weaknesses from which modern ethics suffered: the illogicality of the version of utilitarianism which she was the first to call 'consequentialism'; and the bankruptcy of its alternative, rule-governed deontology pursued in a non-religious context. She ended by concluding briefly and forcefully that in ethics today 'philosophically there is a huge gap', which calls for 'an account of human nature, human action, the type of characteristic a virtue is, and above all of human "flourishing" '.[65]

Anscombe's proposal of, in effect, returning to Aristotle was slow in being taken up, but once started – and notably popularized by Alistair MacIntyre in his study of moral theory, *After Virtue*[66] – it quickly gained impetus to become the powerful modern movement of 'virtue ethics' which is espoused and widely deployed today by major philosophers.[67] Duncan Richter judges that 'virtue theory is a new and somewhat welcome development, and one that can be traced directly to Anscombe's paper'.[68]

Basically, modern 'virtue ethics' began as a protest movement in the favour of concentrating attention on the person of the moral agent, in contrast to centuries of having pursued act-and law-centred ethics and emphasizing the constituents of the individual moral act. This previous moral focusing on isolated pieces of behaviour had found its religious origin in the Torah, or the Mosaic Law in the Hebrew Bible, and on its central legal feature of mainly forbidding numerous types of human actions and occasionally of enjoining the contrary. This was taken up by Jesus and the early Christian writers in the New Testament, who radically modified, but still maintained, the Jewish legal approach to Christian moral living as to a large extent one of avoiding forbidden sinful acts.

As the Christian Church later developed its discipline of the auricular confession of sins, this had the growing effect of concentrating attention on individual sinful acts, and spawned the growing literature of confessors' manuals. These catalogued types and degrees of sinful acts and their differing circumstances thus enabled the confessor to impart sacramental forgiveness while allotting a canonical penance appropriate to the act(s) which had been confessed.[69] In addition, the growing emphasis on natural law as the major non-revealed source of moral information focused on identifying various types of act as contradicting or frustrating the basic innate inclinations which God had inserted at creation into human nature. In addition, moral theology as a rule-based discipline concentrating on acts rather than their agent was greatly influenced by the systematic application of what became the classical analysis of individual human acts offered by Thomas Aquinas, comprising their three essential variable components of object, circumstances and intention.[70]

This Catholic focus on the morality of individual acts in moral and pastoral theology survived the Reformation, lasting well into modern times, and it has been reinforced in modern times, perhaps unconsciously, by the continuing controversy within the Catholic Church on the issue of whether certain actions, notoriously contraception, and later, homosexual activity, must be considered as always inherently bad, morally speaking, regardless of the agent or of their motive or of the circumstances.[71] The rancorous tone of the controversy has not been helped by the regular use of the term 'evil', including 'intrinsically evil', rather than 'bad', to classify such actions morally, careless of the fact that in ordinary English usage today, the term 'evil' is reserved to denote a particularly wicked or heinous situation or person.[72]

Outside the Catholic Church, act-based morality found a new rationale in the Enlightenment abandonment of metaphysics to favour the concentration on epistemology and moral knowledge. This culminated in the moral calculations of Kant's deontology and Bentham's utilitarianism, which were contrived in order to identify and distinguish in moral acts between those which are right or wrong, or good or bad.

The great advantages identified with a return to Aristotelian virtue theory thus included the moving away from an impersonal and static legal approach of calculating moral acts, to a person-centred concern for the moral agent, that is, to the individual human person with her or his unique moral history, assets and liabilities, facing personal moral choices. The return to the virtue approach to morality went behind the question 'what must I do, or how should I behave, here and now?' to the basic consideration, 'what sort of person do I, or should I, want to be, or to become?'; that is, the positive cultivation of estimable personal qualities, in place of avoiding forbidden pieces of moral behaviour or of performing obligatory ones. With this approach to morality, moral education becomes viewed not as inculcating obedience to authorities and to factual codified instructions, but as pursuing the formation of character, in order to be, or become, the bearer of morally desirable qualities, dispositions and aptitudes, which themselves can also have a heuristic role in disposing their owner to identify and pursue appropriate personal moral behaviour.

The modern popularity of virtue ethics has served to downgrade, and even to eclipse, consideration of moral behaviour by way of rules, laws and cases. The reaction is understandable when one considers the almost obsessive and exclusive concern which moral theology has traditionally shown with acts, and the often-justified criticisms of law-centred morality listed earlier. Explaining the appeal and popularity of virtue ethics, Nicholas Austin noted in a Thomist context that 'the balance of some Thomistic moral theology had tipped towards a narrow focus on law and sin'.[73] It is the contention of this study, however, that this does not have to continue to be the case; and to the extent that it does, such a focus is unfaithful to the trajectory of Aquinas's moral thinking.

In fact, as we have seen earlier, Thomas's presentation of morality even in terms of law is remarkably flexible, while also being theologically creative and visionary. His philosophically qualified approach to legal precepts and moral commandments, following Aristotle, can, as we have seen, be summed up in his brief statement that 'universal moral statements are less useful, since actions involve particulars'.[74] More broadly, this statement entails Thomas's further teaching, which we propose to examine in our next chapter, on the moral flexibility to be met with in the bible, the Aristotelian virtue of epieikeia, and the wider systematic recognition that all legislation can and must apply only 'for the most part'. The modern philosopher, Richard Miller, expresses the same corrective approach when he writes that 'the language of moral rules is open-textured, requiring interpretation and clarification in the process of connecting them to facts or cases . . . . One purpose of rules is to identify not a single, unique action but a class of similar actions'.[75]

The unsurprising conclusion to these reflections on the recent revival of virtue and agent-centred ethics, often in protest to legalistic act-centred ethics, is that both virtue ethics and act and rule ethics are equally required for an adequate examination and pursuit of a person's moral life, and that they must balance each other in people's conduct. This balance is precisely what Aquinas achieved, as Jean Porter observed, in writing that

> over the past several years, a number of scholars have attempted to appropriate Aquinas's account of the virtues as a basis for a contemporary virtue ethic, which would provide an alternative to a more legalistic ethic based on concepts of law or rules. It should be noted, however, that Aquinas consistently holds the ideas of virtue and law together in his moral thought.[76]

In confirmation of this we can note that, on the one hand, Thomas does more than justice to virtue theory, and to virtue ethics in general, in his *Summa*, *Prima pars*, questions 55–67, as well as to the individual theological and moral virtues, as he proceeds through much of the *Secunda Secundae*, not to mention his particular interest in the Aristotelian virtue of epieikeia and in the Spirit-instilled virtue and Gift of wisdom which we have been exploring in this chapter. To balance this strongly, however, we also find in Thomas a detailed analysis of human and moral acts in the *Prima Secundae*, questions 18–21, and in his superb treatise on law and moral observance in the *Prima Secundae*, questions 90–108, which we have been unpacking in this chapter. The rich climax of Thomas's moral teaching must then, happily, be the 'new law of the Gospel' (question 106), as consisting primarily in the presence and power of the Holy Spirit of God himself within the agent's mind and heart, imparting the wisdom to read and apply the external law personally in the individual person's unique circumstances. In our following chapter, we shall examine in detail how Thomas envisages this power of the Holy Spirit as being regularly and flexibly at work in the process of human decision-making.

## NOTES

1. *ST* I-II, 106–8.
2. J. Mausbach, *Die Katholische Morale, ihre Methoden, Grundsätze und Aufgaben* (Koln, 1901), 78.
3. J. Lecuyer, 'Docilité au S. Esprit', in *DSp* III (Paris: Beauchesne, 1967), col. 1488.
4. E. Hamel, *Loi naturelle et loi du Christ* (Desclée de Brouwer, 1964), 146.
5. W. Van Roo, 'Law of the Spirit and the Written Law in the Spirituality of St Ignatius', *Gregorianum* 37 (1956) 432–3.
6. *ST* I-II, 106.1. Emphases added.
7. *ST* I-II, 106.1. Emphasis added.
8. *Human Values,* 76.
9. See below, pp. 131–139.
10. Pesch, p. 203.
11. *In Rom.* 8, lect. 1 (M 602).
12. *In Gal.* 5, lect. 4 (M 308).
13. *In Heb.* 8, lect. 2 (M 404).
14. *ST* I-II, 106 1 ad 2.
15. See above, pp. 71–75.
16. See above, pp. 55.
17. *ST* I-II.106. 2.
18. *ST* I-II.68.1. Emphasis added.
19. *ST* II-II.52.1. obj 3 et ad 3.
20. *ST* II-II.52.1.
21. Cf Van Roo, 438.
22. *ST* II-II.52.2 ad 1.
23. *ST* I-II, q.90, prologue; above p. 42.
24. *In 2 Cor.* 3, lect. 3 (M 112).
25. *In Gal.* 5, lect. 7 (M 337).
26. *In Rom.* 8, lect. 5 (M 690).
27. Ibid (M 691).
28. *In Rom.* 8, lect. 5 (M 693).
29. See below, pp. 121–123.
30. *In Joan.* 18, lect. 4, 2 (M 2321). Cf *In Rom.* 1, lect. 5 (M 80).
31. *ST* II-II, prologue. Cf II-II. 52.1 ad 1.
32. Lecuyer, coll. 148–9.
33. M.-D. Chenu, *Mélanges Auguste Pelzer* (Louvain, 1947), 161–2.
34. J. Mahoney, *The Making of Moral Theology. A Study of the Roman Catholic Tradition* (Oxford: Clarendon, 1989), 202–10.
35. *ST* I-II, 93.1.
36. *ST* I-II, 91.
37. *ST* I-II, 3.2.
38. *ST* II-II, 19.7, emphasis added.

39. Eleonore Stump, 'Wisdom: Will, Belief, and Moral Goodness', in MacDonald, Scott & Stump, Eleonore, *Aquinas's Moral Theory, Essays in Honor of Norman Kretzmann* (Ithaca and London: Cornell University Press, 1999), 51–2.
40. *ST* I-II,100.11.
41. On Thomas's teaching on the Gifts of the Spirit, see above pp. 69–75.
42. *ST* II-II, 45.1.
43. *ST* I-II, 111.4 ad 4.
44. *ST* II-II, 45.3 ad 1.
45. *ST* II-II, 45.2.
46. Pinsent, *The Second-Person*, 40–1.
47. Sherwin, p. 170.
48. *ST* II-II.45.3. Emphasis added.
49. *In III Sent*, d. 35, q. 2, a. 1, sol. 3.
50. *ST* II-II, 45.3 ad 3. Emphasis added. Cf. K. Conley, *A Theology of Wisdom. A Study in Saint Thomas* (Dubuque: Priory Press, 1963), 128–30.
51. H. Rackham, trans., Aristotle *Nicomachean Ethics,* (Harvard: Loeb Classical Library, 1999), 337.
52. Thomas Gilby, *Aquinas, Summa Theologiae*, vol 36, Prudence, Blackfriars, Eyre & Spottiswoode (London, 1974), xiv.
53. H. McCabe, *God Still Matters* (London: Continuum, 2002), 152.
54. *ST* II-II, 45.2.
55. See above, pp. 24–26.
56. *ST* II-II, 60.1 ad 2.
57. *ST* II-II, 45.4.
58. *ST* II-II, 45. 3 ad 1.
59. *In Col.* 3, lect. 1 (M 139).
60. *In duo praecepta*, 3 (M 1148).
61. *ST* II-II, 24.1 ad 2. Emphasis added.
62. *Monumenta ignatiana, Epist.*, IX (Madrid, 1909), p. 176.
63. Fergus Kerr, 'The Varieties of Interpreting Aquinas', in idem, *Contemplating Aquinas*, 38.
64. G. M. Anscombe, 'Modern Moral Philosophy', *Philosophy* 33 (1958), 1–18. The Aristotelian expert, G. J. Hughes, intriguingly argues in 'The Function of Aristotle's Virtues', in *Bidragen*, International Journal in Philosophy and Theology, 66 (2005), 196–212, that Aristotle was not a 'Virtue Ethicist'.
65. Anscombe, 18.
66. Alistair McIntyre, *After Virtue* (London: Duckworth, 1981).
67. See Duncan Richter, *Ethics After Anscombe. Post "Modern Moral Philosophy"* (Dordrecht: Kluger, 2000). Among many authors exploring the topic, see, with specific reference to Aquinas, Jean Porter, *The Recovery of Virtue. The Relevance of Aquinas for Christian Ethics* (Louisville/Westminster: John Knox, 1990).
68. Richter, 147.
69. Mahoney, *The Making of Moral Theology*, Chapter 1, 'The Influence of Auricular Confession'.

70. Cf *ST* I-II, 18.4.

71. Mahoney, *The Making*, p. 260, n. 2.

72. See Nenad Polgar & Joseph Selling, edd., *The Concept of Intrinsic Evil and Catholic Theological Ethics* (Lanham, MD: Lexington/Fortress Academic, 2019).

73. Nicholas Austin, 'Spirituality and Virtue in Christian Formation: A Conversation between Thomistic and Ignatian Traditions', *NB* 97, 1068 (March 2016), 203. For an original analysis of virtue theory in Thomas in the light of Aristotle's four causes, see Austin's *Aquinas on Virtues: A Causal Reading* (Washington, D.C.: Georgetown University Press, 2017).

74. *ST* II-II, prologue.

75. Richard B. Miller, 'Rules', in Gilbert Meinander & William Werpehowski, edd., *The Oxford Handbook of Theological Ethics*, (Oxford: Oxford University Press, 2005), 221.

76. Porter, Jean, 'Virtues and Vices', in Davies, Brian and Stump, Eleonore, eds, *The Oxford Handbook of Aquinas* (Oxford: Oxford University Press, 2012), 272. Cf also her *The Recovery of Virtue: The Relevance of Aquinas for Christian Ethics* (Louisville, KY: Westminster/Knox Press, 1990).

*Chapter 4*

# Moral Decision-Making in the Spirit

In the past chapter, we examined how Thomas regards the primary and secondary aspects of the New Law of the Gospel as internal and external sources of moral awareness which proceed from the one Spirit; and we showed a further unity between these two sources by examining them as differing and complementary manifestations of the one wisdom of God according to which the Holy Spirit directs all human creatures individually to God as their common and final end. In this chapter, we propose to consider how Thomas showed how this process was, and could be, instantiated in individual moral cases and questions of conscience, a review which should help to confirm and refine his theoretical teaching. As we shall see, his examinations of such cases, while varying greatly in the degree of detailed explanation, appeal regularly to the themes which we have come to appreciate as basic to his teaching on the guidance of God's children by God's Spirit: wisdom and all that it implies; connaturality or natural affinity; the 'promptings' of the Holy Spirit; and, above all, the 'spirituality' of those who have received God's Spirit. We can usefully begin with Thomas's study in his commentary on Second Corinthians of Paul's resorting to the apparently immoral behaviour of boasting, in commending to his Corinthian converts, his personal qualifications to preach the Gospel, and his consequent appeal, 'I wish you would bear with me in a little foolishness' (2 Cor. 11.1).

In setting out to justify Paul's apparently wrongful behaviour, Thomas points to the inadequacy of moral precepts to cover or envisage all possible situations. He also invokes two technical phrases, drawing on Aristotle, of which the first is acting *praeter*, or 'despite', a law; and the second is recognizing at times a situation as a *casus emergens*. In the former phrase, the Latin preposition '*praeter*' means 'alongside', or 'beyond', and when it is applied, following Aristotle and the Greek version, *para nomou*, to a law or a regulation, it refers to an action which is not in accordance with a law, but also, more importantly, one which is not against the law and is thus forbidden. The action in question disregards the law, or places it to one side as irrelevant in this particular situation, as Thomas is now about to explain in justifying Paul's behaviour as only apparently immoral. Secondly, this sort of thing, he argues, can happen *'cash emergente'* (literally, 'with a situation emerging'). This term might appear to be associated with the English 'emergency', calling for a rapid response; but this need not be the case, since the Latin means only that a special situation has occurred. It seems appropriate, therefore, to convey the meaning of the phrase as something 'cropping up', or as some contingency arising which was not foreseen nor envisaged by the law.

Accordingly, on Paul's appeal to the Corinthians, Thomas explains:

> We should know that moral precepts relate to things which have to be done, and since these are particular and variable they cannot be determined indefinitely in a single common reason and rule. *It is sometimes necessary, when something crops up, to act despite, or regardless of, the common rule.* When something like this happens despite the common rule, wise people are not upset, because they know the reason for doing this, and they do not consider it an unwise action. However, those who cannot tell the difference and who are less wise [cf 2 Cor. 11. 23], do not consider the reason for this happening, and they are upset and consider it 'foolishness'.[1]

Having given his line of reasoning, Thomas now applies it to Paul's current situation. The normal moral law is that one should not commend oneself, as Prov. 27.2 enjoins, 'Let another praise you, and not your own mouth'. But it can happen that in some case, despite this general law, a person does commend him or herself, and does so justifiably, even though undiscerning people consider this behaviour blameworthy. So, when such a situation was arising in which Paul would have to commend himself, he exhorted his readers not to blame him, but to tolerate his behaviour. In other words, the 'un-wise', or the foolish, in Corinth lacked the wisdom which would enable them to rise above the formulation of general rules and to judge all human actions, including Paul's, in their full context, that is, according to the higher perspective of God's wisdom or of the eternal law. It was God's wisdom and will for the here and now that Paul should commend himself in this way in order, Thomas explained, to guarantee the integrity of the Gospel that he was preaching against the false teachers at Corinth (2 Cor. 10–11).[2] As Thomas points out elsewhere, 'Judgement about human values (*bonis*) ought not to be accepted from the stupid but from the wise, just as judgement on taste should be accepted from those who have a healthy taste'.[3]

Thomas's examination of the disapproving reaction of the Corinthians which Paul feared would happen exemplifies two aspects of un-wisdom (*insipientia*): (a) not realizing that cases can occur when one can, or should, act despite a general legal prohibition; and (b) not realizing or appreciating that the present situation is precisely such a case. As Thomas explains elsewhere, in human actions, some things are so explicit that, given a modicum of consideration, they can be immediately either approved or disapproved in the light of the primary moral precepts. 'But there are some human actions where judgment requires a lot of consideration of the different circumstances, which cannot be considered by just anyone, but only by wise people'.[4]

Another unpretentious, but not untypical, example of this is to be found in Thomas's commentary on Matthew 1, where Ruth, the Moabite who married Boaz, figures in the genealogy of Jesus (Mt. 1.5; Ruth 2–4). In his exegesis, Thomas faces the objection drawn from the Mosaic Law that 'no Moabite shall be admitted into the assembly of the Lord' (Dt. 23.3). As he responds,

> We reply with Paul in Galatians 5.18 that 'if you are led by the Spirit, you are not subject to the law'. In a law the intention ought always to be observed rather than the words. What was the cause of the Lord prohibiting the Moabites from entering the assembly? Because he found idolatry among the Moabites and did not want them to lead the Jews astray into their idolatry. But Ruth was already a convert to Judaism and not an idolater. Therefore, she was not subject to the prohibition.[5]

In fact, far from having a baneful influence on the Jewish people, Ruth was already converted to their faith, so, within the meaning of the law, she was no Moabite, and in fact was, as Thomas points out, being led by the Spirit with the result that she was 'not under the law'. It was only a true appreciation of the Law and its purpose, as well as of Ruth and her personal situation, that could enable one wisely to appreciate that, despite appearances, the Law simply did not apply in her case.

In one sense, the wisdom to read the law and the wisdom to read the situation to which the law might apply are complementary, since, as we have pointed out, the law itself is a factor in the total situation which confronts the individual. Yet, in another sense, the wisdom to read the law is the more basic, because if one does not admit nor realizes that in principle situations actually can 'crop up' when one can, or should, act in spite of the law, one is hardly in a position to acknowledge when precisely such a situation may occur, or may have occurred.

Parallel to admitting that cases can occur when the law may or should be ignored is the wisdom required to know what the law actually means or covers, or what its purpose is; and Thomas reflects on this elsewhere in connection with the classic case of the allegedly scandalous behaviour of Jesus and his disciples on the Sabbath day.

His Pharisaic opponents thought that Jesus was breaking the Sabbath (Mk 3.1–6) because they thought that the Sabbath law (Ex. 20.8–11) forbade even beneficial or health-promoting works. But this, Thomas observed, was 'against the intention of the law'. 'Jesus appeared to be breaking the Sabbath according to the superstitious understanding of the Pharisees, but in reality and truth he was not in fact doing so'.[6] Nor were the disciples breaking the law of the Sabbath in satisfying their hunger by picking and eating corn on that day (Mk 2.23–8), any more than were the Maccabees when they were fighting to defend their lives on the Sabbath (1 Macc. 2. 41) – nor even Elijah when he was fleeing for his life from Jezebel (1 Kgs 19.1–4)![7] Again, Jesus himself was not breaking the law when he reached out and actually touched a leper appealing to him, although he did appear to be acting illegally (Mt. 8.3). This was not true, Thomas retorted, because the aim of the law (Lev. 5.3) was to prevent contagion; and so, when Jesus was concerned, 'because he could not be infected, he was able to touch'.[8] Again, when Paul called the Galatians foolish (Gal. 3.1), even although Jesus himself had forbidden such language in the Sermon on the Mount (Mt. 5.23), Thomas sided with Augustine in explaining that one should look at Paul's reasons for using this term: Was it his intention actually to insult the Galatians, or was it to correct them?[9]

An instructive distinction which Thomas introduces when he is dealing with an apparent infringement of the law by Jesus in healing on the Sabbath is the distinction between how things appear and how they actually are. When Jesus retorted to his critics, 'Do not judge by appearances, but judge with right judgement' (Jn 7.24) he was asking them, Thomas commented, not to come to a negative conclusion on first impression, nor to contravene Isaiah's warning 'not to judge by what their eyes see' (Isa. 11.3). They should reach a judgement, Thomas explains, only 'after diligent enquiry', when, as the Vulgate Job 29.16 recalled, 'the cause which I knew not, I searched out most diligently'.[10]

Peter, too, caused some moral puzzlement to later readers of the Acts of the Apostles when he denounced Ananias and Saphira (Acts 5.1–9) without first admonishing them privately, as Jesus himself had decreed should be done in the church in such cases (Mt. 18.15–17). Among various suggested reasons for this unexpected yet proper behaviour, Thomas included the advice of the Holy Spirit that Peter should do so in order to assert his authority in the early church.[11]

A case where Thomas makes much of the difference between appearance and reality occurs in his treatment of Esau's selling his birthright to his younger brother, Jacob (Gen. 25.29–34). Simony! the mediaeval ecclesiastic would cry. Yes and no, Thomas typically replied, quoting Mal. 1.2–3, 'I have loved Jacob, but I have hated Esau' (Mal. 1.2–3), a cumbersome Jewish idiom which simply meant that God preferred Jacob to Esau. This being the case, Thomas judged, on the one hand Esau certainly committed simony in selling his birthright; but, on the other hand, Jacob only appeared to do so, because he knew through the Holy Spirit that the birthright was his, in fact.[12]

Of even greater moral concern to the mediaeval scholastics was the way in which Jacob, the founder of Israel, seemed on his mother's advice to be telling a lie to his dying father, Isaac, in claiming to be the elder brother Esau and, as a consequence, being blessed as Isaac's heir (Gen. 27.1–9). Thomas's approach was to follow the traditional line, and explain that Jacob's statement was not a lie, because he spoke 'according to the prompting and understanding of the Holy Spirit'.[13] Moreover, when Isaac later realized that he had been mistaken (Gen. 27. 30–7) he was taught by the Holy Spirit that he could not reverse the situation: hence Thomas concludes, 'on the advice of the Holy Spirit, Esau was rejected'.[14]

## THE HOLY SPIRIT AND THE UNEXPECTED

To the reader of Thomas's Scripture commentaries especially, it might appear that he was concerned regularly to excuse, or to explain away, the unexpected and apparently immoral behaviour recorded in Scripture of many otherwise estimable people. This appears notably the case in what were for the mediaeval moralist the three notorious instances in the history of Israel of apparently admirable people behaving appallingly, and doing so actually at Almighty God's express command: namely, Abraham's willingness to kill his son (Gen. 22.2); the prophet Hosea's having sexual intercourse with a harlot (Hos. 3.1, the text being understood historically); and the Israelites' robbing the Egyptians of their belongings as they fled from them into the desert (Ex 12.36) – all actions which appeared flagrantly to be serious violations of three of the ten commandments of the Decalogue which God had made a point of solemnly imposing on his chosen people.

In discussing whether one can be dispensed from the obligation of obeying the precepts of the Decalogue, Thomas is categorical in stating that they are 'entirely indispensable', or morally non-negotiable, those of the second table expressing God's intention to establish a relationship (*ordo*) of justice which is to be strictly observed between human beings, and which thus absolutely rejects murder, adultery and theft.[15] What *is* negotiable, however, Thomas observes, is whether this or that piece of behaviour actually meets, or fulfils, the description of the forbidden act, that is, the definition of murder, or of adultery, or of theft; and is as such forbidden by the appropriate relevant divine commandment. Now, since the issue in all the notorious three cases under consideration involved relationships which are governed by justice, Thomas noted, he proceeded to explain neatly that, in the case of Isaac, God as Lord of life and death could dispose of the child's right to life; in the case of the harlot, God as author of marriage could give the woman to the prophet Hosea; and in the case of the Egyptians' property, God as universal judge could transfer their right of ownership to the Israelites.[16] Having occasion later to return to the behaviour of Abraham and of Hosea, Thomas further explained this 'solution' that he had offered to these famous cases:

> Fornication is said to be a sin as it is against right reason, and a person's reason is right insofar as it ruled by the divine will, which is the first and highest rule. Therefore, what one does by the will of God, in obeying his command, is not against right reason, although it may appear to be against the general order of reason; in the same way as what happens miraculously by the divine power is not against nature, although it is against the general course of nature. And therefore, just as Abraham did not sin in willing to kill his innocent son, although, considered in isolation, this is generally against the rightness of human reason; so also, Hosea did not sin in committing fornication by a divine precept. Nor should such a sexual relationship be strictly said to be fornication, although it is called fornication with reference to the general course of behaviour.[17]

It can be seen, then, that although Thomas holds firmly to the immutability of moral commands, whether of natural or of divine law, he also gives himself considerable room for moral manoeuvre regarding the application of such absolute moral principles in actual practice. He concentrates on whether particular instances fulfil the definition of the wrongful deed, asking what the essential constituent elements are of a specific wrongful act, which combine to make it, for instance, an act of murder, or one of adultery or of robbery. If one or more of those required essential constituents is lacking, or is different, in a particular action that is being considered, then the latter does not meet the description of that wrongful act, and is therefore judged not to be, for instance, a forbidden act of murder, or one of adultery or of robbery. As Thomas explains, 'So the actual precepts of the Decalogue are unchangeable as far as concerns the idea of justice which they embody. But so far as concerns some determination by way of application to individual acts, namely, whether this or that is killing, or theft, or adultery, or not – that *is* changeable'.[18]

In his tightly argued examination of 'Aquinas on Exceptions in Natural Law', which considers these infamous cases, John Boler distinguished between claiming that there are 'exceptions' to allegedly unchangeable precepts of natural or divine law, and analysing such precepts and interpreting them as on occasion not being applicable in a precise situation which is being considered.[19] Exceptions to a moral rule can be identified, Boler remarks, by appealing to a 'higher-order goal', as Thomas does in the example he gives which we shall consider later, of opening a besieged city's gates against the law in order to admit people in danger outside who are essential to the city's safety.[20] (Boler is correct in observing that Thomas is 'not lavish with examples'![21]) By contrast, the process of analyzing an absolute moral precept and deciding when it does or does not apply requires much more deliberation, as Boler notes: 'It is not enough, of course, just to claim that an act is not really stealing (or whatever); one must give reasons to show why the formal conditions of an action of that kind have not been met. And the whole enterprise depends on a system of agreed-upon definitions or specifications of actions.' He refers to Aquinas, *ST* Ian IIae. 6–21,[22] and rightly concludes that, in cases which are reliant on the meeting or not of definitions, 'I would not then be asking that an *exception* be made'.[23]

The moral strategy of definition and interpretation which is invoked by Thomas on occasion as a means to identify and justify moral diversity is legitimate enough; although it might be derided by some critics, and dismissed as 'mere semantics,' or just a matter of words, designed to evade the accusation of moral relativism. This reaction, however, would be to ignore the often-crucial significance of language in moral matters and in moral discourse, and the need to reflect on, and carefully identify and delineate, the frequent complexity of moral situations. Logically, then, one can see and appreciate the point of Thomas's approach to the famous three Old Testament cases which we have been considering. However, such instances have also to pass the test of simple credibility and to rebut the charge of being counterintuitive. It is difficult to exonerate Thomas here from the charge of engaging in casuistry of an implausible kind, especially in the light of modern biblical scholarship, which, among other consequences, renders it today unnecessary, as Milton put it in *Paradise Lost*, 'to justify the ways of God to men'.

In mitigation of Thomas's approach, one might suggest that he may have been following his own maxim that in the absence of clear indication of anyone's wrongness, we should consider them good, and interpret what may be doubtful in their favour.[24] More to the exegetical point, in his approach on such occasions, Thomas followed Augustine in considering that the actions of some people in Scripture are shown as examples of virtue, and we must not think that they told lies, for instance, when they spoke in either a figurative or prophetic sense. But he also goes on to explain that there are some people who are commended in Scripture not for their perfect virtue but for some element of virtue which was, however, followed by undesirable actions; and this does show that he was not concerned to justify all the embarrassing behaviour of Israel.[25] What Augustine, and Thomas after him, was attempting was to catch some glimmering behind unexpected human behaviour of what

God's mysterious and providential ways are, and what God's wisdom for a particular person or group has been in individual situations.

For Thomas, the 'Master of the Sacred Page', 'whose thought is grounded in scripture',[26] and for whom 'theology is largely the explication of scripture', as Healy observed,[27] the role of the theologian is not to apologize for, nor to accommodate, Scripture, but to accept it and learn from it as containing the primary data of their science of theology; and the cases where Thomas invokes the influence of the Spirit on human behaviour are cases where he considers that the presence of the Spirit can be discerned directing human activity according to the wisdom of God and not just human wisdom, and in the light of godly rather than merely human principles. Such cases are seen by him not as embarrassments but as the springboard of theological reflection, and he would not have agreed with his master Albert that the counsels of the Holy Spirit would be respected more by silence than by 'the rashness of disputants'.[28] They are, for Thomas, the very stuff of any theology of moral behaviour. The Holy Spirit is his own best interpreter, to paraphrase Augustine; and that this was a cardinal principle of Thomas can easily be seen from the way in which in the *Summa* and elsewhere he will regularly accumulate one text of Scripture with others in order to build up the message of the Spirit and Thomas's theological argument. He will also introduce the surprising behaviour of those who are considered guided by the Spirit to illustrate how the wisdom contained in the letter of Scripture may, or may not, relate to their behaviour.

This intimate personal guidance and direction of individuals by the Holy Spirit in their moral actions is found by Thomas throughout Sacred Scripture, as well as in history. When Paul wrote of the Gentiles who 'have not the law' that they 'do by nature what the law requires' (Rom. 2.14–5), Thomas explained that this could be understood in the sense that such people are acting under the grace of Christ, and that they show the work of the law written on their hearts, not in ink, but principally and primarily by the Spirit of the living God (cf 2 Cor. 3.3), by whom they are alive and by whose teaching they are instructed.[29] And just as it was at the leading of the Spirit that Ruth became one of the people of Israel, it was also at the prompting of the Holy Spirit that Deborah (Judg. 4.4–5) did not actually teach the people publicly (which Paul was to forbid women to do, 1 Tim. 2.12) but gave advice to them privately.[30] Again, it was through the Holy Spirit that Job understood the reason for his unfortunate situation, and was able to rebut his false accusers (Job 16).[31]

The difficulty for scholastic thinkers of why the young Jewish girl, Mary, should have decided to enter the state of marriage, which is ordained for the physical continuance of the human race, even although we are told that she intended to remain a virgin (Lk. 1.34), was solved by Thomas in terms of 'an intimate prompting of the Holy Spirit',[32] just as it was the interior prompting of the same Holy Spirit that made the birth of Jesus known to Simeon and Anna (Lk. 2. 26–7, 37–8). As Thomas explained, it is usual for the just to be taught by the interior prompting of the Holy Spirit without any outward sign, whereas others must be led by external signs, as the shepherds were led by the angels and the Magi by the star. 'That is why the birth of Christ was made known to Simeon and Anna through an interior prompting of the Holy Spirit'.[33] Yet we should also believe that when the Magi had the wisdom to show reverence to the infant Christ they were inspired to do so by the Holy Spirit.[34]

When John began his campaign of baptizing,[35] when the children acclaimed Jesus,[36] when the woman inexplicably anointed the hair of Jesus,[37] when Mary looked into the empty tomb:[38] all these actions and many others described in the New Testament were explained by Thomas as the result of the interior guidance of the Spirit, and they more than instantiate his general remark that 'from this it can be gathered that all the actions and movements of the Apostles were in accordance with the prompting of the Holy Spirit'.[39] As Jerome wrote, it did not matter that the Apostles were unlettered when they were sent out to preach, since what normally came to others through practice and daily meditation on the Law was suggested to the Apostles by the Spirit:[40] and the words of the Apostles were to be respected as the commands of Jesus himself because they came from an intimate revelation from the Holy Spirit as well as from Christ.[41]

## ROOM FOR LEGAL AND MORAL MANOEUVRE

It is natural for Thomas, then, in his handling of Scripture to explain the correct but sometimes unexpected moral behaviour of various individuals in the theological terms of their being moved, inspired or prompted by the Holy Spirit. And this not-infrequent phenomenon, taken generally, gives credence to the observation of Philip Keane that 'we know that there is need to deal with the unforeseen and unforeseeable things God has in store for us as Church through the Spirit's work in the life of the Church and the world'.[42] On other occasions and in other contexts, Thomas is to be found explaining such or similar events, not in scriptural or theological terms, but now in more philosophical terms, by appealing regularly to his philosophical mentor, Aristotle. In some cases of unexpected action, Thomas can point, from a theological viewpoint, to the Spirit's initiative in imparting the degree of wisdom required to make the right decision diverging from the ordinary standard of behaviour or the common expectation. From the rational and philosophical viewpoint, by comparison, the regular ability to make the right decision in problematic cases affecting laws was considered important enough by Thomas, following Aristotle, to recognize the existence of a special virtue, known as *epieikeia*, which corrects anomalies in legal justice.⁴³

Replying to the question whether such epieikeia is a virtue, that is, a desirable moral aptitude to be cultivated, Thomas explains that human actions, with which the law is concerned, consist in an infinite variety of individual situations, with the obvious result that it is impossible to draw up a law which would cover every possible contingency. As a result, lawmakers must consider what happens most often, and to legislate for that. Then, however, in some cases to obey the law would offend fairness or justice, and would be contrary to the common good, which the law aims to promote. For instance, the law requires that some belonging which someone has deposited should be returned to them, because for the most part, this is the just thing to do. Yet, this could sometimes be harmful, as when a madman deposits his sword, and demands it back in a rage; or someone asks for their deposit of a sum of money to be returned, in order to use it against their native country.

In these and similar cases, it would be bad to follow the law in question, but it is good to ignore the words of the law and pursue what is required by justice and the common benefit. This, Aquinas concludes, 'is what *epieikeia*, which we call equity, exists for, and it is a virtue, as a matter of fact'.⁴⁴

> The point of epieikeia is well stated by Finnis when he writes of it as the radical justice of equity (aequitas, *epieikeia*) which departs from the common rule in its common (usual) meaning in order to uphold the rule in its true sense, all things considered. . . . [A]s Aquinas himself makes clear, acting 'for the common good [according to right reason]' is sometimes by no means the same as acting 'according to a common [or general] rule'.⁴⁵

Aristotle himself put it elegantly when he observed that the adapting of the law to the facts in this way is like the leaden rule used by stonemasons in Lesbos, which is not rigid, but flexible, adapting itself to follow the contour of the stone it is measuring.⁴⁶

Elsewhere, Thomas directly addresses the question whether one should strictly follow the wording of a law regardless of the harm which might result, and he is quite clear that 'if a case crops up when observing a law would be harmful to the common good, the law should not be observed'. He instances the case when a town under siege passes a law that its gates be kept permanently closed, with the unfortunate result that some citizens who are necessary for the town's safety are locked outside and are in mortal danger from the enemy unless the gates are opened to let them in. Thomas is quite clear that in such a case, and others like it, the purpose of the law, which is to preserve the common good, is undermined by actually obeying it, whereas its aim is fulfilled by ignoring the law and opening the gates.[47]

Thomas is clear that ignoring the law in this way is not criticizing the law, but only judging on the law's applicability in certain instances.[48] He also faces the objection that anyone acting in this way is usurping the authority of the lawgiver who alone can interpret the law. His reply is that in doubtful cases, interpretation is indeed called for, but if this is not allowable, then the words of the law should be ignored without the decision of the authorities. 'In obvious cases', he sums up, 'there is need not for interpretation, but for execution'.[49] Finnis observes that 'there is a legislative intent – what the legislature would have enacted [would have intended {intendisse}] had it envisaged the circumstances in question – which should be followed, at least where it is obvious. To act on this intention is to prefer equity (*epi[ei]keia*; *aequitas*) to the words or form of the law.'[50]

Elsewhere, however, in acknowledging that it is sometimes permissible for the subjects of a law to act despite it, Thomas adds an important caveat which is not to be found in Aristotle:

> But it must be considered that, if observing the law literally does not entail a sudden danger which must be immediately dealt with, it is not for just anyone to interpret what is useful for the state and what is not. This pertains only to leaders, who have the authority to dispense from the law in such cases. But if there is a sudden danger which does not permit the delay of having recourse to someone higher, 'necessity carries its own dispensation, not being subject to law'.[51] In such sudden cases of necessity 'it is obvious from the evidence of harm that the lawmaker would have intended otherwise'. Otherwise, 'if there is doubt, one ought either to act in accordance with the words of the law or consult one's superiors'.[52]

Thomas's teaching on epieikeia applies not just to civil law in society, but also to ecclesiastical law in the church, as can be seen in his comments on the church's law on fasting, that is, eating less as a penance at certain times during the liturgical year. In establishing common obligations, the lawmaker has in mind what happens usually and with most people, and if for some special reason something is found which goes against a person's observing a rule, the lawmaker does not intend to oblige that person to observe it.

> But this calls for a distinction: if the reason is obvious, the person can lawfully decide for themselves to ignore observing the law, especially if there is a custom to that effect, or if they could not easily have recourse to a superior. But if the cause is doubtful, one ought to have recourse to a superior, who has the power

to dispense in such cases. This is to be observed in fasts set up by the Church, to which all are generally obliged, unless they have some special impediment.[53]

Aquinas's teaching on *epieikeia*, following Aristotle, has not gone without its critics. One such was Edouard Hamel, who published a study of the varied history and use of Aristotelian *epieikeia* in moral theology and canon law following its introduction by Albert the Great, Thomas's teacher.[54] He quotes with approval the judgement of M. Wittman that Aquinas failed to give full weight to *epieikeia* as a virtue, leaving a marked gap between his statement of the doctrine and his applying of it, with the latter being considerably less generous than the former. For Hamel likewise, Thomas's teaching of the theory is full and dynamic and specifically Aristotelian, but his application is cautious, and it appears limited to legislation concerning society and the criterion of the common good. Moreover, Thomas also introduces restrictions in its use which are not to be found in Aristotle nor, for that matter, in Albert. In legitimizing the use of *epieikeia* only in serious and sudden social matters, Hamel concludes, Thomas seems inspired by a fear of detracting from the majesty of the law, or from the authority of the legislator, in a tightly structured legal environment; and all of this, coupled with a certain lack of confidence in the judgement of the subject, provides, according to Hamel, a witness to Platonic influence.[55] He comments, 'We know that for Plato *epieikeia* is not a correction of the law [as it was for Aristotle] but more of a diminution or deviation from the true law. These traces of Neo-Platonism would have prevented Thomas from giving its full value to the virtue of *epieikeia*.'[56]

It is interesting, therefore, to compare these strictures of Hamel on Thomas's teaching on the practical role of *epieikeia* in legal matters with what we have seen of Thomas's approach to similar types of situation within the more theological and spiritual context of his teaching on the role of the Spirit's wisdom in moral matters. In his study of *epieikeia*, Hamel expresses surprise that Thomas appeared not to know of the scriptural classical instances of *epieikeia* to which Albert had referred.[57] In fact, as we have seen earlier, Thomas did show in his scriptural commentaries, and elsewhere, that he was familiar with such cases and how to deal with them, but he did so in the theological context of wisdom rather than the philosophico-legal context of *epieikeia*; and moreover, showing in the former considerably more moral flexibility – even if he felt obliged to – than he did, according to Hamel, on *epieikeia*.

As we have already seen, Thomas explained in the wider perspective of wisdom that general moral commandments are like laws in being limited to what usually happens, and do not claim to cover all contingencies. In legal emergencies, Thomas resorts to a somewhat restrictive application of *epieikeia*, according to Wittman and Hamel; whereas, in more general moral dilemmas, he seems more generous in regularly invoking the internal prompting of the Holy Spirit as helping the individual spiritual person how best to understand and deal with the only seemingly pertinent moral command in question. The interesting systematic point here may be that in a secular legal context laws and commands issued by superior authorities are the product of wisdom, each in their own way expressions of the eternal law of God which is the supreme wisdom governing all creation; while it is only in the general sphere of morality that Thomas develops his more generous teaching on two complementary created wisdoms, the wisdom contained in the law and the wisdom operative in the individual subject, both interacting in a creative dialogue under the guidance of the Holy Spirit. This complementarity finds expression in Thomas's basic attitude that

> the law of the Holy Spirit is superior to every human law, and therefore, to the extent that spiritual people are led by the law of the Holy Spirit, they are not subject to human law when it clashes with their being led by the Holy Spirit. Nevertheless, it is part of the guidance of the Holy Spirit that spiritual people be subject to human laws. As 1 Peter 2.11 enjoins, 'for the Lord's sake, accept the authority of every human institution'.[58]

In this pneumatological context, the attitude of the Christian to the law could hardly be further removed from the idea of a duel between two wills, that of the legislator to dominate and that of the subject to be free, which later theology was to develop under the voluntarist influence of the Jesuit, Francis Suarez.[59] For Thomas, both legislator and subject were engaged harmoniously in a common pursuit, which was that of elucidating the wisdom of God, that is, the determinations of the eternal law, both for the community collectively and for each individual in it. Neither was to seek the mastery, for both were servants of divine wisdom, and if individual subjects were in doubt about God's will for them or were not so wise as to be able to discern for themselves the teaching of the Spirit in the law on a particular occasion, the wise thing to do, when feasible, was to avail themselves further of the community wisdom of the legislator.

## CONCLUSION

We have been considering instances illustrating the doctrine of Aquinas on how the Christian makes moral decisions driven and led by the Holy Spirit, teaching those whom Paul calls 'spiritual' people exteriorly through the external law of the Gospel, and also enlightening them interiorly on what they ought to do in the here and now. Since both of these influences come from the same Spirit, they cannot be discordant, but must be complementary; and indeed, Thomas teaches that the Spirit internally helps us to particularize and personalize in our current situation what he also presents to us externally as a general principle, thus giving order and direction to the use of that grace of the Spirit in which the New Law principally consists. We know in general from the record of the Lord's teaching how to pray and what to pray for, just as we know in principle what is conducive to our salvation and perfection, but what we should ask for and do, here and now, and in what frame of mind, comes to us only from the Spirit in us who helps our weakness and impels us.[60]

We have also aimed to discern in Thomas's works what factor other than the Holy Spirit may be considered common to those two complementary sources of moral knowledge, and we have been impressed to uncover such a factor in Thomas's teaching on Christian wisdom, particularly the Gift of wisdom imparted to the children of God to make them sensitive to the Spirit's promptings. Since the eternal law of God for all creatures is an aspect of that wisdom by whose contemplation God makes all things,[61] all other laws worthy of the name are reflections of that eternal law and wisdom, whether they are formulated directly by God or by that human wisdom which is itself a reflection of divine wisdom. But the wisdom refracted in the formulations of the laws can be grasped adequately in its reality only by those who are themselves wise, or are made wise, and thus realize that all things must be judged in the light of divine principles. Lacking that interior wisdom, which is imparted by the Spirit, one is in danger of accepting appearance for reality, letter for spirit; and one is unable to see that things, or actions, or rules or principles, are not always to be taken at face value. With the wisdom of the Spirit, however, the spiritual person who is made 'one spirit' with God through charity has an affinity, which Thomas calls connaturality, with 'what pertains to wisdom' and is enabled to discern the wisdom in the law and in one's own and other people's situations, as the Corinthians could not. 'Connaturality with divine matters is brought about by love, which unites us to God: 1 Cor. 6.17 "anyone united to the Lord becomes one spirit with him" '.[62] As there is one Spirit of God and one eternal law of God, so there is one wisdom of God which is offered to God's children from outside and which is also at work in the Spirit's prompting them from the inside.

To ask which for Thomas is the more important, law or grace, is in one way a foolish question. Both are grace. And although in some cases the Holy Spirit has worked on people only interiorly, yet the normal dispensation of divine providence is, and has been, to buttress the Christian from within and without by the grace of the Spirit; that is, to influence their intellect by the general formulation of the law and also by the refining of that formulation through the internal illumination of the Spirit. Expressing the same idea in another way, we might note that between the general principle and the particular situation there is a psychological gap which the individual is able to fill adequately only by the internal prompting of the Spirit, just as it is only by the influence of the Spirit that they will acknowledge the existence of that gap, and not attempt to make principle and particular invariably and absolutely identical or coterminous.

This 'realistic' attitude to the general formulations of the Gospel Law Thomas finds frequently contained and taught in the Gospel itself, where the Spirit inspires the 'saints' to show us how we should learn to interpret the letter of the Gospel. It would be ridiculous, of course, to conclude that the Holy Spirit always, or even in most cases, prompts the Christian to act 'despite' the general formulation of the law or moral precept, or apparently at variance with them. The unexpected is by definition unusual, and the reason why Thomas pays attention to such cases is because they do appear so unusual. In the majority of cases, the course of events runs smoothly and nothing 'crops up' to the contrary, and the general principle is recognized as applying exactly to the situation under consideration. Emerging contingencies are, again, by definition unusual and exceptional; if not, Thomas concludes, where human law is concerned, the law should be amended to deal with 'some change in people'.[63]

It is interesting that we have thus found Thomas applying three different strategies to consider how general statements of right behaviour relate to particular instances in which such statements might appear to apply, each of them in its own way acknowledging the incompleteness of general directives when it comes to considering specific occasions. We have found Thomas dealing with this, first, in exploring Paul's instruction on how to pray and when and what to pray for.[64] Secondly, Thomas's basic approach is similar when he considers the philosophical application of the Aristotelian virtue of *epieikeia* in legal matters; and thirdly, we have found a similar line of thought in Thomas's rich theological development of the wisdom of the Holy Spirit in the legislator, calling for the supplementary Gift of wisdom in the subject.

Much that we have been exploring about this role of the Holy Spirit enlightening the children of God both exteriorly and interiorly and driving them in their moral action, inevitably, and regularly, raises the critical question of how we can discern and identify the presence and dynamism of the true Spirit of God at work. This will be the subject of our next chapter.

## NOTES

1. *In 2 Cor.* 11, lect. 1 (M372). Emphasis added.
2. *Ibid.*

3. *ST* I-II.2.1 ad 1.
4. *ST* I-II.100.1.
5. *In Matth.* 1, lect. 2 (M 49). Kimball, 19–20.
6. *ST* I-II.107.2 ad 3.
7. ST II-II.122.4 ad 3.
8. *In Matth.* 8, lect. 1 (M 685). Kimball, 317.
9. *In Gal.* 3, lect. 1 (M 114). Cf *ST* II-II.72. 2 ad 2.
10. *In Joann.* 7, lect. 2, 11 (M 1050).
11. *In 4 Sent.*, d. 19, q. 2, a. 3, sol.1 ad 1.
12. *In Hebr.* 12, lect. 3 (M 692). Cf *ST* II-II.100. 4 ad 3.
13. *In 3 Sent.,* d. 38, a. 3, obj 1 et ad 1.
14. *In Hebr.* 12, lect. 3 (M 692).
15. *ST* I-II.100.8.
16. *ST* I-II. 100, 8 ad 3.
17. *ST* II-II. 154.2 ad 2. Cf I-II.94.5 obj 2 et ad 2.
18. *ST* I-II 100.8 ad 3. Emphasis added.
19. John Boler, 'Aquinas on Exceptions in Natural Law', in S. MacDonald & E. Stump, *Aquinas's Moral Theory* (London: Cornell University Press, 1999), 161–204.
20. Boler, 178. See below, pp. 119–120, *ST* I-II.96.6. See also *ST* II-II.51.4.
21. Boler, 167.
22. Boler, 180, n.62.
23. Boler, 181, emphasis in original. See also ibid., p. 182.
24. *ST* II-II.60.4.
25. *ST* II-II.110. 3 ad 3.
26. Healy, Nicholas H., *Thomas Aquinas Theologian of the Christian Life* (Aldershot: Ashgate, 2003), viii.
27. Healy, 3.
28. Albert, *In 3 Sent.*, d.38. a. 4; *Opera omnia*, ed Borgnet, 28, 726.
29. *In 2 Cor.* 3, lect. 1 (M 83).
30. *In Matth.* 1, lect. 2 (M 49). Kimball, 19–20. p. 105. On Deborah see *In 1 Tim.* 2, lect. 3 (M 80).
31. *In Iob* 16, lect. 1.
32. *ST* III, 29, 1 ad 1.
33. *ST* III. 36.5.
34. *ST* III, 36.8.
35. *ST* III, 38.2.
36. *In Ps.*8, lect. 2.
37. *In Joan.* 12, lect. 2, 1 (M 1609).
38. *In Joan.* 20, lect. 2, 1 (M 2494).
39. *In Gal.* 2, lect. 1 (M 55).
40. *ST* II-II.188.5.
41. *In 1 Cor.* 14, lect. 7 (M 886).
42. Philip Keane, 'The Role of the Holy Spirit in Contemporary Moral Theology', *Catholic Theological Society of America Proceedings* 51 (1996) 234.
43. Aristotle, *Eth. Nic.*, lib. V, 10 (1137a-8).

44. *ST* II-II.120.1.
45. J. Finnis, *Aquinas, Moral, Political, and Legal Theory* (Oxford: Oxford University Press, 1998), 216–17.
46. *Eth. Nic.,* V, 10 (1137b).
47. *ST* I-II.96.6.
48. *ST* II-II.120. 1 ad 2.
49. ST II-II.120.1 ad 3.
50. Finnis, *Moral*, 257 n19.
51. *ST* I-II.96.6.
52. *ST* I-II.96.6 ad 2.
53. *ST* II-II.147.4.
54. E Hamel, 'L'usage de l'épikie', *Studia moralia*, III (1965), Rome, pp. 48–81.
55. Hamel, p. 59, quoting M. Wittmann, *Die Ethik des hl. Thomas von Aquin,* Műnchen, 1933, 350–2.
56. Hamel, 60.
57. Hamel, 60.
58. *ST* I-II.96 5 ad 2.
59. Hamel, 68–9.
60. Above, pp. 86–87.
61. *In Ethic.*, lib. X, lect. 12 (M 2123).
62. *ST* II-II.45.2.
63. *ST* I-II.97.3 ad 2.
64. Above, pp. 86–87.

*Chapter 5*

# Constants of the Holy Spirit

In previous chapters of this study of the role of the Holy Spirit in human moral behaviour, we have examined Thomas's understanding of the influence of the Spirit on the minds and the wills of God's children, as they formulate and decide on moral acts. We have also considered his thought on the ways in which moral decisions are generated from the complementary exterior and interior influences of the Holy Spirit imparting God's wisdom to moral agents. In this chapter, we study more closely three of the outstanding characteristics which Aquinas assigns to the Spirit in that activity.

Thomas does not consider the Spirit as some shapeless force in the Christian life. On the contrary, he sees regularly manifested in the Holy Spirit's activity what we can identify and call three Constants of the Holy Spirit: first, the Spirit never contradicts himself in the Christian's life, for he is one and the same Spirit who has been ever, and remains, active in salvation history; second, the Spirit never contradicts Christ, or the written law of Christ, since he is the Spirit of Christ; and finally, the Spirit never contradicts the church, for the church is, in a striking term applied by Thomas, 'the Church of the Holy Spirit'.[1]

## THE SAME SPIRIT

Of the leading characteristics which can be discerned in Thomas's writings on the activities of the Holy Spirit, the first and most obvious underlying all the perfecting of humans in their being and their activity is that it is one and the same Holy Spirit who has been, and remains, at work in salvation history. As Job's friend, Elihu, quoted in his rebuke to Job, 'the Spirit of God has made me, and the breath of the Almighty gives me life' (Job 33.4); on which

Thomas remarks, 'Since "the Spirit of God made me", it is not surprising if he moves and perfects what he has made, which is why he adds, "the breath of the Almighty gives me life"; namely, he moves and perfects me to living works'.[2]

Following Augustine, Thomas invoked the same principle to explain apparent anomalies in Scripture and, as Spicq pointed out, Thomas used this principle as a hermeneutical rule which saw the sacred writings as a totality inspired by the one Spirit, and which enabled Thomas to explain one passage of Scripture by another, since one and all were inspired by the same Spirit who cannot contradict himself.[3] As Thomas observed, accepting it as a principle of interpretation, 'the Scriptures are explained by the same Spirit who produced them'.[4] Of course, Thomas was well aware of the differences of style, temperament and purpose in the several human writers, but he followed the remark of St Jerome (as he thought) in his commentary on the prologue to the Book of Jeremiah, acknowledging beneath the personal characteristics of all the sacred writers 'the unity of the Spirit inspiring them'.[5]

It was with a conviction of this truth that Thomas included in his inaugural lecture at the start of his teaching career in Paris University the observation that one reason for the authority of Scripture was that all who had handed on sacred doctrine had taught the same thing, having one Master, one Spirit ('Did we not walk with the same Spirit?' 2 Cor. 12.18 Vg), and one heart.[6] This applied even when there were lacunae in the sacred writings, for 'it is the Holy Spirit's will that what one wrote another should pass over in silence',[7] or when there was a literal discrepancy in accounts of the same event. For Thomas, it mattered little, for instance, whether John the Baptist was reported as saying that he was unworthy to carry Jesus's sandals (Mt 3.11) or to untie them (Mk 1.7): both phrases express John's humility before Jesus, and that was all that the writers, divine and human, intended to express.[8] Even when the Evangelists were quoting the Old Testament, which the Spirit had inspired, 'it did not have to be word for word, but sometimes sense for sense in our tongue, as the Holy Spirit gave them'.[9]

Given the purpose of the Holy Spirit in inspiring humans to write in the first place, it is natural that the same Spirit who inspired the sacred writers of the Old Testament and the 'saints' of the New Testament would also inspire others to understand and to interpret what they had written, as Augustine had explained. Indeed, Thomas remarks, the name of 'prophet' is not reserved only to the person who first utters a prophecy; 'it can also be applied to one who explains prophecies in the same Spirit and in the same way in which they were delivered'.[10] Likewise, Thomas observes:

> According to Augustine, the sayings and commands of Scripture can be interpreted and understood from the deeds of the saints, since it was the same Holy

Spirit who inspired the prophets and other authors of Sacred Scripture who moved these saints to act. For, according to 1 Pet 1.21 'men and women moved by the Holy Spirit spoke from God'; and Rom. 8.14 tells us that 'those who are God's sons and daughters are driven by the Spirit of God'. So, Sacred Scripture is to be understood according as Christ and the other saints observed it.

The written Scripture and the general moral precepts it contains are not the only teaching of the Holy Spirit that we possess on how we should behave. This teaching also includes the actions of Jesus and of the 'saints', of the Old as well as the New Testaments, which are undertaken under the influence of the very same Spirit. Commenting on 2 Cor. 12.18 where Paul rhetorically asked his Corinthian readers about his fellow apostles, 'Did we not conduct ourselves with the same spirit?', Thomas explained this as 'prompted by the same Spirit to behave well and rightly?'.[11]

Not everyone reads Scripture in the same way, of course, and not everyone hears the voice of the Spirit (cf Jn 3.8). But this, Thomas explains, again following Augustine, is because the Spirit speaks with a twofold voice. He speaks to us exteriorly in Scripture and in sermons, and this everyone hears, including unbelievers and sinners. But he also speaks interiorly in the human heart, 'and this only the faithful and the saints hear: "Let me hear what God the Lord will speak" (Ps. 85.8)'.[12] It is this internal voice of the Holy Spirit which attunes humans to recognize the Spirit's voice in the sound of Scripture, and to profit from it in their moral lives; and the two voices of the one Spirit can never conceivably contradict each other, since not only do they issue from the one Spirit, but they are both aimed at the same purpose of universal sanctification. 'Although the habitual gifts which are in the soul of Christ differ from those which are in us, nevertheless it is one and the same Holy Spirit who is in him, and who fills all those who are to be sanctified'.[13]

## THE SPIRIT OF CHRIST

The second 'constant of the Holy Spirit' which pervades Thomas's teaching on the Spirit's dynamism in the moral life is, in one sense, the ground of the Spirit's continuity and consistency of action, and, in another sense, the supreme instance of that action: namely, the relationship between the Holy Spirit and Jesus Christ, the incarnate Son of God. Because Jesus is the Son of God and the Eternal Truth, the Spirit who proceeds from him, conjointly with the Father, is characteristically the Spirit of the Son and the Spirit of Eternal Truth, and in his temporal missions, he cannot but communicate and clarify the Son who proclaimed himself to be Truth (Jn 14.6, 16–7; 16.13–5). On the other hand, because Jesus is also man, and *the* Son of God *par excellence*, it is in the 'driving' of this particular child of God by the Spirit of God (Rom. 8.14) that we find best exemplified Thomas's teaching on the universal action and purpose of that same Spirit.

This can be witnessed, firstl, in Thomas's teaching on the activity of the Holy Spirit on, and in, the human Jesus; secondly, in his teaching on the relationship of the Spirit to Christ as God; and finally, in Thomas's teaching on the role of the Spirit of the risen Christ in the moral behaviour of God's adopted children. Dominic Legge makes it clear that for Thomas 'just as the incarnation of the Son always points us back to the Father . . . , so it also always brings the presence and action of the Holy Spirit, both to the humanity that the Word assumes, and to the [people] Christ comes to save'.[14] Further, in his aim to rebut the views of theologians who accuse Thomas of 'forgetting about the Holy Spirit's presence in Christ's life and ministry',[15] Legge develops explicitly how 'Christ as man is also moved by the Holy Spirit' and how 'St Thomas does not hesitate to give the full sense to this scriptural witness',[16] not just seeing the Spirit 'move' Christ through the gift of charity, but also *par eminence* through the Spirit's own seven Gifts.[17]

For Thomas, the relationship between the human Jesus and the Holy Spirit is found most richly expressed in the three scriptural metaphors of the *fullness* of the Spirit which Jesus received, of Jesus's being *anointed* by the Spirit, and on the *resting* of the Spirit on him; and significantly, Thomas sees all three ideas as expressing not only the power of the Spirit in and on Jesus but also the precise purpose for which Jesus received the Spirit. These three themes are brought together by Thomas in his exegesis of Jn 3.34 'He whom God has sent speaks the words of God for he gives the Spirit without measure.' Thomas explains how Jesus's own prior receiving of the Spirit as man was unmeasured and sanctified him, and Thomas confirms this by citing the prophetic words of Isaiah (61.1) 'The Spirit of the Lord God is upon me, because the Lord has anointed me'.[18] The fullness of the grace of the Holy Spirit which Jesus received, and of which all of us have received (cf Jn 1.14,16), was not just a fullness sufficient for his own personal outstanding actions, such as Stephen possessed when, full of the Holy Spirit, he witnessed to the Lord Jesus (Acts 6.3–5; 7.55–60). Nor was it only the fullness of grace which Luke informs us that Mary possessed (Lk 1.28 Vg), excelling that of all the saints. 'There is also a fullness of effectiveness and outpouring which applied only to Christ as a human being, as the author of grace. This is why, to show that Christ had this unique fullness of redundancy and effectiveness, the Evangelist added "from his fullness we have all received" (Jn 1.16).'[19]

What Thomas here refers to as an outflowing fullness of the grace of the Spirit from Christ is most richly developed by him in his examination of the biblical symbolism of oil as applied to the dynamic outpouring of the Spirit on the human Jesus, and through this Anointed One to all who receive the unction of the Spirit. Jesus was anointed with the oil of the Holy Spirit above all the other saints, of course, and the latter are said to be anointed because whatever is possessed of that oil, which is the grace of the Holy Spirit, overflows from Christ to them.[20]

Paradoxically, Thomas sees the idea of the Spirit being on, or resting on, Jesus as a concept which is no less dynamic in expressing the purpose of the Spirit's influence on and through Jesus. The key text here is, of course, Isa. 11.2, which prophetically describes the 'resting' of the Spirit of the Lord upon the Christ, and Thomas is faithful to the context of that verse in seeing it as a preparation of the restorer of Israel by the Spirit of the Lord.[21] It was this messianic mission of Jesus, as Thomas explains, which was made manifest in his baptism when the dove descended and 'rested' upon him,[22] and when he inaugurated his active life under the influence of the Gifts of the Spirit which he received.[23]

Thus panoplies in the possession and power of the Spirit, Jesus was 'most perfectly moved by the Holy Spirit' in his every action, as was only to be expected of him who was pre-eminently the Son of God (Rom. 8.14). It was in the Spirit of God and by the finger of God that Jesus cast out demons, thus inaugurating the kingship of God;[24] and to ascribe this activity of the Holy Spirit through Jesus to the work of Satan was to blaspheme against, not Christ, but the Holy Spirit himself at work. His enemies accused Jesus not only of performing miracles in Satan's name but also of 'having a demon', using Satan's very words in his teaching (Jn 10.19–21), 'as if they were saying: "He is not speaking from the Holy Spirit but from an evil spirit" .' But, as Thomas retorted, 'such conduct on the part of Jesus's adversaries was, as usual, not surprising, for they were "animal persons, unable to perceive the things of the Spirit" (1 Cor. 2.14)'.[25]

It *was* from the Holy Spirit that Jesus spoke, as well as performing his miracles, Thomas commented, and it was the power of the Spirit which gave efficacy and success not only to Jesus's actions but also to his teaching. He himself claimed that his teaching was not his own, but from God (Jn 7.16); and Thomas does not shrink from applying to the teaching ministry even of Jesus the axiom of Ambrosiaster that 'all truth, no matter who utters it, is from the Holy Spirit' (*omne verum, a quocumque dicatur, a Spiritu Sancto est*);[26] just as he elsewhere points out with Chrysostom that when Jesus spoke to promise the Eucharist he claimed that his words were 'spirit and life' (Jn 6.63); 'that is, they have a spiritual meaning, and understood in this way they have life. Nor is it surprising that they have a spiritual sense: they come from the Holy Spirit'.[27]

We might sum up Thomas's teaching on the Holy Spirit's influence on Jesus in his human nature by suggesting that if, as Thomas said, Jesus's soul was most perfectly moved by the Holy Spirit, and, indeed, was actually driven (*acta*) by the Spirit in reverential affection towards God,[28] – even to 'the eternal Spirit' being the cause of Jesus's shedding his blood (Heb. 9.14) 'at whose movement and prompting, namely, through his love for God and neighbour, he did this' – then Thomas would also apply to all the human activity of Jesus his reflections on Matthew's description (4.1) of the Spirit leading Jesus into the wilderness to be tested: that this was an instance of Jesus's soul being 'most perfectly accustomed to be driven (*agebatur*) by the Spirit throughout his life and his death'.[29]

> People are 'led by the Holy Spirit' when they are moved by charity in such a way that their movements come, not from themselves but from another, since they follow the thrust of 'the charity of God which urges them on' (2 Cor. 5.14). Thus, the children of God are driven (*aguntur*) by the Holy Spirit in order that by the power of Christ they may pass victorious through this life, which is full of temptations.[30]

It should not surprise us that Thomas moves here from the idea of the drive of the Holy Spirit to the idea of the active power of Christ himself, for not only did the Spirit work in and on Jesus; he also worked, and works, through him; and here we begin to come closer to what Thomas means by 'the Spirit of Christ'. It is recognized that Thomas was greatly influenced in his Christological teaching by the idea of the Greek Fathers, that Jesus's humanity was the instrument of his divinity; and in his Scripture commentaries, as in his more systematic works, Thomas provides abundant references to the flesh of Jesus, or his humanity, acting as an instrument of, or in virtue of, his divinity. As he wrote of the Eucharistic discourse in John 6, 'the flesh [of Christ] is life-giving, since it is the organ of his divinity; and, since an instrument acts by virtue of the agent'.[31] We have seen enough of Thomas's thinking on instrumental causality to appreciate that his teaching on Jesus's humanity and human activity as subordinate and instrumental to his divinity, far from lessening the validity and value of Jesus's human nature and activity, serves rather to set them in their true context and perspective, and contributes to a fuller understanding of their role and purpose.[32] In discussing in the *Summa* how Jesus in his human nature can be called the 'head' of the church (Col 1.18), Thomas explains that this can be ascribed instrumentally to Jesus as man insofar as his humanity was 'the instrument of his divinity'.[33] This was how, as we have seen, Thomas exploited Augustine's repeated answer to the question of how the children of God could be themselves active if they were so thoroughly 'driven', or acted upon, by God's Spirit, with the phrase 'they are so acted upon as to be themselves active'. In an interesting twist to the phrase, Thomas in the *Summa* explains Jesus's need for habitual sanctifying grace by pointing out that his humanity was an instrument of his divinity 'as an instrument animated with a rational soul which acts in such a way that it is also acted upon (*ita agit quod etiam agitur*)'.[34]

In the Scripture commentaries, this somewhat mechanistic instrumental analogy acquires flesh and blood from more obviously biblical categories, and three of these categories are of most interest in our present context. In a remarkably rich passage in the commentary on John, Thomas explains what Jesus meant in saying 'for their sake I sanctify myself' (Jn 17.19).[35] Jesus began to sanctify his disciples when he sanctified himself in the Incarnation. In his divine nature, he was, of course, already essentially holy. But in his human nature, Jesus is holy by the grace which derives from his divine nature to his human nature; and this holiness of grace in his human nature was to proceed from the human Jesus to his disciples, who would thus all receive from his human fullness, in accordance with Jn 1.16, 'from his fullness we have all received'.[36] We find this same theme of Jesus's 'instrumental' sanctification linked with that of instrumental causality in the *Summa* where Thomas explains that because Jesus's humanity is like an instrument of his divinity it is at the same time both 'sanctified and sanctifying'.[37] Of course, Thomas is using the idea of instrumentality as a metaphor, and he frequently carefully qualifies it with such terms as 'just like', or 'a sort of'. As he explained of metaphorical language, 'in metaphorical speech we should not look for likeness in every respect, since then it would not be a likeness, but the reality'.[38]

The second biblical image which places Jesus's human nature in an instrumental role between his divinity and other humans is, not surprisingly, that of his anointing as Messiah. This anointing of Jesus is with the oil of the Holy Spirit, and it is an anointing which pertains to Jesus's humanity and not his divinity, since in fact it proceeds from his divinity.[39] Thomas follows patristic tradition in seeing the description of the oriental abundance of oil which flowed from Aaron's head to his beard and thence to the hem of his robe (Ps. 132 (133), 2) as representing the spiritual oil which descended from Christ's divinity to his humanity, and thence to us.[40]

Finally, Thomas sees Christ as the distributor of the Gifts of the Holy Spirit, 'bringing about grace and truth through the gifts of the Holy Spirit which he gave to humans'.[41] Jesus alone received the gift of the Spirit without measure, in the sense that he alone received all graces of the Spirit to the full capacity of his human nature, but it is from his fullness that all have received, in the sense that his is the power to give or not to give, or to give only so much.[42] Yet what Christ gives above all is not the gifts of the Spirit or the manifestations of the Spirit, but the Holy Spirit himself, because although the gifts of the Spirit which are in Jesus differ in number and intensity from those which are in us, nevertheless it is one and the same Spirit who is in him who also fills all those who are to be sanctified.[43]

It is because Thomas thus develops, and sees expressed in Scripture, the idea of Christ's humanity as the instrument of his divinity that he can answer the objection taken from Augustine that Christ as man could not give the Holy Spirit.[44] As man, Thomas replies, it is true that Christ cannot give the Spirit with authority, or as the Spirit's source, but he can give the Spirit as the minister and the instrument of his divinity; and on Paul's authority (Gal 3.5), Thomas points out that even other humans can be said to give the Holy Spirit.[45] This latter occurs when ministers confer the church's sacraments, but it is a manner of speaking which is neither customary nor to be extended.[46] There are, of course, enormous differences between Christ's giving of the Spirit and other people's giving of the Spirit through the ministry of the Sacraments, the fundamental difference being that the Spirit given is the Spirit of Christ; of Christ as God, and of Christ as man, but in profoundly different senses.

If Christ's humanity is the instrument of his divinity, then in some sense, and (for Thomas) always within the confines of the doctrine of appropriation, Christ's humanity is also the instrument of the Holy Spirit. We may be helped to understand this to some extent by recalling how Thomas regards the bodies of the saints as the temples and instruments of the Holy Spirit dwelling in and working in them;[47] but, of course, the body of Christ is not so much just a temple as the 'holy of holies', the *sanctum sanctorum*, of the Holy Spirit. 'It was the Holy Spirit, proceeding from the Eternal Word, which formed the body of Christ'.[48] Yet the power of the Spirit did not cease then, for 'between' the two poles of Jesus's divinity and divine action, on the one hand, and his humanity and human activity on the other, Thomas locates the power of the Spirit who proceeds from Christ in his divinity and who sanctifies and influences Jesus's every human activity of intellect and will. In other words, the Spirit who proceeds from Christ in his divinity is communicated by Christ to his humanity, and through that humanity to us, his sisters and brothers.[49]

It is only by some such theological construction that Thomas could attempt to do justice to the texts of Scripture which describe the influence of the Holy Spirit, who is the Spirit of the Word, on Jesus as man. It may be fanciful to see in Thomas's remark that Jesus's rational soul acts in such a way that it is also acted upon an oblique reference to the driving of God's children by the Spirit of God in Rom. 8.14;[50] but he does write explicitly elsewhere of 'Christ's soul being moved in a kind of reverential love for God, being driven by the Holy Spirit'.[51] He repeats significantly that Jesus possessed in the most perfect way the gifts of the Holy Spirit: 'he gives them as God and receives them as man, which is why Gregory says that "the Holy Spirit never left the humanity of Christ, from whose divinity he proceeds" '.[52] And it is perhaps in this teaching that we have Thomas's clearest statement of the power of the Spirit issuing from the divinity of Christ to perfect his humanity in action.

We may sum up our enquiry thus far into what Thomas means by the Spirit of Christ by recalling the Christological climax of his exegesis of Rom. 8.14.[53] All God's children, but above all God's only begotten Son in his human nature, are driven by the Spirit of God; that Spirit of the Son who proceeds from Father and Son, who proceeded from the Eternal Word and who formed in Mary the bodily expression of that Word, and who continued thereafter throughout Christ's human life to ensure that Jesus in his human nature and activity would in all things faithfully and most perfectly express the Eternal Word of God and his Spirit. It is against this theological background that one can fully understand all that Thomas says of the influence and the power of the Spirit of Christ manifested in the messianic activity and preaching of Jesus.

If such is the role of the Spirit of Christ in the life of Jesus himself, then the same Spirit who is communicated through the ministry and the instrumentality of Jesus, as we have seen, cannot but have an analogous role in the life of all those who belong to Christ as his brothers and sisters and as the adopted children of God. The purpose of the Spirit who proceeds from the divine Christ and who communicates himself to us through the ministry of the risen human Jesus is to teach all truth and to make us daughters and sons of God, because he is the Spirit of Truth and the Spirit of *the* Son of God.

Commenting on Jn 14.17, Thomas explains, 'He is the Spirit of truth because he proceeds from the truth and speaks the truth . . . . Just as in us when we conceive and consider the truth, there follows a love of that truth, so in God, when the truth is conceived, namely, the Son, then Love proceeds. And just as it proceeds from the truth, so it leads to a knowledge of it; which is why Ambrose says that "every truth, regardless of who speaks it, comes from the Holy Spirit"'.[54]

Not only that. When Jesus went on to tell his disciples that the Holy Spirit he would send 'will teach you everything and remind you of all that I have said to you' (Jn 14.26), Thomas explains that

> it is the Son who gives us the teaching, since he is the Word; but it is the Spirit who makes us capable of receiving his teaching. The Spirit 'will teach you all things', because whatever a person teaches from the outside works to no purpose unless the Holy Spirit provides understanding from the inside. The words of a teacher are otiose unless the Spirit is present in the heart of the listener, for, as Job says (Vg 32.8), 'It is the Spirit of the Almighty that gives understanding'. *And so true is this, that even the Son himself, speaking through the instrument of his humanity, is powerless unless he is also at work from within through the Holy Spirit.*[55]

The Spirit of Christ 'makes us know all things by inspiring us from within, by directing us, and by raising us up to spiritual things. For just as one whose taste is infected has no true knowledge of flavours, likewise whoever is infected with a love of the world cannot taste divine things. "The animal person does not perceive those things which are of the Spirit of God (1 Cor. 2.4 Vg)"'.[56]

The gentleness and intimacy of the influence of the Spirit in the hearts of Christ's faithful could hardly be more delicately and yet profoundly expressed than in these words of Thomas which faithfully reflect the atmosphere in which John shows Christ talking to his friends about his Spirit that he is promising to give them. It is the Spirit of the risen Christ who gently and smoothly disposes all Christ's friends to receive Christ's teaching; which is only another way of saying that Christ's Spirit leads them individually to the truth which is Christ himself, from whom the Spirit of Truth proceeds, to give power and efficacy to the words of truth in the heart of the individual. And the Trinitarian cycle, which is no more than adumbrated here, is completed elsewhere by Thomas when he explains that Christ is the Truth of the Father, and so the Spirit of Truth which proceeds from Christ inspires those to whom he is sent with the truth of the Father.[57]

This Spirit whom we receive is the Spirit of charity who adopts us as God's children,[58] and who is, in fact, the 'spiritual seed' of the Father, through which some people are generated as God's children, as I John indicates ('God's seed abides in them', 1 Jn 3.9).[59] Here again Thomas considers the roles of the Son and his Spirit in the interplay of their influence on the Christian, for although Jesus has taught us that God is our Father, it is the Spirit who brings that teaching home to us in filial affection and makes us live the truth that we are God's offspring.[60] 'Among other things, the Holy Spirit moves us to have a childlike attitude towards God (Rom. 8.15). And because it is proper to piety to manifest duty and respect to one's father, it follows that the piety through which we manifest duty and respect to God as Father by the prompting of the Holy Spirit is a gift of the Holy Spirit'.[61]

But we cannot become adopted sons and daughters of God unless we receive a resemblance to him who is God's Son by nature, and this family likeness to Christ we receive through Christ himself, receiving his Spirit who makes us resemble him.[62] We are reborn as sons and daughters of God in the likeness of God's real Son, a likeness which we have from receiving his Spirit.[63]

Whether the Holy Spirit is considered, then, as the Spirit of Truth or as the Spirit of the Son, he has but one basic role, to conform us to Christ who is both Truth and Son.[64] It is important to realize, however, that for Thomas, it is not Christ in his human nature who is the final model to which the Spirit of Christ conforms us. Nor indeed was it Jesus's own intention or teaching that conformity to his humanity should be the final result of the power of the Spirit at work in God's adopted children. Jesus's humanity, as he himself said, is only the 'way' (Jn 14.6), not the destination, and Thomas observed in his commentary on Matthew, 'I do not want you to remain on the way, namely the humanity, but to go further, to the divinity';[65] which was, of course, for Thomas the controlling idea of the *Tertia Pars* of his *Summa*, in which 'Our Savior Our Lord Jesus Christ showed us in himself the way of truth through which by rising again we may reach the happiness of immortal life'.[66]

We may conclude this examination of what Thomas means by the phrase 'the Spirit of Christ' by citing a passage in which we see the idea of the power of the Spirit of Christ conforming us to Christ expressed in terms of what it is to be a Christian.

'One is called a Christian for belonging to Christ. And one is said to belong to Christ not just from having faith in Christ, but also from proceeding to deeds of virtue by the Spirit of Christ'.[67]

## 'THE CHURCH OF THE HOLY SPIRIT'

Along with the constants of the same Spirit and of the Spirit of Christ which occur frequently in Thomas's writings on the power and influence of the Holy Spirit in Christian moral action, a third highly significant constant which is identifiable involves the intimate relationship between the Holy Spirit and the church, whether this relationship is expressed in Pauline terms of the manifestations and communications of the Spirit to benefit the church (cf 1 Cor. 12.7), or more simply, yet much more profoundly, in the Thomistic phrase 'the Church of the Holy Spirit' (*ecclesia Spiritus Sancti*). Thomas nowhere appears to provide any source for this phrase, but he may possibly be influenced by Acts 20.20 in the Vulgate, which refers to 'the entire flock in which the Holy Spirit has made you bishops to rule the church of God'. In the third century, Tertullian had used the phrase 'the church of the Spirit (*ecclesia spiritus*)' in disparaging contrast to the church 'of the bishops' in his polemical defence of Montanism, the Spirit-focused heresy; but Aquinas shows no awareness of this.[68] In modern times, the Orthodox theologian Nicholas Afanasief gave his study of the church the title of *The Church of the Holy Spirit*, but he made no mention in it of Aquinas's use of the term.[69]

A dramatic theological controversy in which Thomas was engaged, and which enabled, and perhaps led him, to develop his thinking on the relationship of the Holy Spirit to the church, involved Thomas's detailed refutation of the fanciful theology of the Holy Spirit and the church which had been devised and propagated a century earlier by Joachim of Fiore, and to which Thomas, unusually, dedicated a separate article in the *Summa*, asking 'Will the New Law last until the end of the world?'.[70]

The length of this study has precluded our doing justice to the historical context in which Thomas lived and worked, but it is essential to any just appreciation of his work and achievement to be aware of him as Brother Thomas, the impressive Dominican friar from Aquino, in southern Italy, acting and reacting in mediaeval Europe. The age in which Thomas lived has been rightly termed the golden age of scholasticism, and it was an age which produced scholars with golden reputations like Dominic and Francis, Albert and Bonaventure, and Thomas himself, each in his own freedom of the spirit an example of the power of the Holy Spirit and of the wisdom of Christ and of God. But it was also an age remarkable for the way in which charity had grown cold, and which consequently savoured, if it did not relish, human rather than godly matters, producing such contrasting phenomena as the Franciscans and the Flagellants, the sombre devotion of the *Dies irae* and the blusterings of the *de periculis novissimorum temporum* ('The perils of the last days'), each work in its own way expressing and feeding a near-hysteria of apocalyptic speculation which itself was part-result of what has been called the theological geometry of the twelfth-century Cistertian abbot, Joachim of Fiore.

In his *History of Christianity*, Diarmaid MacCulloch writes of 'the wild underworld of thirteenth-century religion',[71] and in the previous century, Joachim had fed into this by his calculated juggling with the generations of Scripture, through which he felt empowered to compute the future, and create a theology of history which has not been without reverberations even into modern times.[72] His devout adherents, including a deviant group of 'Spiritual' Franciscans, preached the 'Eternal Gospel' drawn from Joachim's writings, and predicting the arrival in history of a culminating and definitive 'third age' of the Holy Spirit. This, they held, was destined to succeed the age of the Father which was chronicled in the Old Testament, and the age of the Son and his church which were described in the New Testament. This third age of the Holy Spirit was due to begin in 1260, and was going to be administered by monastic 'spiritual men';[73] and there was no shortage of enthusiasts advocating that these would be the members of one or other of the new religious orders, later not excluding the Jesuits!

Surveying the origin and spread of Joachism, Mark Bloomfield and Marjorie Reeves proposed that Joachim's speculations on the third *status* of the Holy Spirit lay dormant for some considerable time after his death and found its first explosive expression only in the teaching of the Franciscan Gerard of Borgo San Donnino at Paris in 1256.[74] It was therefore a topical and highly controversial subject in Paris University, clearly calling for comment by Brother Thomas, and nowhere more appropriately than in the *Summa* in his detailed and original treatment of the New Law of the Holy Spirit. Thomas taught in Paris from 1256 to 1259 and started writing the unfinished *Summa* a few years later, in 1265.

Thomas attacked Joachimism head on by asking whether the New Law of the Gospel would last until the end of the world,[75] addressing the argument that, in spite of Jesus's promise to his disciples that the Holy Spirit would teach them all truth (Jn 16.13), the church in the 'state of the New Testament' did not yet know all truth; with the consequence that 'another state is to be expected, in which all truth will be made clear through the Holy Spirit'.[76] Thomas's expert handling of his sources is seen in his detailed response to this objection, recalling that such 'nonsense' (*vanitas*) had been already entertained in Augustine's day by the Montanists, as well as by the Manicheans. Neither of these accepted the Acts of the Apostles, in which it was clear that the promise of an imminent gift of the Spirit had been repeated in Acts 1.5: 'you will be baptized with the Holy Spirit not many days from now', and then duly fulfilled by the descent of the Spirit at Pentecost (Acts 2). Moreover, Jn 7.39 taught that the Spirit had not yet been given because Christ had not been glorified, 'from which it follows that when Christ came to be glorified in the resurrection and the ascension, the Holy Spirit was immediately given, which excludes the folly (*vanitas*) of those who say that another time of the Holy Spirit is to be expected'. Moreover, Thomas concludes for good measure, with a nice ad hominem argument against Joachimite prophecies, 'the Holy Spirit taught the Apostles every truth that is relative to what is needed for salvation, namely, what is to be believed and what actions are to be performed. But he did not teach them about all future events, since this was not for them to consider, as Acts 1.7 points out, "It is not for you to know the times or periods that the Father has set by his own authority"'.[77]

Going back to the source of Joachism, Joachim's biblical calculations, Thomas then addressed the claim that since, in the Trinity the state of the Old Law, in which men focused on generating, was appropriate to the Father; and since similarly the state of the New Law 'in which clerics focused on wisdom are in charge' is appropriate to the Son, there will then come a third epoch, one of the Holy Spirit, in which, of course, 'spiritual' men will be in charge. Thomas easily dismisses this by summarily pointing out that the Old Law belongs to both the Father and the Son, since the latter is symbolized in it and also explained that Moses had written about him (Jn 5.46). Moreover, the New Law belongs to both Christ and the Holy Spirit, being 'the law of the Spirit of life in Christ Jesus' (Rom. 8.2). Therefore, Thomas concluded, no other Law which would be the Holy Spirit's is to be expected.[78]

Thomas reserves his obvious ire for the last Joachimite argument that he dismisses, one based on Jesus's prophecy that the Gospel of the Kingdom would be preached throughout the world, and that then the end would come (Mt 24.14). It was being claimed by the Joachimites that although the Gospel of Christ had long been preached throughout the world, yet the end had not arrived. And they concluded, 'So, the Gospel of Christ is not therefore the

Gospel of the *Kingdom*, and there is still another one to come, the Gospel of the Holy Spirit as another Law'. To which Thomas retorted in exasperation, 'It is the height of stupidity (*stultissimum*) to say that the Gospel of Christ is not the Gospel of the Kingdom. At the very beginning of preaching the Gospel, Christ proclaimed that "the kingdom of heaven has come near" (Mt 4.17).'[79]

Beryl Smalley commented that this sustained refutation of Joachism by Aquinas was a 'quiet dismissal', to be accounted for by Thomas's change of attitude towards the spiritual sense of Scripture which had formed the basis of Joachim's imaginary calculations, and she added that this made a detailed refutation of Joachism by Thomas unnecessary.[80] Yet, it is difficult not to see Thomas's verdict that Joachism was 'empty nonsense' (*vanitas*) and 'the height of stupidity' (*stultissimum*) as much more expressions of theological irritation on Thomas's part. The religious orders, Franciscans and Dominicans, were clinging on to their University chairs of Theology at Paris University in the teeth of bitter opposition from the secular, or diocesan, clergy, led by the ironically named William of Holy Love, and Thomas had felt constrained to write a spirited pamphlet defending religious life, which included two opening chapters justifying members of religious orders in lecturing publicly on theology.[81] It was difficult enough for them, he no doubt felt, to be fighting for their right to lecture precisely on the Gospel of Jesus Christ, without some fellow religious idiots (*stultissimum*!) propounding a completely different 'gospel', and claiming to be teaching what Healy has described as 'massive distortions of orthodox Christian doctrine'![82]

What the Spiritual Franciscan and other Joachimite advocates did not appreciate, as Thomas expounded in the body of the article on the real New Law, was the nature of the church, and how everything in the New Law of the Gospel which is not the internal grace of the Holy Spirit is ordered to either receiving the Spirit's grace or to putting that grace into effect.[83] All this had nothing to do with neurotic calculations of where and when Antichrist would be born, or when the emperor would die.

It was commonplace at one time for Thomist scholars to note, regretfully, in many cases, that Aquinas does not provide a systematic ecclesiology, nor envisage one in his unfinished *Summa* of Theology. However, in recent years, this apparent ecclesiological gap in Thomas's writings began to be filled in, as Christopher Baglow noted, 'beginning with the work of Grabmann and reaching its highpoint with the work of Congar'.[84] To these can now be added Baglow's own work, since the major part of his study is a detailed exegesis of Thomas's commentary on the Pauline letter to the Ephesians, which Baglow identifies as containing a prolonged examination of what Thomas identifies as a major theme in Ephesians: namely, the church and its unifying role. Stressing the Christological emphasis and centrality of the original letter, and therefore of Thomas's commentary, Baglow also recognizes 'that Thomas' ecclesiology is a predominantly pneumatological one',[85] even though Thomas has little to say on this in his commentary on Ephesians.[86] As Baglow explains, 'the pneumatological principle of the church's existence is an essential element, yet one that is also subordinate to Christ's work and centered upon it'.[87]

More prominence on Thomas's teaching on the relationship of the Holy Spirit to the church was provided by Vauthier in his textual study of 'The Holy Spirit as Principle of Unity of the Church according to Thomas Aquinas'. In this, Vauthier shows how Thomas regularly describes the Holy Spirit as the 'soul' of the church, giving unity to the body of which Christ is the head (Col 1.18)[88] and he includes Thomas's succinct statement in his commentary on Jn 6 that 'the unity of the Church is brought about through the Holy Spirit'.[89]

It is clear, then, that the academic world is accumulating, and becoming increasingly sensitive to, evidence of Thomas's theological awareness of the church and of his general approach to it, especially in its relation to Christ, its founder. This provides a valuable theological context for further reflection on our part from Thomas's writings of how intimately he considers God's Spirit to be associated with the life and the inner working of the church, and for crowning Thomas's ecclesiology by introducing two further identifying marks of the church which for him intimately identify it with the Holy Spirit. The first such mark is that of the church being in Thomas's considered view the *ecclesia Spiritus sancti*, that is, 'the Church of the Holy Spirit', providing in just three Latin words a compendious and remarkably promising pneumatic ecclesiology.[90] The further mark of the church we propose is identified by Thomas, in the light of Christ's headship of the church he founded (Eph. 1.22), as his describing the Holy Spirit as the 'heart of the Church', thus providing not only unity to the body of the church but a shared life to all its members.[91]

Identifying the church as 'the Church of the Holy Spirit' can be seen as providing a launching pad and at the same time a theological setting for Thomas's frequent references to 'the prompting (*instinctus*) of the Holy Spirit' as a recurring refrain on his part to account for various deeds and actions which historically took place at the Spirit's instigation in the Bible and within the Christian community up to the present day. In this connection, in an ingenious piece of casuistry which Thomas adopts from Bede, he explains why, after Judas had died, Jesus's disciples cast lots to fill the vacancy in the apostolic college from one of the two shortlisted candidates, 'and the lot fell on Matthias' (Acts 1.15–26).

The morality of drawing lots was a subject to which Thomas returned several times and to which, during one vacation, he devoted the little essay *de sortibus* (on lots) for the benefit of a friend.[92] Basically, Thomas held, 'using lots is just an attempt to discover some indication of God's will in a particular situation'; and although in itself this is not wrong, it can become so in certain circumstances.[93] Hence, Thomas cites Bede as explaining that before the fullness of the Holy Spirit had been poured out on the church at Pentecost, it was lawful for the Apostles to cast lots to discover a successor for Judas. However, after the descent of the Holy Spirit, as we can see from the appointment then of the seven deacons not now by lot, but by election (Acts 6.3–7), it was no longer permissible to use lots for this ecclesial purpose. Thomas's verdict is that now 'doing so is unjust to the Holy Spirit. For *we must believe that the Holy Spirit provides his Church (ecclesiae suae) with good shepherds*'.[94]

Indeed, Thomas is quite clear that 'the Holy Spirit is not lacking in anything which is useful for the church',[95] and more specifically, his background thinking here appears to be that elections in the church ought to happen 'at the inspiration of the Holy Spirit' directing the electors in their knowledgeable and free choice,[96] which, as we have seen, is the Spirit's characteristic and regular way of dealing with human agents.[97] To use lots among a defined set of candidates in such matters is to usurp the rights of the Holy Spirit by narrowing the Spirit's own range of choice, and also eliminating his normal interaction with humans. As Thomas further remarks in his commentary on the Psalms, using lots is not permissible in spiritual matters, because in such matters, one is directed by the Holy Spirit;[98] and, as he points out, 'it would be an injustice against the Holy Spirit who instructs the human awareness to judge rightly, in accordance with 1 Cor. 2.15, "Those who are spiritual discern all things"'.[99] In other words, election by lot is fundamentally at variance with Thomas's idea of the Holy Spirit acting through the instrumentality of humans, and it is also profoundly counter to that connaturality to the things of the Spirit which the Holy Spirit confers on spiritual people. 'Men are to be promoted to Church dignities by an agreement of choice which is brought about by the Holy Spirit'.[100]

Elsewhere Thomas expands this by opining that there is nothing wrong in using lots for secular elections; but it is different in ecclesiastical appointments: 'doing this is doing an injustice to the Holy Spirit *who is firmly believed to be in the Church* or in Colleges'.[101] It may be worth noting that the temptation to cast lots even in ecclesiastical appointments must have been increasingly strong in the church around the time when Thomas was writing his *de sortibus*, when the College of Cardinals was going to take two years, nine months and two days from 1268 to 1271 to elect the future Pope Gregory X,[102] and at a time when, as Roland observes, the whole thirteenth century was rife with squabbles over episcopal elections.[103]

Thomas's opposition to manipulating the Spirit by drawing lots and forcing the Spirit to make a decision on demand for hic et nunc is equally strong in his condemnation of simony, or bribery in ecclesiastical appointments, a practice so named after Simon the former magician who offered Peter and John money in return for the gift which they possessed of actually conferring the Holy Spirit (Acts 8. 9–25). Thomas follows Gratian's *Decree* in condemning this behaviour for turning the Holy Spirit into a slave to be bought and sold by selling his gifts, and as constituting an attempt to dominate the Spirit rather than to serve him.[104]

The power of the Holy Spirit in his own church, then, is not to be usurped nor constrained, far less bought and sold. For he is as free as the wind (Jn 3.8), as we saw in chapter 1; and this freedom of the Spirit must be acknowledged everywhere, but particularly in his church, since the whole institutional church, its scripture, law, authority, *magisterium* and sacramental system, is 'the Church of the Holy Spirit', and constitutes part of the secondary element of the New Law, whose purpose, as we have seen, is to dispose its members either to receive the grace of the Spirit of Christ or to exercise that grace.[105] This is why, for example, Thomas recalls that when the conditions for conferring the Sacrament of Confirmation are being considered (a topical issue, even then), one should bear in mind 'the practice of the Church, *which is governed by the Holy Spirit*'.[106]

Also interesting in this connection is Thomas's reflection on the practice in the church of his day that it did not impose the obligation of fasting on those who had just been baptized at Easter, until they had received the fullness of the Spirit in the Sacrament of Confirmation at Pentecost. 'This showed that they are not required of necessity to undertake difficult actions before they are prompted interiorly by the Holy Spirit to take them on of their own free will'.[107] This statement of Thomas seems to bring out in a remarkable way his constant teaching not only that the New Law is not a heavy burden but that it must not be made so. As we have already seen, the primary element which makes the burden which Christ offers light is the power of the Spirit to enable one to bear it with love; but it must be recognized that it is materially light also, and this is well expressed in Thomas's comparison between the requirements of the Old Law and the New Law of the Gospel. The Old Law had many more external actions regulated. In contrast, 'the New Law, apart from the precepts of the law of nature, added very few in the teaching of Christ and the Apostles, although some were later added by some of the Fathers. In these too, Augustine said there should be moderation, in case the behaviour of the faithful became burdensome'.[108]

The New Law is more difficult, however, Thomas recognizes, in forbidding not just external actions but also internal, of which only a few were expressly forbidden in the Old Law. Obedience, then, is very difficult for a person who does not possess virtue, whereas it is made easy by virtue. As the First Letter of John teaches (5.3), 'his commandments are not burdensome', and Augustine explains that 'they are not burdensome to one who loves, but burdensome to one who does not love'.[109] Thomas himself, in his commentary on the opening chapter of First Timothy, explains that 'what is imposed on someone is imposed as a burden, but the law is not imposed on the just like a burden, because an inner habit inclines them to what the law commands and it is therefore not a burden to them – "they are a law to themselves" (Rom. 2.14)'.[110] And when Paul wrote (Gal. 5.18) 'if you are led by the Spirit you are not subject to the law', this could mean that

> spiritual people are not subject to the law because they voluntarily fulfil the law through the love that the Holy Spirit pours into their hearts. It might also mean that the acts of a person who is driven by the Holy Spirit [cf Rom. 8.14] are said to be more acts of the Holy Spirit than of that person. And since the Holy Spirit is not subject to the law, it follows that acts of this kind, insofar as they are from the Holy Spirit, are not subject to the law, in accordance with 2 Cor. 3.17, 'where the Spirit of the Lord is, there is freedom'.[111]

In his commentary on the same passage, Thomas spells out the mutuality of the relationship between the just person and the Spirit when he observes that 'the just are not subject to the law, because the movement and prompting of the Holy Spirit who is in them is their own prompting, since love inclines one to the same object that the law commands'.[112]

Augustine's monition mentioned earlier in the text that moderation is called for in the increasing of church obligations for the faithful, to prevent making their life unduly burdensome (cf Mk 7.1–13), had obvious implications for those in authority; and Thomas offers a rich exegesis of Mt 20.25–28 along these lines, where Jesus is showing his disciples how authority is abused among the Gentiles by some of these lording it as tyrants over others, climaxing with Jesus's strong conclusion, 'this must not be so among you'. This, in turn, leads Thomas to admonish ecclesiastics, the rulers in the church, and to recall their duty both to the church and to the Holy Spirit, concluding that '*If anyone wants to preside in the Church of the Holy Spirit* he should be as a minister, as 1 Pet. 4.10 commands: "Like good stewards of the manifold grace of God, serve one another with whatever gift each of you has received". '[113] As Congar wrote of the government of the church by both the Spirit and by the college of bishops, 'these two governments are adapted to each other, the government by the hierarchy only favoring from the outside the inner deep action of the Spirit of Christ'.[114] All in the church is ordained to this purpose, and by the Holy Spirit of God himself. This confirms Thomas's theology of the church as being a constituent part of the secondary element of the New Law of the Spirit, and as such it bears out Grabman's description of the twofold analysis of the New Law in the *Summa* as being of capital importance in Thomas's concept of the church.[115]

An entirely appropriate confirmation of this consideration which we are proposing as Thomas's third constant of the Holy Spirit, that the church is 'the Church of the Holy Spirit', is to be found in his discussion of the Apostles' Creed, and specifically of its article, 'I believe in the Holy Catholic Church'. Thomas begins his reflections on this by pointing out that 'the Creed is produced by the authority of the whole Church, and this cannot err, because it is "*governed by the Holy Spirit*", who is the Spirit of truth (Jn 16.13)'.[116] Turning to the article concerning the church, Thomas then explains. 'If we say, "in the holy catholic Church", this should be understood as our faith being directed to *the Holy Spirit who sanctifies the Church*, so the meaning is "I believe in the Holy Spirit making the Catholic Church holy"'.[117]

Here, in a phrase, is why Thomas can understand the church which Christ founded as the church of God's Holy Spirit. Of course, ultimately the church, like all creation, is the work of the divine Trinity as a whole, but, as Emery explains, 'The Spirit is sent to the Church by the Father and the Son: this mission expresses and reflects, at the level of the economy, the eternal origin of the Holy Spirit from the Father and the Son'.[118] In fact, the church's sanctification is particularly associated with the Holy Spirit because, as Thomas points out, the Spirit proceeds within the Trinity as Love and as a result he is fittingly seen as the gift which confers holiness.[119] As Emery specifies, 'The Holy Spirit is the gift poured forth by Christ to sanctify the Church and lead her to the Father'.[120] In addition, Paul's description of Christ as 'the head of the Church' (Eph. 1.22) enabled Thomas further to explain by comparison that the Holy Spirit is 'the heart of the Church'. The head is clearly outstanding with respect to the external members of the body, he explains, but 'the heart has a hidden influence. Therefore, the Holy Spirit is compared to the heart, since he invisibly gives the Church life and unity'.[121]

From all this, we can see how in Thomas's ecclesiology, the church is a perfect fit for the Spirit, because it exists precisely to be acted in, and upon, by the Spirit of Christ, as a component of the secondary element of the New Law of the Gospel. And just as every manifestation of the Spirit is for the benefit of the church, so also (and primarily) Thomas's 'Church of the Holy Spirit' as a whole exists as the Holy Spirit's instrument within the dispensation of salvation.

## CONCLUSION

From our examination of what we have suggested are Constants of the Holy Spirit which in Thomas's thought operate consistently in the Spirit's influence in the lives of God's children, it is evident that for Thomas, the Holy Spirit is a spirit of order in a much more profound sense than even Benz, commenting on Joachism, appears to have understood, when he wrote that 'the Spirit is no free, wild inner force; it is committed to history and to the Church, a "Spirit of Order" '.[122] In our following final chapter, we shall explore whether there is one all-inclusive characteristic of the Spirit which can account for all his influence on the moral behaviour and actions of God's sons and daughters, and we shall propose that this is to be found in the Holy Spirit's role within the ordering, imparting and fulfilling of God's all-embracing design of loving wisdom.

## NOTES

1. '*Ecclesia Spiritus sancti*'. See *In Matth*. 20, lect. 2 (M1668), Kimball, 675, and below, pp. xx.
2. *In Job* 33, lect. 1.
3. C. Spicq, *Esquisse d'une histoire de l'exégèse latine au moyen âge* (Paris, 1944), 225–6.
4. *ST* II-II.176.2 obj. 4.
5. *In Hierem, In Prol. B. Hieron*.
6. Principium Fratris Thomae de Aquino quando incepit Parisiis ut baccelarius biblicus, in P. Mandonnet, *Opuscula Omnia* (Paris 1827), IV, p. 482.
7. *In Matth*. 1, lect. 6. (M 159). Kimball, 57.
8. *In Matth*. 3, lect. 1 (M 278). Kimball, 99.
9. *In Matth*. 2, lect. 4 (M 225). Kimball, 79.
10. *In Tit*. 1, lect. 3 (M 30).
11. *In 2 Cor*. 12, lect. 5 (M 505).
12. *In Joann*. 3, lect. 2, 1 (M453).
13. *In Joann*. 1, lect. 10, 1 (M 202).
14. Dominic Legge, *The Trinitarian Christology of St Thomas Aquinas* (Oxford: Oxford University Press, 2017), p. 132.
15. Legge, p. 3.
16. Legge, pp. 201–2.
17. Legge, pp. 202–4.
18. *In Joann*. 3, lect. 6, 4 (M 543).
19. *In Joann*. 1, lect. 10, 1 (M 201).
20. See above, pp. 33–35.
21. *In Is* 11, lect. unic.
22. *In Joann*. 1, lect. 14, 4 (M 272–3).
23. *In Is*. 11, lect. unic.
24. See above, pp. 35–36.
25. *In Joann*. 10, lect. 5, 1 (M 1429).

26. *In Joann.* 7, lect. 2, 4 (M 1037). On the phrase from Ambrosiaster, see Migne *PL* 17, 245, and Alszeghy, *Nova Creatura*, 194–8.
27. *In Joann.* 6, lect. 8, 5. (M 992).
28. *ST* III, 7, 6.
29. *ST* III.7.5.
30. *In Matt.* 4, lect. 1 (M 310). Kimball, 112.
31. *In Joann.* 6, lect. 6, 7 (M 959). Cf *Comp theol,* cap 212 (M 420). On this Christological theme in Thomas, see B. Lonergan, 'St Thomas' Theory of Operation', *TS* 3 (1942) 391ff; H. Dondaine, 'A propos d'Avicenne et de saint Thomas. De la causalité dispositive à la causalité instrumentale', *RevThom* 51 (1951) 441–53; Y. M.-J. Congar, *Esquisse du Mystère de l'Eglise* (Paris, 1953), 76–7.
32. See above, pp. 56–58, especially 58.
33. *ST* III, 8.1 ad 1.
34. *ST* III, 7, 1 ad 3. Cf *De Verit.*, q.29, a, 1 ad 9.
35. NRSV 'I consecrate myself'.
36. *In Joann.* 17, lect. 4, 3 (M 2231).
37. *ST* III.34.1 ad 3.
38. *ST* III.8.1 ad 2. See above, p. 23.
39. *In Matth.* 16, lect. 2 (M 1374). Kimball, 561. Cf *In Joann.* 6, lect. 8, 10 (M 1004).
40. *In Joann.* 17, lect. 4 3 (M 2231).
41. *ST* II-II.14.2 ad 3.
42. *In Eph* 4, lect. 3 (M 205).
43. *In Joann.* 1, lect. 10, 1 (M 202).
44. *ST* III, 8, 1, arg. 1.
45. *ST* III, 8, 1 ad 1.
46. *In Gal* 3, lect. 2 (M 127).
47. *ST* III.26.6.
48. *ST* III, 6, 6 ad 3.
49. *In Joann.* 17, lect. 4, 3 (M 223).
50. *ST* III, 7, 1 ad 3.
51. *ST* III, 7, 6.
52. *ST* III, 7, 5 ad 2.
53. See above, p. 53.
54. *In Joann.* 14, lect. 4, 3 (M 1916).
55. *In Joann.* 14, lect. 6, 6 (M 1958–9). Emphasis added.
56. Ibid.
57. *In 1 Cor.* 2, lect.2 (M 100). Cf *In Joann.* 14, lect. 6, 6 (M 1957).
58. *In Rom.* 8, lect. 3 (M 643).
59. *In Rom.* 8, lect. 3 (M 636).
60. *In Rom.* 8, lect. 3 (M 644).
61. *ST* II-II.121.1.
62. *In Gal* 4, lect. 2 (M 209).
63. *In Joann.* 3, lect. 1, 4 (M 442).

64. *In Joann.* 15, lect. 5, 7 (M 2062).
65. *In Matth.* 28 (M 2465). Kimball, 964, mistakenly omits 'not'.
66. *ST* III, prologue.
67. *ST* II-II.124.5 ad 1.
68. Tertullian, *de pudicitia,* XXI, 17, *PL* 2, 1026. Cf. David Rankin, *Tertullian and the Church*, Cambridge (Cambridge University Press, 1995), 115.
69. Nicholas Afanasief, *The Church of the Holy Spirit* (Notre Dame, Indiana: University of Notre Dame Press, 2007).
70. *ST* I-II, 106, 4.
71. Diarmaid MacCulloch, *A History of Christianity. The First Three Thousand Years* (London: Penguin, 2010), 410–11.
72. The literature on Joachim and Joachimism is considerable. An informative recent study is Marjorie Reeves, *Influence of Prophecy in the Later Middle Ages: A Study in Joachimism*, new ed. (University of Notre Dame Press, 1993). See also, Warwick Gould and Marjorie Reeves, *Joachim of Fiore and the myth of the eternal evangel in the nineteenth and twentieth centuries,* ed. rev and enlarged (Oxford: Oxford University Press, 2001). For earlier studies, see F. Russo, *Bibliografia Gioachimita* (Florence, 1954). An excellent study is to be found in chapter 3 of R. Manselli's *La "Lectura super apocalipsim" di Pietro di Giovanni Olivi. Ricerche sull' escatologismo medioevale* (Rome 1955), 82–134. See also the informative article by M. J. Bloomfield, 'Joachim of Flora. A critical Survey of his Canon, Teaching, Sources, Biography and Influence', in *Traditio* 13 (1957) 249–311; and H. Richard Niebuhr, 'The Doctrine of the Trinity and the Unity of the Church', *Theology Today* 3 (1946) 371–84.
73. MacCullough, 410.
74. M. W. Bloomfield and M. E, Reeve, 'The Penetration of Joachism into Northern Europe', *Speculum* 29 (1954) 772–3.
75. *ST* I-II.106.4.
76. Ibid, obj. 2.
77. *ST* I-II.106.3 ad 2.
78. *ST* I-II.106.3, obj 3 et ad 3.
79. *ST* I-II.106.3, obj 4 et ad 4.
80. Smalley, 292.
81. Aquinas, *Liber contra impugnantes Dei cultum et religionem*; trans. John Procter, O.P., *An Apology for the Religious Orders* (London: Sands & Co., 1902).
82. Healy in Weinanty, and so on, 8.
83. *ST* I-II.106.1. Cf above, pp. 82–83.
84. Baglow, Christopher T., *"Modus et Forma": A New Approach to the Exegesis of Saint Thomas Aquinas with an Application to the* Lectura super Epistolam ad Ephesios (Rome: Pontifical Biblical Institute, 2002), *Analect.a Biblica* 149, 10. See also M Grabmann, *Die Lehre des heiligen Thomas von Aquin von der Kirche als Gotteswerk* (Regensburg: C. J. Manz, 1903); Yves Congar, *Thomas d'Aquin: sa vision de la théologie et de l'Eglise* (London: Variorum Reprints, 1984); and O.-H. Pesch, 'Thomas Aquinas and Contemporary Theology', in Kerr, *Contemplating,* 185–216.

85. Baglow, 148.
86. Baglow, 180.
87. Baglow, 239.
88. Vauthier, E., 'Le Saint-Esprit principe d'unité de l'Église d'après saint Thomas d'Aquin', *MScRel* 5(1948) 175–96; 6 (1949) 54–80.
89. *In Joann.* 6, lect. 7.
90. *In Matth.* 20, lect. 2 (M1668), Kimball, 675; *In Eph* 1, lect. 4 (M 33).
91. *ST* III.8.1 ad 3.
92. *De sortibus ad Dominum Jacobum de Burgo,* in *Opuscula Theologica*, vol. 1 (Torino: Marietti, 1954), 157–67.
93. *In Ps.* 30, lect. 12.
94. *In Eph* 1, lect. 4 (M 33). Emphasis added. For further detail, and on Bede, cf *ST* II-II.95.8.
95. *ST* II-II.177.1.
96. *ST* II-II.95.8.
97. See above, pp. 72–3.
98. *In Ps.* 30, lect. 12.
99. *De sortibus*, cap 5 (M 670).
100. *De sortibus,* ibid.
101. *Quodl.* 12, q. 23, a.1. emphasis added.
102. A. Dondaine – J. Peters, 'Jacques de Tonengo et Gifredus d'Anagni auditeurs de saint Thomas', *Archivum Fratrum Praedicatorum*, Rome, 29 (1959), 66.
103. E. Roland, 'Election des évêques', in *DTC*, t. 4/2, coll 2269–72.
104. *In Joann.*, 2, lect. 2, 6 (M 388); *ST* II-II.100.1 obj 1 et ad 1.
105. See pp. 82–83.
106. *ST* III.72.12. *sed contra*. Emphasis added.
107. *ST* II-II.189.1 ad 4.
108. ST I-II.107.4.
109. Ibid.
110. *In 1 Tim* 1, lect., 3 (M 23).
111. *ST* I-II.93.5 ad 1.
112. *In Gal* 5. Lect. 5 (M 318).
113. *In Matth.* 20, lect. 2 (M 1668). Emphasis added. Kimball, 675.
114. Y. M.-J, Congar, *Esquisses du mystère,* 88, n. 2.
115. *ST* I-II.106.1. Grabman, *Die Lehre*, 11, 89–90, 97–8, 158–60 and so forth.
116. *ST* II-II.1.9 *sed contra*. Emphasis added.
117. *ST* II-II.1.9 ad 5. Emphasis added. Cf Ch. Journet, *L'Eglise du Verbe incarné* (Desclée de Brouwer, 1951), II, 595, n. 2.
118. Gilles Emery, The Holy Spirit, in P. McCosker and D.Turner, edd., *The Cambridge Companion to the Summa theologiae* (Cambridge: Cambridge University Press, 2016), 131.
119. *ST* I, 43, 7.
120. Emery, 134.
121. *ST* III.8.1 ad 3.
122. Benz, *Joachim-Studien*, 88.

*Chapter 6*

# All-Embracing Wisdom

In addition to the three 'constants' of God's Holy Spirit through which we have found Aquinas regularly expressing the Spirit's activities, there is one theme which finds a central and universal significance in all his writings on human moral behaviour, and that is the wisdom of the Holy Spirit, as he expresses, shares and fulfils God's loving purpose in creation. In this final chapter of our study, we aim to explore how Thomas identifies and understands this loving dynamism of the Holy Spirit in human moral action, in terms of God's all-embracing and interlocking wisdom.

## 'DISCERNING WISDOM'

The modern study of Christian spirituality has stressed the importance of some means of verifying, and authenticating, the influence of the Holy Spirit at work in the minds and wills of God's children, and thus distinguishing between the 'good spirits' and the 'bad spirits', by exercising the 'discernment of spirits', to invoke the traditional terminology based on the biblical injunction to 'test the spirits to see whether they are from God (1 Jn 4.1; cf 1 Cor. 12.10).[1] This need was particularly felt within the Catholic Church during the controversy in the 1950s over the movement of 'situation ethics' which stemmed from existentialist thought and to which Pope Pius XII took serious moral exception.[2] As Josef Fuchs wrote at the time, 'If moral theology is to take the religious importance of the "situation" seriously, it will have to work on developing the doctrine of the discernment of spirits'.[3]

Systematic rules to discern and separate 'good spirits' from 'evil, or bad, spirits', or influences, as these operate in the individual's mind and feelings, were developed from the inclusion by Paul of 'the discernment of spirits' in his list of charismatic gifts given by the Spirit 'for the common good' (1 Cor. 12.4–12); and they have become an established feature of modern spiritual theology. As is clear from Mark McIntosh's historical survey, Aquinas had no such rules, in the sense in which that term is understood today.[4] Nor, interestingly, does Thomas ascribe any particular spiritual significance to the classic biblical texts which were later commonly cited and applied in developing the science of the discernment of spirits: namely, John's advice 'not to believe every spirit but to test the spirits' (1 Jn 4.1); Paul's warning that Satan can turn himself 'into a spirit of light' (2 Cor. 11.14); and Paul's listing of 'the discernment of spirits' among the Spirit's charisms given to the church (1 Cor. 12.10).

In all these passages, Thomas tends in his Scripture Commentaries to be faithful to their context and to accept them in their literal sense of referring only to visible or audible apparitions, without extrapolating them into spiritual principles, as many others have done. It appears, in fact, that for Thomas the wisdom which we have found the Spirit of God regularly communicating externally and internally to all God's children requires no further authentication, especially if Paul is to be accepted that the spiritual person judges all things and is personally to be judged by no one else (1 Cor. 2.15). From this perspective, the whole purpose of the wisdom of the Spirit is to be discerning, rather than to be discerned.

On the other hand, Thomas does have a remarkably rich doctrine of the idea of discernment in moral behaviour, an activity which he traces directly from the virtue of wisdom and the Holy Spirit's Gift of wisdom which we have already considered.[5] Well away from the whole context of spirits and visions, whether good or malign, his commentary is revealing on the instruction contained in 1 Tim. 5.21 to 'test everything', holding fast to what is good and abstaining from every form of evil.

> When he says, 'test everything' he shows how they should behave towards everything, simply using discernment in everything. As Rom.12.1–2 (Vg) puts it, 'reasonable worship . . . so that you may discern what is the will of God – what is good and acceptable and perfect'. In this matter, there should be diligent examination, choice of the good, and rejection of the bad.[6]

Thomas's confirmatory citing here of Rom.12.2 about being transformed in order to get to discern the will of God is richly developed in his Commentary on Romans, where he notes that with the beginning of chapter 12, with its famous 'therefore' in 12.1, Paul is moving systematically from his doctrinal theology to his moral theology. Having expounded the themes of the need, and the power and the origin of grace in the earlier part of his letter, Paul now turns with chapter 12 to 'moral instruction', guiding his readers on how to 'use' that grace in their moral behaviour.⁷ The reference to 'using' grace cannot but recall for us Thomas's systematic development in the *Summa* of the New law of the Gospel in which the secondary aspect of the new law is to enable us either to 'receive' or to 'use' the grace imparted to us by the indwelling presence of the Holy Spirit which is the primary element of that law. As he writes there, 'the new law has some elements which dispose us for the grace of the Holy Spirit, and which refer to the use of this grace, and these are as it were secondary in the New Law'.⁸

And the parallel continues. Christians, for Paul, were not to be *con*formed to this world but to be *trans*formed in seeking to receive or to make progress in the grace of the Holy Spirit, so that, thus equipped, they might 'test', or 'probe', what was the will of God for them. There is a very strong causal connection, for Thomas. between this re-formation of a person's mind through the grace of the Holy Spirit, and what it enables that person subsequently to do; and he invokes a favourite parallel of the discerning, or discriminating, quality of healthy taste to illustrate this connection. 'So, whoever has a right and healthy affect, with their sense renewed through grace, has a right judgement about what is good'. Hence, those who are spiritual 'discern all things' (1 Cor. 2.14). They do not have to apply any rules of discernment to pass judgement or to discern the goodness or badness of a course of action, because for Thomas, this power of discernment is precisely the spiritual person's reaction to a given situation, and it derives 'naturally', or rather, 'co-naturally', from the grace of the Holy Spirit which the person possesses. As Thomas went on to explain, Paul said they were to be transformed in order to test, 'that is, in order to know by experiencing' what was God's will and what was good; 'in other words, he wants us to will what is truly good, and he points us towards this by his commandments'.

It is different for those whose spiritual taste is defective; they do not possess a correct judgement of flavours, but at times, they detest sweet things and enjoy distasteful things, whereas the person who has a healthy taste has a right judgement of flavours. So, the one whose desire is corrupted and conformed to worldly things does not have a right judgement of what is good; whereas, the one whose desire is right and healthy, having one's reason renewed through the grace of the Holy Spirit, has a right judgement of what is good.⁹

Here, in summary, is what Thomas conceived to be the general teaching of 'the Apostle' on Christian moral behaviour. The child of God whose mind is renewed by the grace of the Holy Spirit acquires thereby a taste for God's will, and can recognize it by its sweet flavour. By contrast, the person whose mind is not thus renewed lacks this healthy taste for wisdom and finds God's will bitter to the taste. Eccl 6.21 Vg. sums it up beautifully for Thomas's purpose. 'How bitter wisdom is to the untaught!'.¹⁰

Not just one's spiritual taste, however, but also one's sense of spiritual sight is refined by the influence of the Spirit, thus enabling one now to see everything in the light of the final purpose of all creation; that is: seeing and sharing God; judging everything in the light of God's own wisdom; and then deciding and acting accordingly. In the foundation biblical text of the Gifts of the Spirit in Isaiah 11, it was promised of the Messiah that 'he shall not judge by what his eyes see' (Isa. 11.3), and this became further applied by Thomas to all who are driven by the Spirit. This would enable them to heed the warning of Jesus not to judge by appearances, but to have a right judgement (Jn 7.24). For, as Thomas explains, the person who is wise has insight, and is able to penetrate through superficial, or surface, appearances to the underlying reality, to those causes which give rise to actions and events.[11] Interestingly, Dietrich Bonhoeffer in his *Ethics* has a useful expansion of this insight, when he characterizes the wise person 'as one who sees reality as it is, and who sees into the depths of things. . . . To recognize the significant in the factual is wisdom'.[12]

Thus, the 'sense of discernment' is to be found in Thomas's moral theology, particularly in his teaching on the discernment which comes from wisdom; and, as we have seen, he likes to develop his thought on discerning wisdom in terms of the analogy of healthy and unhealthy taste, judging the term *sapientia*, wisdom, to derive from *sapĕre*, which means to savour, and *sapor*, which means 'taste'. These terms relating to the sense of taste provide him with an alternative means of conveying the special character of sapiential knowledge and experience, as contrasted with rational activity; while the inherent connections between the sense of taste and the state of one's good or bad health or palate which influences one's taste give scope to express his thinking on connaturality and its discerning, or discriminating, 'natural' consequences in considering possible choices in moral behaviour. 'Judgement about what is good in human affairs', he maintains, 'should not be taken from the foolish, but from the wise (*sapientibus*); just as judgement about flavors (*saporibus*) is taken from those whose sense of taste is in good order'.[13]

## FOOLISH 'UNWISDOM'

That is all in theory. It is sadly to be conceded, however, that, whatever the ideal is with regard to the qualities and characteristics of the Holy Spirit's discerning wisdom, which is found in the church's members, these are too often absent, rather than present in reality. Men and women are not all, or not always, 'spiritual'; and to disregard the significance of this fact of life in Thomas's theology would be to run the danger of distorting his heady doctrine of the freedom of God's family into one of undiscerning licence.

Bernard Lonergan is categorical in expressing a view of Thomas with which not all the latter's admirers would agree, that 'in estimating human nature St Thomas was a whole-hearted pessimist. With conviction he would repeat, *numerus stultorum infinitus* (the number of fools is infinite, Eccl 1.15 Vg)'.[14] Other students of Thomas would prefer to align themselves with Eleonore Stump, when she opines that 'Aquinas has an essentially optimistic attitude towards human beings and human nature'.[15] Lonergan's sweeping generalization may not be warranted by Thomas's writings as a whole, yet Thomas does observe in passing that 'the wise are small in number',[16] and he is well aware that people are capable of 'for ever opposing the Holy Spirit' (Acts 7.41) or 'quenching the fervor of the Spirit', whether in themselves or in others (1 Thess. 5.19).[17] Looking back to the Old Testament case of Jephthah, for instance (Judg. 11.29–40), who vowed, in gratitude for his victory over the Ammonites, that he would sacrifice to God the first living thing he would meet, and who then felt constrained, on first meeting his daughter, to sacrifice her, Thomas agreed with the traditional verdict ascribed to Jerome that 'Jephthah was a fool (*stultus*) to make the vow, and a knave (*impius*) to keep it'.[18] In a society highly sensitive to the making and keeping of vows, it must have been satisfactory to his Dominican and other students to hear from the learned Brother Thomas that it is praiseworthy to be inspired to make a vow by the prompting of the Holy Spirit: 'the Spirit of the Lord *was* on Jephthah' (Judg. 11.29). But in the formulation that his vow actually took, Thomas continued, Jephthah was 'following his own spirit': he was lacking in discretion to make such an indiscriminate promise, to sacrifice what he should not have sacrificed.[19]

The term 'foolish' which Thomas regularly uses in some situations – he condemned the views of the Joachists as 'the height of foolishness' (*stultissimum*) – does not express just an exasperated dismissal on his part; it is a theological judgement on diagnosing in Jephthah and the like the absence of the wisdom of the Holy Spirit.[20] So, when it came to Herod in his turn incautiously offering his daughter whatever she wanted, with disastrous results for John the Baptist (Mt 14.7–10), Thomas returned a similar verdict of foolishness and a total lack of discernment in making a wrongful promise, as well as subsequent 'perjury' in keeping it.[21] Jesus himself, Thomas observed, was much wiser in teaching us to be more circumspect in making promises. When the mother of James and John approached him to ask for 'something', and Jesus asked her what it was (Mt 20.20–1), he showed in his action as well as his teaching that he was 'wiser than all the others' and that someone was here greater than Solomon and Solomon's wisdom! For even Solomon had granted a vague request from his mother, but at least he later had the good sense to revoke his rash promise (1Kgs [LXX 3 Kgdms] 2.19–24), because he did possess some wisdom, after all.[22]

Interestingly, Thomas systematically inserts the resistance to the power of the Holy Spirit into his teaching on wisdom, in exploring the existence and prevalence of human 'unwisdom', technically *in-sipientia*, or foolishness (*stultitia*). Following his treatment of the Gift of wisdom in the *Summa*, he devotes a formal question to foolishness, which he says is 'opposed to wisdom', probably influenced by Gregory the Great's comment that wisdom is given to counter foolishness.[23] In this, he also drew heavily on Isidore of Seville, the sixth- and seventh-century bishop whose encyclopaedic work, the *Etymologies*, provided the scholastics with copious classical material on the derivations and associations of individual words. As Thomas thus explains, 'Stupidity is fittingly contrasted with wisdom, because, as Isidore says, "wisdom (*sapientia*) is taken from savor (*sapor*)", because, just as our taste is suited to distinguishing the flavors of food, similarly the wise person is suited to discriminating between things and causes'.[24]

How, then, do the unwise fit into Thomas's scheme of things? According to Isidore, the un-wise person (*in-sipiens*) contrasts with the wise person in lacking the taste for discernment. So, unwisdom seems to be the same as foolishness.[25] Not all foolishness is sinful, of course, Thomas explains. Some arises from a natural indisposition to make a judgement, as in the case of those out of their minds (*amentes*).

> But it can also happen that a person so immerses their attention in earthly matters that they become unsuited to appreciate godly matters. 1 Cor. 2.14 (Vg) observes that 'the animal person does not perceive matters which belong to the Spirit of God', just as sweet things do not taste so to someone with an infected taste. That kind of stupidity is a sin.[26]

It is worth recalling here Thomas's treatment of 2 Cor. 11, justifying Paul for his boasting, which we have already considered in connection with the New Law of the Gospel, since it brings out very well in this new context the connection between foolishness and the lack of discerning wisdom, and its moral significance.[27] Paul decides to commend himself, although he realizes that in general it is morally wrong to do so, and he is wrestling with the dilemma, and with what the Corinthians will think of his apparently sinful behaviour. Thomas explains:

> Moral precepts are concerned with actions to be performed. But since these are individual and variable, they cannot all be specified by one general common statement and rule. Sometimes in an emergency one has to act in spite of the general rule. *Now, when something is done in this way despite the general rule, those who are wise consider the reason for this and are not disturbed. Nor do they think it unwise behaviour. But those who have no discernment, and are*

*less wise, do not consider the reason for this being done, and they are upset and think it foolish behaviour.*

For instance, "thou shalt not kill" is a moral precept; and yet sometimes it is necessary to kill bad people. When this happens, those who are wise approve, or at least do not think it a wrong action; whereas those who are foolish or heretical condemn it, saying it is a bad action.

Now, in this case the general moral law is that a person should not commend themselves, since Proverbs says (27.2), 'Let another praise you, and not your own mouth'. But it can happen in some case that one does commend oneself despite this general rule, and that he or she does so praiseworthily, and yet *those who are undiscerning consider this unwisdom.* Consequently, since a case had arisen in which Paul had to commend himself, he pleads with them not to reckon it to him as unwisdom.[28]

'Those who have no discernment, and are less wise, do not consider the reason for this being done, and they are upset and think it is foolish behaviour'. In this observation, we have in a nutshell Thomas's teaching on discerning wisdom; that wisdom which he saw Paul advocate to the Romans as the centre of his moral teaching on the 'use' of grace, but which Paul appears to have found sadly lacking in his Corinthians, as is evident from the above passage. Thomas's final word on unwisdom might be considered his observation that 'human wisdom is wisdom, as long as it is subject to divine wisdom. But when it withdraws from God, then it turns into unwisdom (*insipientiam*)'.[29]

## THE PRIMACY OF WISDOM

The basis of such wise discernment is to be found, for Thomas, in its intimate connection with his teaching on connaturality. Possessing something in common with what is being considered, one has, as a consequence, the inherent capacity to recognize what one is looking for, whether it be the truth, the good, the right course of action – or even God, since for Christians the pinnacle of such co-natural affinity is what 2 Pet. 1.4 describes as their 'becoming participants in the divine nature'. Pinsent describes this as involving 'a modification of one's own stance towards a thing based . . . on a sharing or participation of God's stance towards the same thing'.[30]

In the light of this conclusion that wise 'discernment', deriving from connaturality with the Holy Spirit, occupies a central position in Thomas's moral doctrine, it is worth being aware that this meaning of the Latin term *discretio*, that is, 'discernment', seems to have been overshadowed recently by some modern Thomist studies which focus on the transferred meaning of *discretio* as 'discretion', or as individual discreet judgement, with a view to seeing this as an early equivalent of the virtue of prudence more readily connected with Aristotle. This is argued for by Deman in his commentary on Thomas's treatise on prudence;[31] and later, Dingjan's historical study, entitled *Discretio*, researched the use of the term in patristic and monastic sources, and concluded that in time, the idea of *discretio* understood as discretion, came to be replaced historically by the Aristotelian term 'prudence' as 'the idea of prudence was definitively chosen in preference to discretion, which was finally eliminated'.[32]

Deman's wish to establish a historical succession from *discretio*-as-discretion to prudence seems to have led him to misunderstand several passages where Thomas clearly uses the Latin term in its sense of discernment. This is notably the case for Deman – but not Dingjan[33] – in connection with the liturgical phrase, 'the salt of *discretio*', which is applied to the lips of baptismal candidates in the course of the ceremony. Thomas had commented in his early *Commentary on the Sentences* that 'the "salt of *discretio*" is placed on the mouth, so that every word of the faithful is seasoned with salt', on which Deman, in turn, explains that Thomas 'calls baptismal salt "the salt of discretion", apparently meaning that its role is a matter for discretion in controlling human wisdom and thus inspiring words which are irreproachable'.[34] However, this interpretation by Deman does not harmonize with Thomas's explicit explanation elsewhere of the use of salt in Old Testament sacrifices ('with all your offerings you shall offer salt', Lev 2.13; cu Mk 9.49–50): that it not only preserves the object from becoming corrupted, but that it also symbolizes the 'discernment of wisdom'.[35] And this, in turn, is confirmed by Thomas's commentary on Paul's appeal to the Romans (Rom. 12.1) to present their bodies as 'a sacrifice, holy and acceptable to God.' As he explains:

> In the preparation of a sacrifice, salt was applied, and it signifies the discernment of wisdom, as Col 4.5–6 teaches. 'Conduct yourselves wisely towards outsiders. Let your speech always be gracious, seasoned with salt, so that you may know how you ought to answer everyone'. And this is why Paul here in Romans speaks of 'reasonable worship', namely, to present your bodies to God as a victim, either by martyrdom or by abstinence or by any work of justice, but always with discernment.[36]

As we then proceed to consult Thomas's Commentary on Colossians on the verse, he cites earlier, we find some of his most informative remarks on the subject packed in there with appropriate scriptural confirmations and expansions from elsewhere. The Colossians, Thomas explains, were to 'walk in wisdom with outsiders', that is, conduct themselves wisely towards unbelievers, for 'God loves no one so much as one who lives with wisdom' (Eccl 6.5 Vg). Moreover, they were not just to walk, but also to talk with wisdom.

Their speech was to be graceful, and it was also to be discerning – which is why Paul described it as 'seasoned with salt'.

> By salt is understood discernment, because every dish which is seasoned with salt is tasty, whereas every undiscerning action is insipid and distasteful, As Jesus said, 'Have salt in yourselves, and be at peace with one another' (Mk 9.49), knowing, that is, as Paul writes, how to answer everyone. For it is one thing to give an answer to wise people, and quite another to answer unwise people (*insipientibus*). As Prov. 21.4 warns us, 'Do not answer fools according to their folly, or you will be a fool yourself'; whereas 1 Pet 3.15 exhorts us, 'Always be ready to make your defense to anyone who demands from you an account of the hope that is in you'. [37]

It seems clear, then, that for Thomas, salt as a scriptural symbol has one fundamental meaning, the discernment, or the healthy sense of taste, which comes to the Christian with wisdom. This the baptismal candidate receives in order to be able to give a good account of their faith, but always in the light of the quality and capacity of those with whom they are speaking, as Paul did, making himself all things to all people (1 Cor. 9.22) and recognizing that the Corinthians, for instance, could stomach only milk, not solid food (1 Cor. 3.1–3). Even then, Paul continues, they were not ready, since they were still of the flesh; that is, Thomas explains, they could not take the things of the Spirit, but had a taste only for the things of the flesh. This discerning wisdom is the salt on our offering of our body to God as a victim, discerning the best means of giving expression to the grace of the Spirit in us, and also, in our acts of virtue, testing and proving by the taste of experiencing the sweetness of God's will and wisdom for each of us here and now.

This primacy of discerning wisdom springs, of course, from Thomas's, and Paul's, whole understanding of 'the spiritual person', which we have already examined.[38] Because he or she is 'one spirit' with God through the charity poured out in their heart by their reception of the Holy Spirit, they see all things from God's point of view, which is why Thomas can note that it is the affective union of the heart with God through charity which causes the affective knowledge and judgement of the mind through wisdom.[39] We might express the continuity of charity and wisdom by saying that charity overflows from the will to the intellect and in so doing it becomes wisdom, contributing its own orientation and discernment to all the other virtues and Gifts which one possesses by the grace of the Holy Spirit. It is by the habit of charity which God's children possess that they have a deep-rooted and fundamental bias towards recognizing in all things, individually and as a whole, their vertical relationship and wise orientation to God, and therefore 'one who has charity has a right judgment, both as regards what can be known as well as what can be done'. Charity cascades from the heart to influence all cognitive activity and all the virtues and Gifts that one possesses, which is why Paul could pray in Phil. 1. 9–10 that the charity of the Philippians might 'overflow more and more' precisely 'with knowledge and full insight', so that they would then approve the better things.[40]

It is by discerning wisdom, then, that God's children can find the wisdom of God in everything, recognizing the eternal wisdom refracted to them in the formulations of law, whether natural, divine or human; and applying that wisdom in a multiplicity of variable and varying situations, with discernment both of the external law and also of the total situation of which that law is just one significant factor.[41] In acting thus, or, better, being acted upon, or 'driven' thus through the prompting of the Spirit of God, God's sons and daughters not only recognize but also create and put into effect that universal salvific will of their Father for all things, individually and collectively, which comprises God's eternal law and the divine wisdom. Starting from the Bible, as one commentator remarked, 'the writings which we know as the Wisdom literature are the fruit of continued and developing reflection in Israel on the raw material of human experience, and of attempts to discern patterns in life, and structures and rules for living'.[42]

## 'THE SPEECH OF WISDOM'

In considering how the Holy Spirit distributes God's wisdom among God's sons and daughters, Thomas finds a further systematic place for the charisms which Paul described as provided by the Spirit to the church 'for the common good' (1 Cor. 12.7). This applies particularly to what Paul lists, according to the Vulgate, as 'the speech of wisdom' (*sermo sapientiae*), and what the NRSV refers to as 'the utterance of wisdom', given to some in the community as a 'manifestation of the Spirit for the common good (1 Cor. 12.8)'.

In his question in the *Summa* devoted to the Holy Spirit's Gift of wisdom, Thomas asks whether this gift is received by everyone who has sanctifying grace, and this query gives him the opportunity to explain that

> the wisdom in question involves a rightness of judgement in the considering and the consulting of godly matters; and from their union with the divine, people receive wisdom with regard to each of these activities in differing degrees. Some people receive as much rightness of judgement [i.e., wisdom], both in contemplating godly matters and in ordering human affairs in accordance with the divine rules, as is necessary for salvation. And this is not lacking to anyone who is, through grace, not in serious sin, since if nature is not lacking

in necessary matters, far less lacking is grace. As 1 John 2.27 teaches us, 'his anointing teaches you about all things'.

'Other people, however,' Thomas continues,

> receive the gift of wisdom to a higher degree, both as regards the contemplating of godly matters, insofar as they know and can make manifest to others some higher mysteries; and also as regards the directing of human matters in accordance with divine rules, *in being able to direct according to these rules not just themselves, but other people too.* That degree of wisdom is not common to everyone who has sanctifying grace; it pertains more to the graces given freely which the Holy Spirit 'distributes as he chooses' according to 1 Cor. 12. 8, 'to one is given through the Spirit the utterance of wisdom'.[43]

In this key passage, Thomas identifies the charismatic grace of the 'word of wisdom' as a further gift with which the Holy Spirit endows some people in a community, precisely for the purpose of enabling them to share their wisdom with others, as these may have need of it. Like all graces freely given, the speech of wisdom is for the benefit of the church, and it comes, of course, from the Holy Spirit, who, as we have seen Thomas declare more than once, is not sparing in anything which pertains to the benefit of his church.[44] Writing of wisdom and of knowledge (1 Cor.12.8; cf Rom.15.14), Thomas explains that these are not counted among the graces freely given, that is, the charisms, insofar as they are numbered among the gifts of the Holy Spirit; namely, insofar as one's mind is easily moved by the Holy Spirit towards matters pertaining to wisdom and knowledge. In this respect, these are gifts of the Holy Spirit.

> But they are counted among the graces freely given [charisms] insofar as they signify a kind of abundance of knowledge and wisdom, so that some people might not just savor godly matters for themselves, but can also instruct others, and refute opponents. So, among the graces freely given, express mention is made of "the word of wisdom" and 'the word of knowledge', because, as Augustine says, in his *de Trinitate* 'it is one thing to know just what a person ought to believe in order to reach eternal life; but it is another thing to know how this can enrich devout people and be defended against the ungodly'.

The function of 'the word of wisdom', then, is to help to influence and persuade people to become aware of godly matters and divine considerations in their lives.[45]

Further light is thrown on 'the speech of wisdom' in Thomas's detailed exegesis in his Commentary on First Corinthians of Paul's list of the charisms which are given by the Holy Spirit to some of the faithful for the common benefit (1 Cor. 12.4–11). Its function is to help achieve the salvation of other people. It is not just wisdom, Thomas, notes, but a 'word of wisdom', or a verbal communication, because it does not operate interiorly, as only God does. Its aim in communicating is to cooperate with the interior prompting of the Holy Spirit experienced by listeners in their hearts, so it requires a talent for verbal persuasion. This, in turn, requires both certainty about principles, and skill in drawing conclusions, Thomas concludes, in those areas in which we have to be persuasive; yet he carefully leaves the initiative always to the Holy Spirit, as we have seen him do in opposing appointments through the drawing of lots or simony,[46] accepting and welcoming Paul's teaching that the Spirit distributes his 'graces freely given' 'to each one individually just as the Spirit chooses' (1 Cor. 12.11).[47]

What we have in the previous chapter identified as three constants of the Holy Spirit that Thomas sees recurring in the moral action of God's children is amply demonstrated in Thomas's understanding of this charismatic speech of wisdom. Our first constant, the same Spirit ever in action, is explicitly recognized by Paul himself in his teaching the Corinthians that 'there are varieties of gifts, but the one Spirit' (1 Cor. 12.4). As Thomas explained on this verse:

> Although the gifts of graces are different, and are possessed by different people, they do not proceed from different sources, as the pagans proposed in attributing wisdom to Minerva and speech to Mercury, and likewise for the others. To exclude this, Paul adds 'but the same Spirit', namely the Holy Spirit who is the source of all graces. Ephesians 4.4 speaks of 'one body and one Spirit' and Wisdom 7.22 tells us of 'a spirit that is unique and manifold' that is, one in substance and manifold in graces.[48]

This is the same Spirit under whose influence and guidance the whole perspective of salvation history has been unfolding, and who can never contradict himself, whether in the wisdom of the law, or in the wisdom of the legislator, or in the wisdom of the individual child of God, or, finally, in the charismatic speech of wisdom.

Secondly, all these graces the Spirit distributes 'as he wills' (1 Cor. 12.11), but never in contradiction to Christ, whose Spirit he is. This is no more a constraint on the Spirit's freedom than is his influence on us a constraint on our freedom. He is the Spirit of Christ and so, as Paul affirmed in listing the Spirit's gifts, 'no one speaking by the Spirit of God ever says, "Let Jesus be cursed!", and no one can say "Jesus is Lord", except by the Holy Spirit' (1 Cor. 12.3). In support of this, Thomas invokes 1 Jn 4.3, that we know the Spirit of God in the confessing of Jesus Christ, to conclude that 'no one can sin against Jesus under the influence of the Holy Spirit'.[49]

Finally, the charism of the speech of wisdom is given by the Spirit to the church of the Holy Spirit, because the latter is not sparing in anything which pertains to the benefit (*utilitatem*) of the church, and the manifestation of the Spirit is given to each 'for the common benefit' (1 Cor. 12.7).[50]

## A SYNTHESIS OF WISDOM

At the beginning of this chapter, we noted that Aquinas does not have a doctrine of 'the discernment of spirits' as this was developing technically. It is now attractive to suggest that his teaching on the Spirit's charism of 'the speech of wisdom' could today be developed and expanded in terms of spiritual guidance and of counselling, at least to complement modern practice. Moreover, since 'the word of wisdom' is a charism given by the Holy Spirit to his church and its members as a help to penetrate and discern in contemporary situations the eternal law, or wisdom, of God, we suggest that developing this could contribute to a method of wise counselling on contemporary issues of moral behaviour.

Such a development would also be an instance of the conclusion to which this study has been progressively advancing, namely, the intellectual satisfaction and the theological significance of discerning *a synthesis of wisdom* presiding over, and pervading, the whole of Thomas Aquinas's moral teaching, or theological ethics. With the locking of the charismatic speech of wisdom into place alongside the other external and internal manifestations of wisdom, a full cycle of wisdom becomes evident as permeating Thomas's whole moral theology of the Spirit of God guiding and driving God's children. All law which deserves the name of law is the product of wisdom, and every formulation of law in human terminology, whether natural, civil or divine, is an attempt to express, however inadequately, that wisdom of God directing God's creatures at every moment and in every situation in their individual lives, which, since Augustine, we call the eternal law. Beside this wisdom refracted and reposing in formulated law, there is also received within the individual sons and daughters of God at baptism the wisdom which is a personal Gift of God's Holy Spirit; and it is this wisdom which enables God's children to discern, and then choose to enact, in every situation in their lives what is the eternal wisdom and will of God specifically for them. These two wisdoms, that of the external law and that in the heart, we have described as *complementary* expressions of the wisdom of the Holy Spirit. They converge in the acts of discernment which are prompted in the believers' minds and wills by the Spirit, as these consider the interplay between, on the one hand, the external wisdom of God expressed in the general social formulations of law, and, on the other hand, the individual's sensitivity and connaturality to

God's wisdom received from the Spirit by God's children. From the interplay, or dialectic, between these two complementary wisdoms, there emerges the act of wise discernment for the here and now which is prompted interiorly by the Spirit. If God's daughter or son recognizes and considers the Holy Spirit in the law, they complete and perfect the work of God's wisdom by applying the final determination to the law in their situation. On the other hand, if they do not discern in the external law, the Holy Spirit guiding them for this particular situation, they ignore the law by acting in spite of it (*praeter legem*), because it is not divinely intended for this situation and it is judged irrelevant to the present circumstances.

However, not every one of God's children is sufficiently equipped with this wisdom of the Spirit to judge and recognize whether or not God's wisdom is to be found in the apparently appropriate general law within every situation; and it is here that other expressions of the wisdom of the Spirit can enter into play, wisdoms which could be termed, not now complementary, but *supplementary*. The first of these is the wisdom of the lawgiver in a society who can spell out the content and implications of the general statement of law for those who are 'less wise', or less naturally equipped, to do it for themselves, as Thomas saw Moses's deputies spelling out the Law of Israel in this way for those of the people of Israel who were in need of it.[51] And, as we have now seen, the other type of supplementary wisdom is on offer from those in the community who possess the charismatic 'word of wisdom', which equips them precisely, according to Thomas, to provide direction in human matters in accordance with godly rules 'not just for themselves, but also for other people'.[52]

Exercising discernment in all one's moral choices, then, appears to evoke for Thomas the whole background panorama of his theological schema of the wisdom of God's Holy Spirit. It should not be thought, however, that such an approach leads to antinomianism, or complete subjectivism; because Thomas's conviction remains true, that 'the fervor of the will is not virtuous unless it is ordered by reason'.[53] It is not enough simply to consult and accede to one's inner awareness or individual feeling of spiritual certainty. Thomas's paradigm of wisdom permeating his whole approach to morality ensures a place for not only objective factors, including the written law, and for subjective factors, including the 'familiar', or intimate grace of the Spirit; but also for seeking wise enlightenment from other people whom the Holy Spirit has raised up in the community and who are at least equally possessed by the Spirit for this purpose, including lawgivers and charismatic counsellors.

Finally, people's ultimate guide in the discovery of religious and moral truth remains their God-given power of human reasoning. And yet, the Holy Spirit also enlightens their minds and directs their decisions by his promptings in such a way, as we have argued, that from beginning to end, the use of one's reason and the free application of one's will are no less dependent on the internal action of the Holy Spirit. Appropriately enough, the pursuit of wisdom, including moral discerning wisdom, is misconceived if it is portrayed as contentious or competing; on all sides, it proceeds from Christ's Spirit of unity who imparts all his gifts for the benefit and good of his church and all its members together.[54]

## 'ORDERING ALL THINGS WELL' (WIS 8.1)

At the end of this study of Aquinas's teaching on the role of the Holy Spirit in the moral acts of God's sons and daughters, we have concluded that Thomas's whole moral theology is centred on the theme of God's eternal dynamic wisdom emanating and deployed throughout the whole of creation, and directing this in its return to its final fulfilment in God. It is satisfying, then, to propose, as a closing confirmation of our conclusion, that Thomas found this all-embracing wisdom expressed universally in a theme which he found centrally present in both the Christian Scriptures and the philosophy of Aristotle: the theme of order *(ordo)*.

As Ménard showed well, the idea of order pervaded the whole culture and life of the Middle Ages;[55] and in this, of course, Augustine was a major source and influence. For him, peace is defined as 'the tranquility of order';[56] and God's eternal law could briefly be described as that through which everything is, as he wrote, 'extremely well ordered' *(ordinatissima)*.[57] After all, God is 'the supremely wise creator of order and supremely just orderer of all natures' *(sapientissimus conditor et iustissimus ordinator)*.[58] Moreover, for Augustine, the original sin of God's human creatures began with self-love and pride distorting the order of being between humanity and God, and resulting instantly in a radical distortion of the order within humanity itself.[59]

In his turn, Thomas followed Augustine in describing God as a supremely wise creator,[60] and he also defined all law as an 'ordering' *(ordinatio)* produced by reason.[61] He saw order as permeating the relationship of all the virtues to one another, providing an orderly connection within individual people as well as in their relationship to others.[62] Outstanding among all the intellectual virtues, of course, and giving order to them, since its object is God, is the very highest cause, namely, wisdom, which enables one to judge all lower causes and relate them in order. In a word, wisdom is an 'architectonic' virtue in relation to all the others.[63] Thomas brings this out well when he explains that

> the person whose mind is illuminated and whose feelings are kept *in order* by the Holy Spirit has a right judgment on individual matters relating to salvation.

On the other hand, the person who is not 'spiritual', also has their mind darkened and their feelings *disordered* about spiritual values; and the 'unspiritual' person cannot judge the spiritual person, just as a person awake cannot be judged by a sleeping person.[64]

Turning from Thomas's major theological source after Scripture, namely, Augustine, to his primary Greek resource, Aristotle, for the latter's teaching on wisdom and on the ordering which is characteristic of it, we find Aristotle famously observing that 'the wise person is concerned with order (*sapientis est ordinare*)'.[65] As the ability to plan, or arrange, or organize things, it is a basic metaphysical maxim which Thomas the Christian theologian found immensely congenial.[66] It is important to note, of course, that Thomas's use of Aristotelian arguments and formulae is almost invariably an a fortiori application: an 'even more so' move in his Christian reflections; and his application of the Aristotelian *sapientis est ordinare* contains riches which 'the Philosopher' could never contemplate. In his commentary on Aristotle's *Ethics*, Thomas expanded Aristotle's succinct description of wisdom by explaining that 'it is the role of the wise person to provide order, since wisdom is the most powerful perfection of the reason, and the point of reason is to be aware of order'.[67]

Thomas also adopts Aristotle's famous illustration from architecture. Since it is for the wise person to provide order and to pass judgements, and since judgement is made by the higher cause in relation to lower causes, then the wise person in any area is the one who considers the highest cause in that area, such as the architect or the master builder in the area of housebuilding (cf 1 Cor. 3.10), as contrasted with the subordinate carpenter or the bricklayer. Accordingly, Thomas continues, 'In the area of the whole of human life the prudent person is called wise insofar as they order human acts to their due end, which is why Proverbs 10.23 says that "wisdom is prudence to a person". So, the one who considers the highest cause of the whole universe, namely, God, is called supremely wise.'[68]

This concept of order (*ordo*), influenced by Augustine and Aristotle, permeates all of Thomas's works, where it is both dynamic and sapiential. The theme of emanation and return, of the process of *exitus* and *reditus*, that is, of everything proceeding from God and designed and destined to return to God, plays an important part in the order of Thomas's *Summa Theologiae*, according to Chenu; and in this, Thomas's debt to the Greek Fathers and to the Neoplatonism of Pseudo-Dennis is obvious (although Duffy is less confident).[69] As Thomas asserted, 'Whatever things come from God are ordered to each other and to God himself.'[70]

Thomas also pointed out that one cannot arrange things in order, unless one knows the relations and proportions that they have to one another. Yet this is not yet Christian wisdom; for it is only two-dimensional, or what we might call 'horizontal' wisdom. For wisdom to be Christian, one needs to introduce a third dimension, the relations and proportions of the components to something higher than themselves, which is their purpose or goal, their shared end. It is this vertical order which dictates and dominates, and which is the purpose of, the horizontal order among all created things. 'To perceive the relationships and the proportion of things to one another [their horizontal order], there is need for knowledge; but to judge according to their highest cause [their vertical order], that requires wisdom'.[71]

Thomas could not ignore the obvious verbal connection between the Latin '*sapite*' (savour) and *sapientia* (wisdom) in Col 3. 2, where Paul exhorts his readers to 'set your minds (*sapite*) on things that are above, and not on things that are on earth.' This referred, Thomas explained, to someone 'ordering their life in accordance with heavenly considerations, and judging everything by that. As James 3. 17 pointed out, "this is the wisdom from above"'.[72]

As well as being sapiential, then, 'order' in Thomas is also a dynamic concept expressing finality; and to consider it as static, to regard the created universe as an enormous still-life painted by God, is to ignore the idea of orientation, or of 'being ordered to', or even 'ordained to', which is essential to Thomas's conception of the created universe, as well as to his concept of *ordo*. For him an important implication of order is *ordo ad*, ordered towards; and the totality of created being, as a whole and in all its hierarchy of parts, is *in ordine ad Deum*, ordered towards God. This ordered universe is the product of God's wisdom,[73] and to perceive that dynamic order holistically and to share creatively in realizing it and actually promoting it is the role of all Christian wisdom. According to Stephen J. Duffy, the structure and theme of Thomas's mindset and aim was 'to articulate the sapiential order of the universe'.[74]

It is precisely because wisdom is the knowledge of God, and because having this enables God's children to judge everything in the light of godly principles, that it is so universal and all-embracing. But, although the Christian virtue of wisdom judges the horizontal relationship of each thing and action, and of all things and actions taken together as a unity, in the light of their vertical relationship to their common end, which is God, this does not mean that wisdom supplants or interferes unduly with any of the other intellectual virtues. It does, of course, have an influence on them, but, as Thomas explains, 'Wisdom can judge all the other intellectual virtues, and *its role is to order all of them*; in fact, it is with respect to all of them an architectonic virtue'.[75] And wisdom's influence also extends to the moral virtues,[76] because while these are directed by prudence, 'prudence itself is not concerned with the highest considerations, as wisdom is; *prudence is a minister to wisdom*, introducing people to it, and opening up the way to it, like an usher into the presence of royalty'.[77]

It is important to acknowledge of the subject matter which Thomas draws partly on Aristotle to elucidate that 'the wisdom with which we are wise is a sharing in the divine wisdom'.[78] It is also worth repeating in the context of 'order' what we have seen him observe elsewhere

> since wisdom is knowledge of godly matters, it is looked at differently by us and by the philosophers. Because our life is *ordered* to the enjoyment of God and is directed by a certain sharing in the divine nature [cf 2 Pet 1.4], which is effected through grace, wisdom according to us is not just considered as being knowledgeable about God, as it is with the philosophers; it is also considered by us as *providing direction to human life*, which is thus directed not only by human considerations but also by godly considerations.[79]

'Ordo', then, is a central concept in Aquinas; and it has been suggested that 'much of contemporary moral theology is unconsciously moving towards a recovery of that dynamic *ordo* which for Augustine and Aquinas was the very basis and context of all human morality'.[80] If order was the regular expression, or manifestation, of wisdom for Aristotle, it was even more, a fortiori, the case for Thomas, as he drew ever more dependently on the Word of God outlining God's 'eternal law' and the divine wise ordering of creation, and so unfolding a purposive principle of divine totality in all the Creator's dealings. As the Vulgate Book of Wisdom itself expressed it, wisdom 'reaches from end to end mightily and disposes everything smoothly', which the NRSV captures as '[wisdom] orders all things well' (Wis 8.1). In other words, God's universe is a well-ordered universe, since God creates all things and their behaviour 'in the contemplation of God's own wisdom'.[81]

The graces which the Holy Spirit bestows on humans are a medium of the Spirit's activity as primary cause operating within and through those humans, as they are given the forms and aptitudes by which they are disposed to do willingly what the Spirit moves them to do. The result is that when the creature proceeds to act with discerning wisdom at the Spirit's prompting, it does so smoothly and effortlessly, in an 'orderly' manner, in accordance with divine wisdom and not, as it were, reluctantly.

By such shared wisdom, extending beyond contemplation to active obedience, God's children themselves have their own divinely ordained ordering function and role in God's universe. They are invited to perceive all created reality not only in its horizontal dimension and ordering, but also, and particularly, in its vertical ordering. Unlike the philosophers, it is for Christians not just to recognize and accept God's order in creation. It is also for God's sons and daughters under God's Spirit to enter individually into the eternal law, the ordered design of God's all-embracing wisdom, and to collaborate, with their wise discernment and actions, to bringing it to fulfilment in and through their lives. Augustine had described how Adam's sin had undone the order between humans and their creator and consequently substituted chaos for the order interior to humans themselves. In the light of this, Dominic Hughes countered, in reverse, 'when the soul has a tranquility of divine order within itself, it is zealous to establish that order in the whole world'.[82]

In introducing this study, we aimed to explore to what degree Thomas Aquinas would share our interest in the role of the Holy Spirit in human moral action; and the conclusion we have reached is that the presence and interior dynamism of the Holy Spirit pervades Thomas's entire moral theology. It is within this holistic, sapiential and dynamic setting which we have explored that we can best appreciate the description offered by Thomas F. O'Meara of Aquinas's moral theology, as this appears in the *Summa Theologiae*, and (as we can now appreciate), as it applies equally in Thomas's Scripture Commentaries. O'Meara wrote:

> Aquinas's moral theology is not a philosophy of virtues, nor a psychology of means to contact a Supreme Being or Goodness. It is not a foundation for offering general principles to casuistry in the sacrament of penance or to a canon law of censures. It is neither an applied moral theology of cases nor a logic or metaphysic of ethical principles. As a part of the entire *Summa theologiae*, the Second Part narrates the journeying Christian life touched by the processions of the Trinity and the emerging of a psychology of the human being existing in salvation-history through a life-principle, which is the gift and presence of the Holy Spirit.[83]

In his essay on 'Recovering the Gifts of the Holy Spirit in Moral Theology', Charles Bouchard concluded that 'a renewed pneumatology would enrich moral theology', by making morality more explicitly theological, by making its study more Scripture-based, and by greatly enhancing Christian anthropology.[84] The results of our enquiry vastly more than substantiate Bouchard's claim, as must now be evident. As we have learned from Thomas Aquinas, God is engaged in creation of an enterprise of love, delighted to share the fullness of divine existence with a multiplicity of created beings, climaxing in humans who are uniquely conscious of themselves as made in God's own 'image and likeness' (Gen. 1.26) and who are thus drawn to 'participate in God's nature' (2 Pet. 1.4). To fulfil this divine enterprise, the Holy Spirit issues lovingly from the Father and the Son, to enter intimately as a further gift into the lives – the minds as well as the hearts and histories – of God's sons and daughters in Christ, catching them up and carrying them forward, in their conscious and free actions, to divine loving fulfilment. This is exactly what morality is, for Aquinas: God's human creatures being desirably 'driven' interiorly by God's Spirit in all their actions, to make their unique contribution of wisely discerning the orderly design of God's eternal loving wisdom, for themselves, their fellows in society and the whole of God's creation; and thus in their decisions freely contributing to the fulfilment of that enterprise of wisdom and love, in partnership with God's own Holy Spirit.

In 1256, in the intellectual powerhouse that was the University of Paris, Brother Thomas, the promising young Dominican friar from Aquino, delivered his inaugural lecture as master, and he chose his topic the verse of the psalmist, 'From your lofty abode you water the mountains; the earth is satisfied with the work of your hands' (Ps. 104.13). Thomas applied the verse to the theme of the powerful living waters of divine Wisdom as these cascade down the mountains to enrich God's whole earth; a wisdom and a favourite image which, as we have seen, Thomas would regularly ascribe to the Holy Spirit.[85] From this divine outpouring, Thomas expounded, faithful to the Dominican mission of 'handing on to others the fruit of contemplation' (*contemplata aliis tradere*), how the divine wisdom flows from its heavenly source into the lofty minds of learned professors, who then communicate it, in turn, to the more lowly minds of their students. And he closed his lecture by advising his academic audience to follow the advice which had been given by James in his Epistle (1.5), 'If any of you is lacking in wisdom, ask God, who gives to all generously and ungrudgingly, and it will be given you';[86] a 'word of wisdom'[87] on Thomas's part which has by no means lost its topicality.

## NOTES

1. See Timothy M. Gallagher, *The Discernment of Spirits. An Ignatian Guide for Everyday Living* (New York: Crossroad, 2005).
2. Pope Pius XII, Instruction of the Holy Office on situation ethics, 1956, *DS* 3918–21. See Mahoney, *The Making of Moral Theology,* 'Subjectivity and "Situation Ethics" ', 202–10.
3. Josef Fuchs, 'Morale théologie et morale de situation', *NRT* 76 (1954), 1084.
4. Mark A. McIntosh, *Discernment and Truth. The Spirituality and Theology of Knowledge* (New York: Crossroads Publishing Company, 2004), Part I. History and Theology of Spiritual Discernment, pp. 3–124.
5. See see above, pp. 90–96.
6. *In 1 Thess* 5, lect. 2 (M 135).
7. *In Rom.*12, lect. 1 (M 953).
8. *ST* I-II. 106.1. Cf above, pp. 87–88.
9. *In Rom.*12, lect.1 (M 967).
10. *In Rom.* ibid.
11. *ST* I-II.100.1; *In Joan* 7, lect. 2.

12. Dietrich Bonhoeffer, *Ethics* (Fontana, 1964), 68–9.
13. *ST* I-II.2.1 ad 1.
14. B. Lonergan, 'St Thomas' Thought on Gratia Operans, III. Habitual Grace as *operans et cooperans*', *Theological Studies* 3 (1942) 69.
15. Stump, Wisdom, p. 62.
16. *CG* 3, cap 154.
17. *In 1 Thess.* 5, lect. 2 (M 133).
18. *In 4 Sent.*, d.38, q. 1, a.1, sol. 2 ad 3.
19. *In Heb* 11, lect. 7 (M 630); *ST* II-II.88.2 ad 2.
20. *ST* I-II.106.4 ad 4. On the Joachists, see above, pp. 131–134.
21. *In Matth* 14, lect. 1 (M 1227, 1230). Kimball, 512–3.
22. *In Matth* 20, lect. 2 (M1655). Kimball, 670.
23. *ST* II-II.46. On Gregory, see *ST* I-II.45.5 arg. 3.
24. *ST* II-II.46.1. For Isidore, see Migne *PL* 82.
25. *ST* II-II.46.1 ad 1.
26. *ST* II-II.46.2.
27. See above, pp. 104–106.
28. *In 2 Cor.* 11, lect. 1 (M 372); 12, lect. 4 (M 485), emphasis added.
29. *In 1 Cor.* 15, lect. 5 (M 968).
30. Pinsent, *The Second-Person,* 41.
31. T.-H. Deman, *La Prudence* (*Somme théologique*, 2a-2ae, Qq. 47–56) (Paris: Desclée, 1949), 398–413 at 408.
32. F. Dingjan, *Discretio. Les origines patristiques et monastiques de la doctrine sur la prudence chez saint Thomas d'Aquin* (Assen: Van Gorcum, 1967), 2–4.
33. Dingjan, 217.
34. *In 4 Sent.*, d. 6, q. 2, a. 1, sol. 3 ad 3. Deman, 409.
35. *ST* I-II.3 ad 14.
36. *In Rom.*12, lect. 1 (M 963).
37. *In Col* 4, lect. 1 (M 187–8).
38. See above, pp. 25–26.
39. *ST* I-II.60, 1 ad 2; 45.4.
40. *In Phil* 1, lect. 2 (M 17).
41. See above, p. 136.
42. J. Mahoney, *The Ways of Wisdom*. An Inaugural Lecture in the Frederick Denison Maurice Chair of Moral and Social Theology, King's College (London, 1987), 4.
43. *ST* II-II.45.5. Emphasis added.
44. See above, p. 136.
45. *ST* I-II.111.4 ad 4.
46. See above, pp. 136–137.
47. *In 1 Cor.* 12, lect. 2 (M 727).
48. *In 1 Cor.* 12, lect. 1 (M 721).
49. *In 1 Cor.* 12, lect, 1 (M 716).
50. *ST* II-II.177.1.
51. *ST* I-II.199.11.

52. *ST* II-II.45.5.
53. *ST* II-II.106.4 ad 2.
54. *ST* II-II.177.1.
55. E. Ménard, *La tradition selon s.Thomas d'Aquin* (Montréal: Desclée de Brouwer, 1964), 164–5.
56. *De civ. Dei.* XIX, 3, 1; *PL* 41, 640.
57. *De lib.arb.*, 1, 6; *PL* 32, 1229.
58. *De civ Dei*, XIX, 13; *PL* 41, 641.
59. Cf. Mahoney, *The Making of Moral Theology*, 74–7.
60. *De Potentia*, q. 1.
61. *ST* I-II.90.4.
62. ST I-II.66.4.
63. *ST* I-II.66.5.
64. *In 1 Cor.* 2, lect. 3 (M 117–8). Emphasis added.
65. Aristotle, *Metaph* 1.2.3, 982a18.
66. Aristotle, *Metaph* 1. 2, 3; 982a18.
67. Aquinas, *Com in Eth*, Bk 1, chap. 1.
68. *ST* 1.1.6.
69. M.-.D. Chenu, *Saint Thomas d'Aquin et la théologie* (Paris, 1959), 128; S. J. Duffy, *The Dynamics of Grace. Perspectives in Theological Anthropology* (Collegeville: Liturgical Press, 1993), 129 and n.12.
70. *ST* I.47.3.
71. *CG* 2, 24.
72. *In Col.* 3, lect. 1 (M 139).
73. See Ménard, 165.
74. Duffy, pp. 124–5.
75. *In Eph* 5, lect. 6 (M 305), emphasis added.
76. *ST* II-II.47.6 ad 3.
77. *ST* I-II.66.5 ad 1. Emphasis added.
78. *ST* II-II.23.2 ad 1.
79. *ST* II-II.19.7. Emphasis added.
80. Mahoney, *The Making of Moral Theology*, 321.
81. *In Ethic*, lib 10, lect. 12; Vivès, t. 26, p. 76.
82. D. Hughes, 'The Gift of Wisdom', in Walter Farrell OP & Dominic Hughes OP, *Swift Victory. The Gifts of the Holy Spirit at Work in Your Soul* Harrison, NY: Roman Catholic Books, 1955), 100.
83. O'Meara, T. F., 'Interpreting Thomas Aquinas. Aspects of the Dominican School of Moral Theology in the Twentieth Century', in Stephen J. Pope, ed., *The Ethics of Aquinas* (Washington, D.C.: Georgetown University Press), 2002, 366.
84. Bouchard, 556–58.
85. On the Spirit as living water, see above, pp. 29–33.
86. *Breve Principium Fratris Thomae de Aquino, quando incepit Parisius ut Magister in Theologia,* in *Opuscula Theologica* (Rome: Marietti, 1954), vol. 1, pp. 441–3.
87. See above, pp. 154–157.

# Bibliography

## 1. WORKS OF AQUINAS

### Collected Works

*Opera Omnia*, ed. Leonina, Romae, 1882–
*Opera Omnia*, tt. 25, Parmae, 1852–1873.
www.corpusthomisticum.org.
St Thomas Aquinas's Works in English: https:/dhspriory.org.thomas

### Individual Works

S. Thomae Aquinatis *De sortibus ad Dominum Jacobum de Burgo,* in *Opuscula Theologica*, vol. 1, Torino: Marietti, 1954, 157–67.

S. Thomae Aquinatis *De veritate, Quaestiones Disputatae,* ed. R. Spiazzi, Turin: Marietti, 1964, vol. 1.

S. Thomae Aquinatis *In Decem Libros Ethicorum Aristotelis ad Nicomachum Expositio*, ed. R.M. Spiazzi, Turin: Marietti, 1949.

S. Thomae Aquinatis *In librum Beati Dionysii de Divinis Nominibus Expositio*, ed. Pera et al., Turin: Marietti, 1950.

S. Thomae Aquinatis *In librum Beati Dionysii de Trinitate*, ed. Leonina, t. 50, 1992.

S. Thomae Aquinatis *Liber contra impugnantes Dei cultum et religionem*; trans. John Procter, O.P., *An Apology for the Religious Orders*, London: Sands & Co., 1902.

S. Thomae Aquinatis *Opuscula Omnia*, tt. 5, ed. Mandonnet, Paris: 1927.

S. Thomae Aquinatis *Opuscula Theologica*, tt. 2, ed. R.A. Verardo, Turin: Marietti, 1954.

S. Thomae Aquinatis *Quaestiones Disputatae*, tt. 2, ed. R.M. Spiazzi, Turin: Marietti, 1949.

S. Thomae Aquinatis *Quaestiones Quodlibetales*, ed. R.M. Spiazzi, Turin: Marietti, 1949 (ed. 8).

S. Thomae Aquinatis *Scriptum super Libros Sententiarum* Magistri Petri Lombardi Episcopi Parisiensis, tt. 4, ed. Mandonnet-Moos, Paris: Lethielleux, 1929–1947.

S. Thomae Aquinatis *Summa contra gentiles,* ed. Leonina, Romae 1918–1930.

Thomas Aquinas *Summa Theologiae*, Latin text and English translation, Introductions, Notes, Appendices and Glossaries, London: Blackfriars-Eyre & Spottiswoode, 1964–73.

## Commentaries on Sacred Scripture

S. Thomae Aquinatis *In Isaiam Prophetam Expositio* [= *In Isa.*], ed.leonina, t. 28, 1974.

S. Thomae Aquinatis *In Jeremiam Prophetam Expositio* [= *In Jer.*], Opera Omnia, Parmae, t. 14.

S. Thomae Aquinatis *Expositio Super Iob ad litteram* [= *In Job*], ed. leonina, t. 26, Romae, 1965.

S. Thomae Aquinatis *In Psalmos [I-LI] David Expositio* [= *In Ps.*], Opera Omnia, Parmae, t. 14.

S. Thomae Aquinatis *In Threnos Jeremiae Expositio*, Opera Omnia, Parmae, t. 14.

S. Thomae Aquinatis *Super Evangelium S. Ioannis Lectura* [= *In Joan.*], ed. R. Cai, Turin, Marietti [= M 1, etc.], 1952 (ed. 5).

S. Thomae Aquinatis *Super Evangelium S. Matthaei Lectura* [= *In Matt.*], ed. R. Cai, Turin: Marietti, 1951 (ed. 5).

S. Thomae Aquinatis *Lectura in Matthaeum* [Mt 1. 22–12.50]. Basel, *Univ. B.V.12.* [*See Appendix* in Kimball, below.]

S. Thomae Aquinatis *Super Epistolas S. Pauli Lectura* [= *In Rom.*; etc.], 2 vols, ed. R. Cai, Turin: Marietti, 1953.

S. Thomae Aquinatis *Catena aurea (Glossa continua) super quattuor evangelia*, ed. A. Guarienti, 2 vols Turin: Marietti, 1953.

## Commentaries on Sacred Scripture: Texts and English translations

Thomas Aquinas, *Commentary on the Letters of Saint Paul,* Aquinas Institute for the Study of Sacred Doctrine, Lauder, Wyoming, 2018.

Thomas Aquinas, *Commentary on the Gospels of John and Matthew*, Aquinas Institute for the Study of Sacred Doctrine, Lauder, Wyoming, 2018.

Thomas Aquinas, *Commentary on the Gospel of Saint Matthew,* trans: P. M. Kimball, Bristol: Dolorosa Press, 2012. Appendix: Transcription of Basel *Manuscript B.V. 12.* [Reportatio Petri de Andria]. Ed. H. Kraml, pp. 971–997.

## 2. OTHER WORKS

Abbott, W. M., ed. *The Documents of Vatican II*, London: Chapman, 1966.

Afanasief, Nicholas. *The Church of the Holy Spirit*, Notre Dame, Indiana: University of Notre Dame Press, 2007.
Alberti Magni *Opera Omnia*, tt. 38, ed. A. Borgnet, Paris: 1890–99.
Alfaro, J. 'Supernaturalitas fidei iuxta S. Thomam,' *Greg* 44 (1963) 501–542, 731–787.
Alszeghy, Z. *Nova creatura. La nozione della grazia nei commentari medievali di S. Paolo* (Analecta Gregoriana, 81), Rome: Univ. Greg., 1956.
Alszeghy, Z. *See* Flick.
Anscombe, G.E.M. 'Modern Moral Philosophy', *Philosophy* 33 (1958) 1–18.
Aristotle. *Ethics*, London: Penguin Classics, 1976.
Aubert, J.-M. *Loi de Dieu Lois des Hommes*, Paris: Desclée, 1964.
Augustine, Saint. *de correptione et gratia PL 44*, 915–946.
Augustine, Saint. *de dono perseverantiae*, PL 45, 993–1034.
Augustine, Saint. *de gestis Pelagii*, PL 44, 319–60.
Augustine, Saint. *de gratia Christi*, PL 44, 359–386.
Augustine, Saint. *de praedestinatione sanctorum*, PL 44, 959–992.
Augustine, Saint. *de spiritu et littera*, PL 44, 199–246.
Augustine, Saint. *In Joannis Evangelium tractatus CXXIV*, PL 35, 1379–1976.
Augustine, Saint. *Sermones, PL* 38–39.
Austin, Nicholas. 'Spirituality and Virtue in Christian Formation: A Conversation between Thomistic and Ignatian Traditions', *NB* 97, 1068 (March 2016), 206–217.
Austin, Nicholas. *Aquinas on Virtues: A Causal Reading*, Washington, DC: Georgetown University Press, 2017.
Baglow, Christopher T. *The Doctrine of the Eucharist in St Thomas Aquinas' 'Commentary on the Gospel of St John'*, Dallas: University of Dallas, 1996.
Baglow, Christopher T. *'Modus et Forma': A New Approach to the Exegesis of Saint Thomas Aquinas with an Application to the* Lectura super Epistolam ad Ephesios, *Analecta Biblica* 149, Rome: Pontifical Biblical Institute, 2002.
Benz, E. 'Joachim-Studien III. Thomas von Aquin und Joachim de Fiore. Die katholische Antwort auf die spiritualistische Kirchen- und Geschichtsanschauung', *Zeitschrift für Kirchengeschichte* 53 (1934) 52–116.
Berkman, John and Titus Craig Steven, eds. *The Pinckaers Reader: Renewing Thomistic Moral Theology*, Washington, D.C.: Catholic University of American Press, 2005.
Bernard, R. *La Vertu*, Somme Théologique, Ed. Revue des jeunes, Paris: Desclée, 1953.
Bierbaum, M. *Bettelorden und Weltgeistlichkeit an der Universität Paris*, Münster, 1920.
Bloomfield, M. J. 'Joachim of Flora. A critical Survey of His Canon, Teachings, Sources, Biography and Influence,' *Traditio* 13 (1957) 249–311.
Bloomfield, M. J. and Reeves, M. E. 'The Penetration of Joachism into Northern Europe,' *Speculum* 29 (1954) 772–793.
Böckle, F. *Grundbegriffe der Moral*, Aschaffenburg: Pattloch Verlag, 1966.
Boismard, M.E. 'La loi et l'Esprit', *Lumiére et Vie* 21 (1955) 345–362.

Boler, John. 'Aquinas on Exceptions in Natural Law', in MacDonald & Stump, pp. 161–204.
Bonaventurae, S. *Opera Omnia*, tt. 10, Quaracchi, 1882–1902.
Bouchard, Charles E. 'Recovering the Gifts of the Holy Spirit in Moral Theology', *Theol Stud* 63 (2002) 539–581.
Bougerol, J.G. *Introduction à l'étude de saint Bonaventure*, Paris: Desclée, 1961.
Bouillard, H. *Conversion et grâce chez s. Thomas d'Aquin*, Paris: Aubier, 1944.
Boyle, J.F. *Master Thomas Aquinas and the Fullness of Life*, South Bend, Indiana: St Augustine's Press, 2014.
Budziszewski, J. *Commentary on Thomas Aquinas's Virtue Ethics*, Cambridge: Cambridge University Press, 2017.
Buytaert, E.M., ed. *St. John Damascene*, de Fide Orthodoxa, *Versions of Burgundio and Cerbanus*, New York: 1955.
Callan, C.J. 'The Bible in the *Summa Theologica* of St. Thomas Aquinas,' *Catholic Biblical Quarterly* 9 (1947) 37–47.
*Catechism of the Catholic Church,* London: Burns & Oates, 2000.
Chenu, M.-D. 'Le dernier avatar de la théologie orientale en Occident au XIIIe siècle, *Mélanges Auguste Pelzer*, Louvain, 1947, pp. 159–181.
Chenu, M.-D. 'Évangelisme et théologie au XIIIe siècle', *Mélanges Cavallera*, Toulouse, 1948, pp. 339–346.
Chenu. M. D. 'Théologie symbolique et exégèse scolastique', *Mélanges J. De Ghellinck* Gembloux, 1951, pp. 509–526.
Chenu. M. D.'Vocabulaire biblique et vocabulaire théologique', *NRT* 74 (1952) 1029–1041.
Chenu. M. D. *Introduction à l'étude de Saint Thomas d'Aquin*, Montréal-Paris, 1954 (ed. 2).
Chenu. M. D. *La théologie au douzième siècle,* Paris, 1957.
Chenu. M. D. *Saint Thomas d'Aquin et la théologie*, Paris, 1959.
Chenu. M. D. *Aquinas and His Role in Theology*, Collegeville: Liturgical Press, 2002.
Congar, Y.M.-J. *Esquisses du Mystère de l'Église* Paris, 1953 (ed. 2).
Congar, Y.M.-J. 'Traditio thomistica in materia ecclesiologica', *Angelicum* 43 (1966) 405–428.
Congar, Y.M.-J. *I Believe in the Holy Spirit*, 3 vols. New York, Seabury Press, 1983.
Congar, Y.M.-J. *Thomas d'Aquin: sa vision de la théologie et de l'Eglise*, London: Variorum Reprints, 1984.
Conley, K. *A Theology of Wisdom. A Study in St. Thomas,* Dubuque, Iowa: Priory Press, 1963.
Davies, Brian. *The Thought of Thomas Aquinas*, Oxford: Clarendon Press, 1992.
Davies, Brian. 'Aquinas and the Academic life', *NB* 83, 977 (July 2002), 336–346.
Davies, Brian, and Stump, Eleonore, eds. *The Oxford Handbook of Aquinas*, Oxford: Oxford University Press, 2012.
De Guibert, J., *Les Doublets de Saint Thomas d'Aquin*, Leur étude méthodique, Quelques réflexions, quelques exemples, Paris: Gembloux, 1926.
Delhaye, Ph. *Pierre Lombard, sa vie, ses oeuvres, sa morale*, Paris: Desclée de Brouwer, 1961.

Delhaye, Ph. *La conscience morale du Chrétien*, Tournai: Gembloux, 1964.
Deman, Th. 'Le *Liber de Bona Fortuna* dans la théologie de saint Thomas d'Aquin', *RSPT* 17 (1928) 38–58.
Deman, Th. *La prudence*, Somme Théologique, Paris: Desclée, 1949.
Deman, Th. *Aux origines de la théologie morale*, Montréal-Paris: Desclée, 1951.
Deman, Th. *Der Neue Bund und die Gnade*, die deutsche Thomas-Ausgabe, Bd. 14, Heidelberg, 1955.
Dempf, A., *Sacrum Imperium*. Geschichts- und Staatsphilosophie des Mittelalters und der politischen Rennaissance, München, 1929.
Denifle, H. 'Quel livre servait de base à l'enseignement des maîtres en théologie dans l'université de Paris?' *RevThom* 2 (1894) 149–161.
Denifle, H., ed. *Chartularium Universitatis Parisiensis*, tt. 4, Paris, 1889–1897.
Diepen, H. 'La psychologie humaine du Christ selon s. Thomas d'Aquin', *RevThom* 50 (1950) 515–562.
Di Marino, A. 'L'epikeia cristiana', *Divus Thomas (Piacenza)* 55 (1952) 396–424.
Di Monda, A. *La legge nuova della libertà secondo San Tommaso*, Napoli, 1954.
Dodds, Michael J. *Unlocking Divine Action. Contemporary Science and Thomas Aquinas*, Washington, D.C.: The Catholic University of America, 2012.
Dondaine, A. *Secrétaires de saint Thomas*, 2 vols, Rome, 1956.
Dondaine, A. & Peters, J. 'Jacques de Tonengo et Gifredus d'Anagni auditeurs de saint Thomas', *Archivum Fratrum Praedicatorum* 29 (1959) 52–72.
Dondaine, H.-F. *La Trinité (Summa theologiae, I. qq 27-43), 2 vols,* Paris: Revue des Jeunes, 1946s.
Dondaine, H.-F. 'A propos d'Avicenne et de saint Thomas. De la causalité dispositive à la causalité instrumentale', *RevThom* 51 (1951) 441–453.
Dondaine, H.-F. 'Les scolastiques citent-ils les Pères de première main?', *RSPT* 36 (1952) 231–243.
Dozois, C. 'Sources patristiques chez saint Thomas d'Aquin' *RUO* 33 (1963) 28\*-48\*, 145\*-167\*; 34 (1964) 231\*–241\*; 35 (1965) 73\*–90\*.
Duffy, Stephen J. T*he Dynamics of Grace, Perspectives in Theological Anthropology*, Collegeville, Minnesota: The Liturgical Press, 1993.
Emery, Gilles. *The Trinitarian Theology of Saint Thomas Aquinas*, Oxford: Oxford University Press, 2007.
Emery, Gilles. 'The Holy Spirit', in P. McCosker and D. Turner, ed., *The Cambridge Companion to the Summa theologiae*, Cambridge: Cambridge University Press, 2016, 129–141.
Epperly, B. G. *Process Theology. A Guide for the Perplexed*, London, Edinburgh: T & T Clarke, 2011.
Eschmann, I. T. 'The Quotations of Aristotle's *Politica* in St. Thomas' *Lectura super Matthaeum', Medieval Studies* 18 (1956) 232–240.
Eschmann, I. T. 'A catalogue of St. Thomas's Works. Bibliographical Notes', in E. Gilson, *The Christian Philosophy of St. Thomas Aquinas*, London: Sheed & Ward, 1957, pp. 381–399.
Evans, C Stephen, ed. *Exploring Kenotic Theology: The Self-Emptying of God*, Vancouver, B.C.: Regent College Publishing, 2009.

Fabri, Cornelio. 'Le 'Liber de Bona Fortuna' de l''Éthique à Eudème' d'Aristote et la dialectique de la divine Providence chez saint Thomas', *RevThom* 88 (4) (1988).

Farrell, Walter, & Hughes, Dominic. *Swift Victory. The Gifts of the Holy Spirit at Work in Your Soul*, Harrison NY: Roman Catholic Books, 1955.

Finnis, John. *Natural Law and Natural Rights*, Oxford: Clarendon Press, 1980.

Finnis, John. *Aquinas, Moral, Political, and Legal Theory,* Oxford: Oxford University Press, 1998.

Flick, M. & Alszeghy, Z. *Il Vangelo della Grazia.* Un trattato dogmatico, Firenze, 1964.

Fuchs, Josef. *Die Sexualethik des heiligen Thomas von Aquin*, Köln, 1949.

Fuchs, Josef. 'Morale théologie et morale de situation', *NRT* 76 (1954) 1073–1085.

Fuchs, Josef. *Lex naturae. Zur Theologie des Naturrechts*, Düsseldorf, 1955.

Fuchs, Josef. 'Éthique objective et éthique de situation', *NRT* 78 (1956) 798–818.

Fuchs, Josef. *Theologia moralis generalis, Pars prima*, ed. 2, Roma, 1963.

Fuchs, Josef. 'Theologia moralis perficienda. Votum Concilii Vaticani II', *Periodica* 55 (1966) 499–548.

Fuchs, Josef, *Natural Law: a theological investigation*, Dublin: Gill, 1965.

Fuchs, Josef, *Human Values and Christian Morality*, Dublin, Gill and Macmillan, 1970.

Gallagher, Timothy M. *The Discernment of Spirits. An Ignatian Guide for Everyday Living*, New York: Crossroad, 2005.

Gardeil, A. 'Les procédés exegetiques de Saint Thomas', *RevcThom* 11 (1903) 428–457.

Gardeil, A. 'Dons du Saint-Esprit', *DTC,* 4, 1728–1781.

Gardeil, H.D. *La Charité*, Paris: Gembloux, 1957.

Garrigou-Lagrange, R. *Perfection chrétienne et contemplation,* t. 1, Saint-Maximin 1923.

Gay, R.M. *Vocation et discernement des esprits*, Montréal, 1959.

Gilby, Thomas, *Aquinas, Summa Theologiae*, vol 36, Prudence, London: Blackfriars, Eyre & Spottiswoode, 1974.

Gilleman, G. *Le primat de la charité en Théologie morale*, Bruxelles-Paris: Aubier, 1952.

Gilleman, G 'Théologie morale et Charité', *NRT* 74 (1952) 806–820.

Gillon, L.-B. 'L'imitation du Christ et la morale de Saint Thomas', *Angelicum* 36 (1959) 263–286.

Gils, P.-M. 'Le manuscrit *Napoli, Biblioteca nazionale I. B. 54* est-il de la main de S. Thomas?', *RSPT* 49 (1965) 37–59.

Gilson, E. 'Wisdom and Love in Saint Thomas Aquinas', Aquinas Lecture 1951, Milwaukee: Marquette University Press, 1951.

Gilson, E. *The Christian Philosophy of St. Thomas Aquinas*, New York: Sheed & Ward, 1956.

Glorieux, P. 'Essai sur les commentaires scripturaires de saint Thomas et leur chronologie', *RTAM* 17 (1950) 237–266.

*Glosa Ordinaria* cum expositione Lyre litterali et morali, necnon additionibus ac Replicis, Basileae, tt. 6, 1506–1508.

Gould, Warwick, and Reeves, Marjorie, *Joachim of Fiore and the myth of the eternal evangel in the nineteenth and twentieth centuries,* ed. rev and enlarged, Oxford: Oxford University Press, 2001.

Grabmann, M. *Die Lehre des heiligen Thomas von Aquin von der Kirche als Gotteswerk*, Regensburg, 1903.

Gratiani *Decretum*, ed. Friedberg, Leipzig, 1879.

Green, J. P., ed. *The interlinear Hebrew-Greek-English Bible*, Peabody, MA: Hendrickson, 2005.

Grelot, P. 'Exégèse, théologie et pastorale', *NRT* 88 (1966) 3–13.

Guillelmus de Sancto Amore. *Opera Omnia*, Constantiae, 1632.

Guindon,, R. '*L'Expositio in Isaiam* est-elle une oeuvre de Thomas d'Aquin "bachelier biblique"'? *RTAM* 21 (1954) 312–321.

Guindon,, R. 'La *Lectura super Matthaeum incompleta* de saint Thomas d'Aquin', *RUO* 25 (1955) 213*–219*.

Guindon,, R. 'Le caractère évangélique de la morale de Saint Thomas', *RUO* 25 (1955) 145–167.

Guindon,, R. *Béatitude et théologie morale chez saint Thomas d'Aquin*, Ottawa, 1956.

Haight, Roger. *The Experience and Language of Grace*, Dublin: Gill & Macmillan, 1979.

Hall, Pamela M. *Narrative and the Natural Law: An Interpretation of Thomistic Ethics*, Notre Dame: University of Notre Dame, 1994.

Hamel, E. *Loi naturelle et loi du Christ*, Paris: Desclée de Brouwer, 1964.

Hamel, E. 'L'usage de l'epikie', *Studia Moralia* III, Rome, 1965.

Hamel, E. 'L'usage de l'Écriture Sainte en théologie morale', *Greg* 47 (1966) 53–85.

Hanigan, James P., 'Conscience and the Holy Spirit', *Catholic Theological Society of America. Proceedings* 51 (1996) 237–246.

Hankey, W. J. *God in Himself. Aquinas' Doctrine of God as expounded in the* Summa Theologiae, Oxford: Oxford University Press, 1987.

Hayent, A. 'Saint Thomas a-t-il édité deux fois son Commentaire sur le livre des Sentences?', *RTAM* 9 (1937) 219–236.

Healy, Nicholas H. *Thomas Aquinas Theologian of the Christian Life*, Aldershot: Ashgate, 2003.

Healy, Nicholas H. Introduction to Weinandy, etc.

Henry, A.-M. *L'Esprit-Saint*, Paris: Desclée, 1959.

Holmes, Jeremy. 'Aquinas' *Lectura in Matthaeum*', in Weinandy, etc.

Hughes, D. 'Grace and the Gifts', in Farrell & Hughes.

Hughes, G. J. 'The Function of Aristotle's Virtues', *Bidragen*, International Journal in Philosophy and Theology, 66 (2005) 196–212.

Hursthouse, Rosalind. 'Virtue Theory and Abortion', *Philosophy and Public Affairs*, 20, 3 (Summer 1991) 223–246.

Ignatius of Loyola. *Epistulae*, Monumenta Ignatiana, Madrid, 1909.

Initiation Theologique, t. III: Théologie Morale, Paris: Gembloux, 1952.

Jenkins, John L. *Knowledge and Faith in Thomas Aquinas*, Cambridge: Cambridge University Press, 1997.

John, Helen James. *The Thomist Spectrum*, New York: Fordham University Press, 1966.
John of Saint Thomas. *The Gifts of the Holy Ghost*, trans., D. Hughes OP, New York: Sheed & Ward, 1951.
John Damascene. *de fide orthodoxa*, Migne *PG* 94.
Johnson, Elizabeth A. *She Who Is: the Mystery of God in Feminist Theological Discourse*, New York, Crossroad, 1992.
Jordan, Mark D. *Ordering Wisdom. The Hierarchy of Philosophical Discourses in Aquinas*, Notre Dame: University of Notre Dame Press, 1986.
Journet, Ch., *L'Église du Verbe incarné*, t. 2, Paris: Desclée de Brouwer, 1951.
Keane, Philip, 'The Role of the Holy Spirit in Contemporary Moral Theology', *Catholic Theological Society of America. Proceedings* 51 (1996) 227–246.
Keenan, James F. *Goodness and Rightness in Thomas Aquinas's* Summa theologiae, Washington, D. C.: Georgetown University Press, 1992.
Keenan, James F. 'Virtues', in McCosker & Turner, 194–205.
Kerr, Fergus, 'Recent Thomistica: I', *NB* 83, 975 (May 2002), 245–251.
Kerr, Fergus, ed. *Contemplating Aquinas. On the Varieties of Interpretations*, London, SCM, 2003.
Kerr, Fergus, 'The Varieties of Interpreting Aquinas', in idem, *Contemplating Aquinas.*
Kerr, Fergus, 'Thomas Aquinas and his Family', *NB* 91, 1031, January 2010, 11–13.
Klooster, Anton ten, *Thomas Aquinas on the Beatitudes,* Leuven: Peeters, 2018.
Knowles, D. *The Evolution of Medieval Thought*, London: Longmans, 1962.
Kretzmann, Norman and Stump, Eleonore, edd. *The Cambridge Companion to Aquinas,* Cambridge: Cambridge University Press, 1993.
Kühn, U. *Via caritatis. Theologie des Gesetzes bei Thomas von Aquin*, Göttingen: Vandenhoeck, 1965.
Labourdette, M. 'Dons du Saint-Esprit, IV: Saint Thomas et la théologie thomiste, *DSp* t. 3, 1610–1635.
Lecuyer, J. 'Docilité au Saint-Esprit', *DSp* t. 3, 1471–1497.
Legge, Dominic. *The Trinitarian Theology of St Thomas Aquinas*, Oxford: Oxford University Press, 2017.
Le Guillou, M.-J. *Le Christ et l'Église: théologie du mystère*, Paris: Desclée, 1963.
L'Enfant, F.D. *Sancti Thomae Aquinatis . . . Biblia sive Collectio et explicatio omnium locorum S. Scripturae quae sparsim reperiuntur in omnibus S. Thomae Scholasticis operibus*, Parisiis, 1659.
Levering, Matthew. 'Wisdom and the Viability of Thomist Trinitarian Theology', *The Thomist*, 64 (2000) 593–618.
Levering, Matthew. *Scripture and Metaphysics. Aquinas and the Renewal of Trinitarian Theology*, Oxford: Blackwell, 2004.
Levering, Matthew. 'A Note on Scripture in the *Summa theologiae*', *NB*, 90, 1030 (November 2009), 652–658.
Lonergan, B. 'St. Thomas' Thought on *Gratia Operans*', *TS* 2 (1941) 289–324; 3 (1942) 69–88, 375–402, 533–578.
Lonergan, B. 'St Thomas' Theory of Operation', *TS* 3 (1942) 373–402.
Lottin, O.,*Psychologie et morale aux XIIe et XIIIe siècles*, tt. 6, Louvain, 1942–1960.

Lottin, O. *Morale fondamentale*, Desclée, 1954.
Lottin, O. 'A propos de la formule "ultra humanum modum" de saint Thomas d'Aquin', *RTAM* 30 (1963) 277–298.
Lottin, O. 'La formule authentiquement thomiste des dons du Saint-Esprit', *ETL* 40 (1964) 413–419.
Lottin, O. Bibliography of Dom Odon Lottin, O.S.B., *RTAM* 32 (1965) 7–19.
Lyonnet, S. 'St. Paul. Liberty and Law', *The Bridge*: A Yearbook of Judaeo-Christian Studies 4 (1962) 229–251.
Lyra, Nicholas of. *See* Glosa.
MacCulloch, Diarmaid. *A History of Christianity. The First Three Thousand Years*, London: Penguin, 2010.
Macdonald, S. & Stump, E. edd. *Aquinas's Moral Theory*, London: Cornell University Press, 1999.
Macierowski, E.M. *Doctrine of the Analogy of Being according to Thomas Aquinas*, Milwaukee: Marquette University Press, 2004.
MacIntyre, Alistair. *After Virtue,* London: Duckworth, 1981.
Mahoney, J. *The Making of Moral Theology. A Study of the Roman Catholic Tradition*, Oxford, Clarendon Press, 1987.
Mahoney, J. *The Ways of Wisdom*. An Inaugural Lecture in the Frederick Denison Maurice Chair of Moral and Social Theology, King's College London, 1987.
Mahoney, J. 'Christian Doctrines, Ethical Issues, and Human Genetics', *TS* December 2003, 719–749.
Mahoney, J. *Christianity in Evolution. An Exploration,* Washington D.C.: Georgetown University Press, 2011.
Mandonnet, P., et Destrez, J. *Bibliographie thomiste*, deuxième edition revue et completée par M.-D. Chenu, Paris, 1960.
Manselli, R. *La 'Lectura super apocalipsim' di Pietro di Giovanni Olivi*. Ricerche sull' escatologismo medioevale, Roma, 1955.
Mausbach, J. *Die Katholische Morale, ihre Methoden, Grundsätze und Aufgaben*, Köln, 1901.
McCabe, H. *Knowing and Naming God*: Summa Theologiae, Vol. 3, Blackfriars-London, 1964.
McCabe, H. *God Still Matters*, London: Continuum, 2002.
McCosker, P., and Turner, D., edd. *The Cambridge Companion to the Summa theologiae*, Cambridge: Cambridge University Press, 2016.
McGuckin, Terence. 'Saint Thomas Aquinas and Theological Exegesis of Sacred Scripture', *NB* 74, 870 (April 1993), 197–213.
McInerny, Ralph M. *Ethica Thomistica*, Washington, D.C.: Catholic University Press, 1982/1997.
McInerny, Ralph M. *Aquinas and Analogy,* Washington, D.C.: Catholic University of America, 1996.
McInerny, Ralph M. *Aquinas on Human Action. A Theory of Practice*, Washington, D.C.: Catholic University of America, 1992.
McIntosh, Mark A. *Discernment and Truth. The Spirituality and Theology of Knowledge,* New York: The Crossroad Publishing Company, 2004,

Meinander, Gilbert & Werpehowski, William, edd. *The Oxford Handbook of Theological Ethics*, Oxford: Oxford University Press, 2005.

Meinert, John M, *The Love of God Poured Out: Grace and the Gifts of the Holy Spirit in St Thomas Aquinas*, Emmaus Academic, Stebenville, 2018.

Ménard, E. *La tradition selon saint Thomas d'Aquin*, Montréal: Desclée de Brouwer, 1964.

Mennessier, A.-I. 'Conseil, Don de, *DSp* t. 2, 1583–1592.

Milbank, John & Pickstock, Catherine. *Truth in Aquinas*, London and New York: Routledge. 2001.

Miller, Richard B. 'Rules', *in* Meinander & Werpehowski.

Molari, C. 'I luoghi paralleli nelle opere di San Tommaso e la loro cronologia', *Euntes Docete* 11 (1958) 371–391.

Mondin, Battista. *The Principle of Analogy in Protestant and Catholic Theology*, The Hague: M. Nijhoff, 1963.

Mussner, F. 'Thomas von Aquin über die Entmythologisierung', *Catholica* (Münster) 19 (1965) 192–198.

Newman, John Henry. *Essay on the development of Christian doctrine*, London: Sheed and Ward, 1960.

Nichols, Aidan. *Discovering Aquinas: An Introduction to His Life, Work and Influence,* London: Darton, Longman and Todd, 2002.

Nichols, Aidan. 'Book Review', *NB* 87, 1012 (Nov 2006), 660–662.

Niebuhr, H.R. 'The Doctrine of the Trinity and the Unity of the Church', *Theology Today* 3 (1946) 371–384.

Novarina. *See* Walz.

O'Connor, Edward. D. St Thomas Aquinas, *Summa theologiae*, vol 24, The Gifts of the Spirit, London: Eyre & Spottiswoode, 1974.

O'Meara, Thomas F. *Thomas Aquinas Theologian*, Notre Dame: University of Notre Dame Press, 1997.

O'Meara, Thomas F. 'Virtues in the Theology of Thomas Aquinas', *TS* 58 (1997) 254–285.

O'Meara, Thomas F. 'Interpreting Thomas Aquinas: Aspects of the Dominican School of Moral Theology in the Twentieth Century', in Stephen J. Pope, 355–373.

O'Neill, C. 'St. Thomas on the membership of the Church', *The Thomist* 27 (1963) 88–140.

Pazdan, Mary Margaret. 'Thomas Aquinas and Contemporary Biblical Interpreters: "I Call You Friends" (John 15:15), *NB* 86, 1005, 465–477.

Pesch, O.-H. 'Thomas Aquinas and Contemporary Theology', in Kerr, *Contemplating*, 185–216.

Peters, J. *See* Dondaine, A.

Pjhilipon, M.M. *Les dons du Saint-Esprit*, Paris: Desclée de Brouwer, 1964.

Pickstock, Catherine. *See* Milbank.

Pinckaers, Servais. *The Sources of Christian Ethics*, Washington, D.C.: Catholic University of America Press, 1995.

Pinsent, A. *The Second-Person Perspective in Aquinas's Ethics. Virtues and Gifts,* New York: Routledge, 2012.

Pinsent, A. 'The Gifts and Fruits of the Holy Spirit', in Davies & Stump, pp. 475–488.
Polgar, Nenad & Selling, Joseph, edd. *The Concept of Intrinsic Evil and Catholic Theological Ethics,* Lexington, Fortress Academic, 2019.
Pollet, J.V.-M. 'Les charismes', *Initiation théologique,* t. 3: Théologie Morale, Paris: Aubier, 1952, pp. 1081–1108.
Pope, H., *St. Thomas Aquinas as an Interpreter of Holy Scripture,* Oxford: Oxford University Press, 1924.
Pope, Stephen J. *The Ethics of St Thomas Aquinas,* Washington, D.C.: Georgetown University Press, 2002.
Pope, Stephen J. 'Theological Anthropology, Science, and Human Flourishing', in Lieven Boeve, Yves De Maeseneer, and Ellen Van Stichel, edd. *Questioning the Human. Towards a Theological Anthropology for the Twenty-First Century,* New York: Fordham University Press, 2014, 13–30.
Porter, Jean. *The Recovery of Virtue; The Relevance of Aquinas for Christian Ethics,* Louisville, KY: Westminster/Knox Press, 1990.
Porter, Jean. 'Virtues and Vices', in Davies & Stump, 265–275.
Procter, John, T*homas Aquinas, An Apology for the Religious Orders,* London: Sands & Co., 1902.
Rankin, David. *Tertullian and the Church,* Cambridge: Cambridge University Press, 1995.
Reeves ,Marjorie, *Influence of Prophecy in the Later Middle Ages: A Study in Joachimism,* new ed., Notre Dame, Indiana: University of Notre Dame Press, 1993.
Reeves, Marjorie, *see* Bloomfield; *see* Gould.
Renard, J. P. 'La Lectura super Matthaeum V, 20-48 de Thomas d'Aquin (Edition d'après le ms. Bâle, Univ. *Bibl. B. V.12)' RTAM* 50 (1983) 153–189.
Richter, Duncan. *Ethics After Anscombe. Post 'Modern Moral Philosophy',* Dordrecht and London: Kluger, 2000.
Roland, E., 'Élection des évêques', *DTC* t. 4/2, 2256–2281.
Rosemann, Philipp W. *Omne agens agit sibi simile*: a 'repetition' of Scholastic metaphysics, Leuven: Leuven University Press, 1996.
Rousselot, P. *L'intellectualisme de saint Thomas,* Paris: Aubier, 1924.
Russo, F. *Bibliografia Gioachimita,* Firenze, 1954.
Salet, G. 'La Loi dans nos coeurs', *NRT* 79 (1957) 561–578.
Schelkle, K.H. *Paulus Lehrer der Väter.* Die altkirchliche Auslegung von Römer 1-11, Düsseldorf, 1956.
Schillebeeckx, E. *Approches théologiques,* I: Révélation et théologie, Bruxelles, 1965.
Seckler, M. *Instinkt und Glaubenswille nach Thomas von Aquin,* Mainz, 1961.
Seckler, M. *Das Heil in der Geschichte.* Geschichts-theologisches Denken bei Thomas von Aquin, München, 1964.
Selling, Joseph A. *Reframing Catholic Theological Ethics,* Oxford: Oxford University Press, 2016.
Selling, Joseph A. ed., *see* Polgar.
Sherwin, Michael, *By Knowledge and By Love: Charity and Knowledge in the Moral Theology of St Thomas Aquinas,* Washington, D.C.: Catholic University of America Press, 2012.

Shooner, H.V. 'La *Lectura in Matthaeum* de saint Thomas', *Angelicum* 33 (1956) 121–142.

Silva, Ignacio. 'Thomas Aquinas Holds Fast: Objections to Aquinas Within Today's Debate on Divine Action, *Heythrop Journal*, 54 (2013) 658–667.

Slee, Nicola. 'The Holy Spirit and Spirituality', in Susan Frank Parsons, ed., *The Cambridge Companion to Feminist Theology*, Cambridge: Cambridge University Press, 2002, 171–189.

Smalley, B. *The Study of the Bible in the Middle Ages*, ed. 2, Oxford: Oxford University Press, 1952.

Smedes, Taede A. *Chaos, Complexity and God: Divine Action and Scientism*, Leuven: Peters, 2004.

Spiazzi, R. *Lo Spirito Santo nella vita cristiana*, Rome, 1954.

Spicq, C. *Esquisse d'une histoire de l'exégèse latine au moyen age*, Paris: Desclée, 1944.

Spicq, C. 'Saint Thomas d'Aquin exégète', *DTC*, t. 15, 694–738.

Stump, Eleonor. *see* Kretzmann.

Stump, Eleonor. 'Wisdom: Will, Belief, and Moral Goodness', in MacDonald & Stump, 28–62.

Stump, Eleonor. 'Biblical Commentary and Philosophy', in Kretzmann and Stump., 252–268.

Synave, P. 'Les commentaires scripturaires de saint Thomas d'Aquin', *La vie spirituelle* (1923) 455–469.

Tascón, Th. 'Note sur la place du don de sagesse dans la Théologie Morale thomiste', *RevThom* 35 (1930) 415–425.

Tertullian. *De pudicitia, PL* 2, 979–1030.

Torrance, T. F. 'Scientific Hermeneutics of Aquinas', *Journal of Theological Studies*, ns 13 (1962).

Torrell, J.-P. *Saint Thomas Aquinas*, vol. 1. *The Person and His Work*, Washington, D.C.: University of America Press, 1996.

Torrell, J.-P. *Saint Thomas Aquinas,* vol 2. *Spiritual Master,* Washington, D.C.: University of America Press, 2003.

Torrell, J.-P. *Christ and Spirituality in St Thomas Aquinas*, Washington, D.C.: The Catholic University of America Press, 2011.

Tromp, S. *Corpus Christi quod est Ecclesia,* III: De Spiritu Christi Anima, Rome, 1960.

Tugwell, Simon. *Albert & Thomas. Selected Writings*, New York: Paulist Press, 1988.

Valkenberg, W. *Words of the Living God: Place and Function of Holy Scripture in the Theology of St. Thomas Aquinas*, Leuven: Peeters, 2000.

Valsecchi, A. *La 'Legge nuova' del cristiano secondo san Tommaso d'Aquino*, Varese, 1963.

van der Ploeg, J. 'The Place of Holy Scripture in the Theology of St. Thomas', *The Thomist* 10 (1947) 398–422.

van Ouwerkerk, C. A. J. *Caritas et Ratio. Étude sur le double principe de la vie morale chrétienne d'après saint Thomas d'Aquin*, Nijmegen, 1956.

Van Roo, W. 'Law of the Spirit and the Written Law in the Spirituality of St. Ignatius', *Greg* 37 (1956) 417–443.
Vatican Council, Second. *Pastoral Constitution on the Church in the World (Gaudium et spes)*; *in* Abbott, 199–308.
Vauthier, E. 'Le Saint-Esprit principe d'unité de l'Église d'après saint Thomas d'Aquin', *MScRel* 5 (1948) 175–96; 6 (1949) 54–80.
Verbeke, G. *Jean Philopon. Commentaire sur le De anima d'Aristote,* Louvain-Paris, 1966.
Vosté, I.-M. 'De investigandis fontibus patristicis sancti Thomae', *Angelicum* 14 (1937) 417–434.
Vosté, I.-M. 'Sanctus Thomas Aquinas Epistularum S. Pauli Interpres', *Angelicum* 19 (1942) 257–276.
Wadell, Paul J. *The Primacy of Love: An Introduction to the Ethics of Thomas Aquinas*, New York/Mahwah: Paulist Press, 1992.
Walz, A., Novarina, P. *Saint Thomas d'Aquin,* Louvain, 1962.
Wawrykow, Joseph P. 'Wisdom in the Christology of Thomas Aquinas', in Emery, Kent, Jr and Wawrykow, Joseph, eds. *Christ Among the Medieval Dominicans: Representations of Christ in the Texts and Images of the Order of Preachers*, Notre Dame: University of Notre Dame Press, 1998, pp. 175–219.
Weaver, Rebecca Harden, *Divine Grace and Human Agency a Study of the Semi-Pelagian Controversy,* Macon GA: Mercer University Press, 2003.
Weinandy, Thomas G., Keating, Daniel A., & Yocum, John P., edd. *Aquinas on Scripture. An introduction to his Biblical Commentaries*, London: T & T Clark, 2005.
Weisheipl, James A. 'The Johannine Commentary of Friar Thomas', *Church History*, 4, 1976, 191.
Werpehowski, William, *see* Meinander.
White, Thomas J. *The Analogy of Being: Invention of the Antichrist or the Wisdom of God?,* Grand Rapids, MI: Eerdmans, 2011.
Wilkins, John, ed. *Considering Veritatis Splendor*, Cleveland, Ohio: Pilgrim Press, 1994.
Williams, Rowan. 'What Does Love Know? St Thomas on the Trinity', *NB* 82 (2001) 260–272.
Woppell, John F. *The Metaphysical Thought of Thomas Aquinas from Finite Being to Uncreated Being*, Washington, D.C.: The Catholic University Press, 2000.

# Index

Abraham ordered to kill Isaac (Gen 22), 107–9
Afanasief, 131
Albert the Great, 1, 2, 8, 32
Alfaro, 53
Alszeghy, 50
Ambrosiaster, 43, 125
analogy: analogical predication, 59–62, 65–66; analogy of being, 62–65
Anscombe, 96–97
Anselm, 13, 50
appropriation of the Holy Spirit, 21–22
Augustine: being acted on is more than being directed, 49–52
Austen, 94
Austin, 56, 89, 96

Baglow, 10, 12, 134–35
Basel University, 5
Bede, 134, 136
Bentham, 98
Bernard, 8, 12
Bloomfield, 132
Bonaventure, 8, 132
Bonhoeffer, 148
Bouchard, 53, 54, 163
Bouillard, 6
Boyle, 7, 12

Cajetan, 32
*casus emergens*, 103–4
*Catechism of the Catholic Church*, 74–75
causality: Aristotelian causes, 56–58; divine causality, 58–59, 61–66
Chenu, 82, 160
Chrysostom, 27, 29, 125
Coakley, 15
Cologne, 2
Congar, 134, 138
Conley, 93

Dionysius. *See* pseudo-Dennis
Dallas, 12
Davies, 7
Deman, 73, 152
Denifle, 9
Dingjan, 152
discernment, 153–54, 157, 164; differs from 'discretion', 151–54
discernment of spirits, 145–48
Dominic, Saint, 1, 132
Dondaine, 21
Dodds, 58–59, 62, 63, 65

Emery, 9, 10, 20, 42, 44, 52, 61, 74, 139
*epieikeia* in legal and moral matters, 99, 111–15

# Index

Esau selling his birthright (Gen 25: 29–34), 106–7
Eschmann, 6
'evil' terminology, 98

Fabro, 73
Farrell, 74
Fossanova, 2
Francis of Assisi, 89, 132
Fuchs, 26, 83

Gardeil, 69, 74
Garrigou-Lagrange, 72
gender issues in translating, 14–15
Gerard of Borgo San Donnino, 132
Gilby, 93
Glorieux, 6
Gloss: Ordinary and Interlinear, 50
*The Good Luck Book* (*Liber de bona fortuna*), 71–75, 84, 85
Grabmann, 134, 139
Gratian, 137
Grelot, 10

Haight, 44
Hamel, 82
Hankey, 20
Healy, 3, 134
Herod, 149
Holy Spirit in triune God, 19–20; Holy Spirit and 'the Church of the Holy Spirit', 131–39; Holy Spirit and appropriation, 21; Holy Spirit as the 'same Spirit', 87–88, 121–23; Holy Spirit as the Spirit of Christ, 123–31; Holy Spirit 'prompting', *instinctus*, 52–54; Spirit as being 'sent', 36–37; Spirit as dove, 37–38; Spirit as fire, 26–29; Spirit as God's finger, 35–36; Spirit as (living) water, 29–33, 52, 58, 67, 164; Spirit as new wine, 38–39; Spirit as oil, 33–35, 124–25, 127
Holy Spirit: the 'grace of the Holy Spirit', 42–44

Holy Spirit: the seven Gifts of, 8, 69–75, 124
Hosea ordered to have sex with a harlot (Hos 3:1), 107–10
Hugh of Saint-Cher, 8
Hughes, 74, 163
Hume, 59

Ignatius Loyola, 90
Isidore, 150
Israelites taking Egyptian possessions (Ex 12:36), 107–10

Jacob lies to Isaac (Gen 27:1–9), 107
Jephthah, 149
Jerome, 122, 149
Joachim of Fiore, 131–34, 149
John Chrysostom, 22
John of Damascus, 55
John of St Thomas, 72
Johnson, 14, 15
Jordan, 4

Kant, 96
Kerr, 6, 10, 11, 15, 96
Kimball, 5
Knowles, 55

The Law of the Gospel, 81–82; The law as external teacher, 85–89; The Spirit as internal teacher, 83–84; The wisdom of the Holy Spirit, 90–96
Lecuyer, 53, 88
Legge, 54, 124
Leonine Commission, 4
Levering, 19
Lombard, 2, 19, 50, 66, 70
Lonergan, 149
lots, morality of drawing, 135–37
Luther, 83
Lyons, 2

MacCulloch, 132
MacIntyre, 97
Macquarrie, 42

Mahoney, 15
Mausbach, 81
McCabe, 93–94
McGuckin, 9
McInerny, 11, 60
McIntosh, 146
Meinert, 12, 44, 53, 54, 69
Menard, 159
Migne, 15
Miller, 99
Mondin, 61
Monte Casino, 1
moral absolutes, 107–11

Naples, 1, 2, 6
Newman, 74
New Revised Standard Version, 14, 15, 24, 49
Newton, 59
Nichols, 3
Novarina, 4

O'Connor, 54, 69, 73
O'Meara, 53, 163
order, *ordo*, 159–63
Orvieto, 2

Pazdan, 3
Pelagius, 50, 55
Pesch, 12, 62, 83
Peter of Andria, 5
Pinsent, 53, 92
Plato, 7
Porter, 99
'*praeter*', 103–4
Pope Gregory IX, 7
Pope Gregory X, 2, 136
Pope Gregory the Great, 8, 20, 70, 128, 150
Pope Pius XII, 145
'practical wisdom' a misnomer, 93–94
prompting (*instinctus*) of Spirit, 52–54
pseudo-Dennis, 22, 23, 26, 60, 62, 160

Rackham, 93

Reeves, 132
Richter, 97
Roccasecca, 1
Roland, 136
Rosemann, 61, 62
Ruth and the Old Law (Dt 23:3), 105

Seckler, 53, 72
Sherwin, 69, 93
Silva, 65
Simony, 137
Slee, 15
Smalley, 4, 8, 134
Smedes, 63
Solomon's wisdom, 149
Spicq, 8, 22, 122
St Paul justifying his conduct (2 Cor 11), 103–5
Stump, 4, 91, 92, 149

Tertullian, 131
Thomas Aquinas (1225–74): life and career, 1–3; scripture commentaries, 3–8
Torrell, 2, 6, 10, 15, 19, 21, 42, 66
Tugwell, 2, 5–7, 9

Valsecchi, 49
Van Roo, 82
Valkenberg, 5
Vatican Council, Second, 63
Vauthier, 7, 135
Verbeke, 2
*via negativa*, 22
virtue ethics, 96–99
Viterbo, 6

Walz, 4
Wisdom, 90–96, 151, 153–54, 157–59; architectonic, 161–62; charismatic 'speech of wisdom', 154–57; divine and human, 162; foolish 'unwisdom' (*insipientia*), 148–51; horizontal and vertical, 161
William of Holy Love, 2, 134

# About the Author

**John A. ("Jack") Mahoney, SJ**, received the doctorate in moral theology *summa cum laude* from the Pontifical Gregorian University in Rome. He lectured in moral and pastoral theology at the University of London for twenty-eight years, first in the Jesuit Heythrop College, where he was also Principal; then at King's College London, as F.D. Maurice Professor of moral and social theology, and founding director of the King's College Business Ethics Research Centre; and finally at London Business School, as the first Dixons Professor of business ethics and social responsibility. When he retired in 1998, he was appointed Emeritus Professor of moral and social theology in London University, and was later awarded an Honorary Doctorate of the University.

Professor Mahoney also lectured in business ethics in Gresham College in London where he was the Mercers' School Memorial Professor of Commerce, and then Emeritus Professor. In Edinburgh, he founded the Lauriston Centre for Catholic Belief and Action and taught occasionally in the university there, as well as in the University of Saint Andrews and Glasgow University. He was subsequently appointed Distinguished Professor at Georgetown University, Washington, D.C., in the Department of Theology. He now resides in London. He has published more than 100 articles and chapters and numerous books, notably *The Making of Moral Theology. A Study of the Roman Catholic Tradition* (1987); *The Challenge of Human Rights: Origin, Development and Significance* (2007); *Christianity in Evolution. An Exploration* (2011); and most recently, *Glimpses of the Gospels* (2019). He was also for five years founding editor of the quarterly *Business Ethics: A European Review* (Blackwell).

He has served as personal Chaplain to the Lord Mayor of London; has been a regular member of the Theology Committee of the Bishops' Conference of England and Wales; was president of the Sector on Collegiality and Co-Responsibility at the 1980 National Pastoral Congress in Britain; and was a member of the International Theological Commission, Rome.

He sang in the Edinburgh Bach Choir and enjoys playing the piano as well as unrequited golf.

www.ingramcontent.com/pod-product-compliance
Lightning Source LLC
Chambersburg PA
CBHW032149010526
44111CB00035B/1414